Linux

PHRASEBOOK

SECOND EDITION

Scott Granneman

♦Addison-Wesley

800 East 96th Street, Indianapolis, Indiana 46240 USA

Linux Phrasebook, Second Edition

Library of Congress Control Number: 2015955629

ISBN-13: 978-0-321-83388-4
ISBN-10: 0-321-83388-0

First printing: December 2015

Trademarks

Many of the designations used by manufacturers and sellers to distinguish their products are claimed as trademarks. Where those designations appear in this book, and the publisher was aware of a trademark claim, the designations have been printed with initial capital letters or in all capitals.

Warning and Disclaimer

The author and publisher have taken care in the preparation of this book, but make no expressed or implied warranty of any kind and assume no responsibility for errors or omissions. No liability is assumed for incidental or consequential damages in connection with or arising out of the use of the information or programs contained herein.

Special Sales

For information about buying this title in bulk quantities, or for special sales opportunities (which may include electronic versions; custom cover designs; and content particular to your business, training goals, marketing focus, or branding interests), please contact our corporate sales department at corpsales@pearsoned.com or (800) 382-3419.

For government sales inquiries, please contact governmentsales@pearsoned.com.

For questions about sales outside the U.S., please contact international@pearsoned.com.

Visit us on the Web: informit.com/aw

Acquisitions Editor	Copy Editor	Technical Reviewer	Compositor
Mark Taber	Anne Goebel	Brian Tiemann	Mary Sudul
Managing Editor	**Senior Indexer**	**Editorial Assistant**	
Sandra Schroeder	Cheryl Lenser	Vanessa Evans	
Senior Project Editor	**Proofreader**	**Cover Designer**	
Tonya Simpson	Laura Hernandez	Chuti Prasertsith	

Table of Contents

About the Author

Scott Granneman is an author, educator, and small business owner. He has written seven books (about Firefox, Linux, Google Apps, and Mac OS X) and contributed to two. In addition, he was a columnist for *SecurityFocus*, one of the largest and most important security-focused sites on the Web, and *Linux Magazine* while it was in print.

As an educator, he has taught thousands of people of all ages—from preteens to senior citizens—on a wide variety of topics, including both literature and technology. He is currently an adjunct professor at Washington University in St. Louis and at Webster University, where he teaches a variety of courses about technology, social media, the Internet, and Web development. With the shift in focus over the past few decades to Linux and other open-source technologies, he has worked to bring knowledge of these powerful new directions in software to people at all technical skill levels.

As a Principal of WebSanity, a website planning, development, and hosting firm with clients in 12 states, he manages the firm's Linux-based servers and infrastructure, researches new technologies, and works closely with other partners on the underlying WebSanity Content Management System (CMS).

Dedication

*This book is dedicated to Linux users,
both old and new. Welcome!*

Acknowledgments for the First Edition (2005)

No one learns about the Linux shell in a vacuum, and I have hundreds of writers, working over decades, to thank for educating me about the awesome possibilities provided by the Linux command line. Books, websites, blogs, handouts at LUG meetings: All helped me learn about bash and the beauty of the Linux command line, and they continue to teach me today. If I can give back just a fraction of what I have absorbed, I'll be satisfied.

In addition to that general pool of knowledgeable individuals, I'd like to thank the people (and animals) who gave me help and support during the writing of *Linux Phrasebook*.

My agent, Laura Lewin, who has been helpful in too many ways for me to recount.

My editors at Pearson, who gave me the opportunity to write this book in the first place and have encouraged me whenever I needed prodding.

Robert Citek provided invaluable help with RPM and was always there if I had a question. That man knows Linux.

My business partner and lifelong buddy, Jans Carton, helped me focus when I needed it, and was a (mostly) willing guinea pig for many new commands and options. Looking back at that day in fifth grade when we met, who'da thunk it?

Jerry Bryan looked over everything I wrote and fixed all the little grammatical mistakes and typos I made. I promise, Jerry: One day I'll learn the difference between "may" and "might"!

My wife, Denise Lieberman, patiently listened to me babble excitedly whenever I figured out something cool, even though she had absolutely no idea what I was talking about. That's true love. Thanks, Denise!

Finally, I must point to my cute lil' Shih Tzu, Libby, who always knew exactly the right time to put her front paws on my leg and demand ear scratches and belly rubs.

Acknowledgments for the Second Edition (2015)

For the second edition, many things have changed (sadly, Libby has gone to that great dog house in the sky), but one thing is the same: Lots of folks helped me during the writing of this book, and they deserve recognition and my gratitude.

Mark Taber at Pearson supported me over a *very* lengthy writing period. I can't thank you enough, Mark. You are why this book exists today.

My wife, Robin Woltman, read through every chapter and made many invaluable edits and suggestions. You did a great job, Robin!

Robert Citek looked over many of the chapters and made suggestions and technical edits that were always right on the nose. He's who I turn to when I need help!

Craig Buchek looked over a chapter or two and made some good points. As the former benevolent dictator for life of the St. Louis Linux Users Group, that was expected.

Tom Kirk loaned me a few laptops from his enormous collection that enabled me to test out things from the networking sections. Tom, you are a lifesaver, and the best hardware guy I know.

In addition to my friends above, the following people emailed to let me know about problems in the first edition.

- Joe Hancharik pointed out a problem in Chapter 1's "Wildcards and What They Mean" that was a very silly mistake on my part.

- William H. Ferguson found another silly mistake I made in Chapter 3's "Copy Files."

- Brian Greer pointed out a problem I should have noticed in Chapter 15's "Troubleshooting Network Problems."

Thank you, gentlemen! It's readers like Joe, William, and Brian that make writing a book fun. Feedback is a great thing, even if it is a bug report. If you see an error, let me know, so I can fix it for the third edition!

We Want to Hear from You!

As the reader of this book, *you* are our most important critic and commentator. We value your opinion and want to know what we're doing right, what we could do better, what areas you'd like to see us publish in, and any other words of wisdom you're willing to pass our way.

We welcome your comments. You can email or write directly to let us know what you did or didn't like about this book—as well as what we can do to make our books better.

Please note that we cannot help you with technical problems related to the topic of this book, and that due to the high volume of mail we receive, we might not be able to reply to every message.

When you write, please be sure to include this book's title and author, as well as your name and phone number or email address.

E-mail: feedback@developers-library.info

Mail: Reader Feedback
            Addison-Wesley Developer's Library
            800 East 96th Street
            Indianapolis, IN 46240 USA

Reader Services

Visit our website and register this book at **www.informit.com/register** for convenient access to any updates, downloads, or errata that might be available for this book.

Introduction

Among key Linux features, the command-line shell is one of the most important. If you run a Linux server, your main interface is more than likely going to be the shell. If you're a power user running Linux on the desktop, you probably have a terminal open at all times. If you're a Linux newbie, you may think that you'll never open up the command line, but you will sometime ... and the more you use Linux, the more you're going to want to use that shell.

The shell in many ways is the key to Linux's power and elegance. You can do things with the command line that you simply can't do with whatever GUI you favor. No matter how powerful KDE or GNOME may be (or IceWM or XFCE or any of the other kajillion windowing environments out there), you will always be able to do many things faster and more efficiently with a terminal. If you want to master Linux, you need to begin by mastering the Linux command line.

The traditional method has been to use the Linux man pages. While man pages are useful, they are often not enough, for one simple reason: They lack examples. Oh, a few man pages here and there have a few examples, but by and large, good examples are hard to come by. This presents a real problem for users at all experience levels: It's one thing to see options listed and explained, but it's another thing entirely to see those options used in real-world situations.

This book is all about those missing examples. I've been using Linux for two decades, and I consider myself pretty knowledgeable about this amazing, powerful operating system. I'm so addicted to the command line that I always have a terminal open. And to top it off, the Linux servers my company relies on don't have GUIs on them (just the way I like it!), so I *have* to use the terminal to work with them. But I'm always lamenting—along with my Linux-using friends, acquaintances, and LUG members—the dearth of examples found in man pages. When I was asked to write *Linux Phrasebook*, and told that it was to consist of hundreds of examples illustrating the most important Linux commands, I replied, "I can't wait! That's a book I'd buy in a heartbeat!"

You're holding the result in your hands: a book about the Linux commands you just have to know, with examples illustrating how to use each and every one. This is a reference book that will be useful now and for years to come, but I also hope you find it enjoyable as well, and even a little fun.

NOTE: Visit our website and register this book at informit.com/register for convenient access to any updates, downloads, or errata that might be available for this book.

Audience for This Book

I've written this book to be useful both to beginners—
the folks that show up to meetings of our Linux
Users Group seeking guidance and a helping hand
as they begin the adventure of using Linux—and to
experienced users who use the shell for everything
from systems administration to games to programming.
If you've just started using Linux, this book will help
teach you about the shell and its power; if you've
been using Linux for years and years, *Linux Phrasebook*
will teach you some new tricks and remind you of
some features you'd long ago forgotten.

There are many shells out there—csh, tcsh, zsh,
to name but a few—but I use the default shell for
virtually every Linux distro: bash, the Bourne Again
Shell. The bash shell is not only ubiquitous, but also
powerful and flexible. After you get comfortable with
bash, you may choose to explore other options, but
knowledge of bash is required in the world of Linux.

I wrote this book using Debian, which is about as
generic a Linux distro as you can get, as well as one
of the most widely used. Even though I used Debian,
the commands I discuss should work on your distro
as well. The only major difference comes when you
run a command as root. Instead of logging in as root,
some distros (like Ubuntu, for instance) encourage the
use of the `sudo` command; in other words, instead of
running `lsof firefox` as root, an Ubuntu user would
run `sudo lsof firefox`.

NOTE: Sharp-eyed readers may note that, in the first edition, I used Ubuntu (or, as I referred to it there, K/Ubuntu—I was trying to emphasis that I was using KDE with Ubuntu). Now I've gone more generic and I just use straight Debian, the distro upon which Ubuntu is based.

In order to appeal to the widest number of readers out there, I showed the commands as though you have to run them as root, without `sudo`. If you see a `#` in front of a command, that's the shell indicating that root is logged in, which means you need to be root to run that command, or utilize `sudo` if you're using Ubuntu or a similar distro.

One final thing: In order to keep this book from being even longer, I've often truncated the outputs of commands. For instance, on your Linux computer, you'd normally see the following output after entering `ls -l`:

```
-rwxr-xr-x 1 scott admins 1261 Jun 1 2012 script.sh
```

You will see that in a few places in this book in which it's appropriate, but often you'll instead find something like this:

```
-rw-r--r-- 1 scott admins script.sh
```

In that case, I cut out the stuff that wasn't important to my point, which helped keep the output to only one line instead of two. You'd be surprised how those lines can add up, which is why I made those changes when it seemed appropriate (or when my editor was about to freak out at the number of pages the book was going to have!!).

TIP: Much of the information I provide about Linux in this book can also be applied to other flavors of UNIX, such as BSD and OS X. Note that I did not say *all* or *most*—I said *much*. As long as you keep that in mind, you'll find *Linux Phrasebook* to be helpful with those operating systems as well.

About the Second Edition

When Mark Taber, my editor at Pearson, first approached me about writing a second edition of *Linux Phrasebook*, I jumped at the chance. I actually use my own book as a reference a few times a month, so over the years, I've noticed errors (wincing every time) and have seen many things that I'd like to change, remove, or add.

My goal has been to make the second edition a must-buy for new readers as well as for owners of the first edition of *Linux Phrasebook*. This isn't some so-called new edition with just a few small changes. Oh no. So here's what I've done that's new or different in this book:

- I split the former Chapter 2, "The Basics," into two chapters: Chapters 2, "Navigating Your File System," and 3, "Creation and Destruction." The old Chapter 2 was ridiculously long, and it crammed together different kinds of commands. The new split makes things far more manageable and sensible (although it did mean every chapter after those two had to be re-numbered).

- I removed Chapters 6, "Printing and Managing Print Jobs," and 16, "Windows Networking," because they just don't seem as vital as they did ten years ago. In addition, most people who need to print or connect to and work on a Windows-based network will have GUI tools that more than adequately do those jobs. However, don't despair—you can still find those original chapters from the first edition on my website, www.granneman.com/linux-redaction.

- I added a new chapter: Chapter 7, "Manipulating Text Files with Filters." There is a *large* amount of great new information there, and I know you will find it very useful!

- I removed sections from the old Chapters 2 (now Chapters 2 and 3), 3 (now 4), 7 (8), 8 (9), 9 (10), 10 (11), and 14 (15). Again, you will find those original sections from the first edition on my website, www.granneman.com/linux-redaction.

- I added new sections in Chapters 1–6 and 8–13. And I almost doubled the size of Chapter 15 by keeping the deprecated commands (since they're still on most distros) while adding all the new ones.

- I moved sections into new chapters where they made sense, which you can especially see in Chapter 8.

- I revised things in every chapter of the book. I fixed mistakes, rewrote parts that were unclear, added additional notes and tips, and improved examples by adding or revising text.

- I mentioned many more commands in passing, like `ssh-agent`, `wput`, `htop`, `dnf`, `pandoc`, `rename`, `whoami`, and `iconv`.

- I provided little tidbits of information about many different things that are good to know about, like variables, `for` loops, cron jobs, arguments, and `sources`. Oh, and there's more H.P. Lovecraft!

Finally, a tip: If any links are broken or don't work any longer, try entering them at the Internet Archive's Wayback Machine, which you can find at https://archive.org, to see if you can still find the content. Then let me know so I can fix that reference in future editions.

Thank you for reading this far, and I really hope you enjoy this new edition of *Linux Phrasebook*!

Conventions Used in This Book

This book uses the following conventions.

- `Monospace` type is used to differentiate between code/programming-related terms and regular English, and to indicate text that should appear on your screen. For example:

  The `df` command shows results in kilobytes by default, but it's usually easier to comprehend if you instead use the `-h` (or `--human-readable`) option.

  ```
  It will look like this to mimic the way text
  looks on your screen.
  ```

- An arrow (➡) at the beginning of a line of code means that a single line of code is too long to fit on the printed page. It signifies to readers that the author meant for the continued code to appear on the same line.

- In addition to this, the following elements are used to introduce other pertinent information used in this book.

NOTE: A note presents interesting pieces of information related to the surrounding discussion.

TIP: A tip offers advice or teaches an easier way to do something.

CAUTION: A caution advises you about potential problems and helps you steer clear of disaster.

Things to Know About Your Command Line

Before you really dig in to your bash shell, you first need to understand a few things that will help you as you proceed throughout this book. These are absolutes that you just gotta know, and some of them are not obvious at all. But after you understand them, some of the ways in which your shell behaves will start making much more sense.

Everything Is a File

On a Linux system, everything is a file—everything, which may seem obvious at first. Of course a text document is a file, and so is an OpenOffice.org document, and don't forget a picture, an MP3, and a video. Of course!

But what about a directory? It's a file, too—a special kind of file that contains information about other files.

Disk drives are really big files. Network connections are files. Hardware devices, too, are represented as files. Even running processes are files. They're all files.

To Linux, a file is just a stream of bits and bytes. Linux doesn't care what those bits and bytes form; instead, the programs running on Linux care. To Linux, a text document and a network connection are both files; it's your text editor that knows how to work with the text document, and your Internet applications that recognize the network connection.

Throughout this book, I'm going to refer to files. If it's appropriate, feel free to read that as "files and directories and subdirectories and everything else on the system." In particular, many of the commands I'll cover work equally well on documents and directories, so feel free to try out the examples on both.

NOTE: Strictly speaking, "Everything is a file" isn't 100% true. It's more accurate, as Linux Torvalds has pointed out, to say "Everything is a stream of bytes." For more on this concept, see the Wikipedia article, "Everything is a file," at http://en.wikipedia.org/wiki/Everything_is_a_file, and How-To Geek's "What 'Everything Is a File' Means on Linux," at www.howtogeek.com/117939/htg-explains-what-everything-is-a-file-means-on-linux/.

Maximum Filename Lengths

People who can look back to using MS-DOS (shudder!) remember that filenames could be no longer than eight characters, plus a three-letter extension, giving you incredibly descriptive names such as MSRSUME1.DOC. Pre-OS X Macs, on the other hand, extended that limit to 31 characters, which was certainly better but could still produce some odd-looking names.

Linux (and UNIX) filenames can be up to 255 characters in length. That's an outrageous length for a filename, and if you're getting anywhere even close to that, your picture should appear next to *verbose* in the dictionary. You're given up to 255 characters, so feel free to be descriptive and accurate, but don't go nuts.

In fact, it's a good idea to keep filenames below 80 characters, because that's the width of your average terminal and your filenames will appear on one line without wrapping. But that's just advice, not a requirement. The freedom to describe a file in 200+ characters is yours; just use it wisely.

Names Are Case-Sensitive

Unlike Windows and Mac OS X machines, Linux boxes are case-sensitive when it comes to filenames. You could find the three following files in the same directory on a computer running Linux:

- `bookstobuy.txt`

- `BooksToBuy.txt`

- `BoOkStObUy.txt`

To the Linux file system, those are three completely different files. If you were on Windows or Mac OS X, however, you would be asked to rename or cancel your attempt to add `BooksToBuy.txt` to a directory that already contained `bookstobuy.txt`.

Case-sensitivity also means that commands and filenames must be entered exactly to match their real command names or filenames. If you want to delete

files by running `rm`, you can't type in `RM` or `Rm` or `rM`.
`rm` is it. And if you want to delete `bookstobuy.txt` and
you instead enter `rm BooksToBuy.txt`, you just removed
the wrong file or no file at all.

The lesson is twofold: Linux forces you to be precise,
but precision is a good thing. At the same time, you're
given a degree of flexibility that you won't find in
other operating systems. That combination of required
precision and flexibility is one of the things that makes
Linux fun to use, yet understandably a bit confusing
for new users.

Special Characters to Avoid in Names

Every operating system has certain no-no's when it
comes to the characters you can use when naming files
and directories. If you use Mac OS X, the colon (:)
isn't allowed; Windows users, on the other hand, can't
use the backslash (\). Linux has its *verboten* characters
as well. Before looking at those, however, here are the
characters that are always safe:

- numbers
- letters (either uppercase or lowercase)
- dots (.)—although making one the first character
  of a file or directory hides it from most command
  line and GUI environments
- underscores (_)

Other items on your keyboard might work perfectly,
others might work but present complications due to
the fact that your shell will try to interpret them in
various ways, and some won't work at all.

/ is never an option because that particular character is used to separate directories and files. Let's say you want to keep a file listing books you want to buy. You somehow manage to name the file `books/to_buy.txt` (with a forward slash) to distinguish it from `books/on_loan.txt` and `books/lost.txt`. Now when you try to refer to your file at `/home/scott/documents/books/to_buy.txt`, your command isn't going to work because your shell thinks that a `books` directory is inside the `documents` directory, but it doesn't exist.

Instead of a forward slash, use an underscore (as I did for the `to_buy` part of the filename), or cram the words together (as in `booksToBuy.txt` or `BooksToBuy.txt`).

You could use a hyphen, forming `books-to-buy.txt`, but I find that underscores work nicely as word separators while remaining more unobtrusive than dashes. If you do use a hyphen, though, do not place it at the beginning of a filename, as in `-books_to_buy.txt`, or after a space, as in `books - to buy.txt`. As you're going to see later, if you're using a command and you want to invoke special options for that command, you preface the options with hyphens. You'll find out in Chapter 3, "Creation and Destruction," the `rm` command deletes files, but if you tried typing `rm -books_to_buy.txt`, your shell would complain with the following error message:

```
rm: invalid option -- b
```

You can use spaces if you'd like, forming `books to buy.txt`, but you have to let your shell know that those spaces are part of the filename. Your shell usually sees a space as a separator between arguments. Attempts to delete `books to buy.txt` confuses the shell, as it would try to delete a file named `books`, then one named `to`, and finally one named `buy.txt`. Ultimately, you won't delete `books to buy.txt`, and you might accidentally delete files you didn't want to remove.

So how do you work with spaces in filenames? Or the `*` and `?` characters, which you'll learn more about in the next section? Or the `'` and `"` characters, which also have special meanings in your shell? You have several choices. Avoid using them, if at all possible, but this is often difficult with spaces. Or escape them by placing a backslash (`\`) in front of the characters, which tells the shell that it should ignore their special usage and treat them as simple characters. It can grow tiresome, however, making sure that `\` is in its proper place all the time:

```
$ rm I\ shouldn\'t\ name\ files\ with\ \*\?.txt
```

Yuck. A simpler method that's a bit less onerous is to surround the filename with quotation marks, which function similarly to the `\`:

```
$ rm "I shouldn't name files with *?.txt"
```

This will work, and it's not too much of a pain to have to use quotation marks. A better solution is just not to use particularly troublesome characters in the first place. Table 1.1 lists some characters and what to do about them.

Table 1.1   **How to Use Special Characters in Filenames**

Character	Advice
/	Never use. Cannot be escaped.
\	Must be escaped. Avoid.
-	Never use at beginning of file or directory name.

Character	Advice
[ ]	Must be escaped. Avoid.
{ }	Must be escaped. Avoid.
*	Must be escaped. Avoid.
?	Must be escaped. Avoid.
'	Must be escaped. Avoid.
"	Must be escaped. Avoid.
<space>	Must be escaped. Often cannot be avoided, but try.

Wildcards and What They Mean

Imagine that you have the following files—12 pictures and a text file—in a directory on your computer:

```
libby1.jpg    libby8.jpg
libby2.jpg    libby9.jpg
libby3.jpg    libby10.jpg
libby4.jpg    libby11.jpg
libby5.jpg    libby12.jpg
libby6.jpg    libby1.txt
libby7.jpg
```

You want to delete these files using the `rm` command (covered in Chapter 3) on your command line. Removing them one at a time would be tedious and kind of silly. After all, one of the reasons to use computers is to automate and simplify boring tasks. This is a job for wildcards, which allow you to specify more than one file at a time by matching characters.

There are four wildcards:

- `*` (asterisk)
- `?` (question mark)

[ ] (square brackets)

{ } (curly brackets, also known as braces, hence the name: *brace expansion*)

NOTE: The curly brackets are different from the others. The translations done by the first three are classified by bash as *filename expansion*, while the curly brackets provide *brace expansion*. The first three simply match existing files; the curly brackets can be used to match existing files, but they can also be used to create new files, as you'll see.

The * matches any character zero or more times. Table 1.2 lists some uses of the * and what they would match.

Table 1.2 The Wildcard * and What It Matches

Command	Matches
rm libby1*.jpg	libby10.jpg through libby12.jpg, as well as libby1.jpg
rm libby*.jpg	libby1.jpg through libby12.jpg, but not libby1.txt
rm *txt	libby1.txt, but not libby1.jpg through libby12.jpg
rm libby*	libby1.jpg through libby12.jpg, and libby1.txt
rm *	All files in the directory

The ? matches a single character. Table 1.3 lists some uses of the ? and what they would match.

Table 1.3   **The Wildcard ? and What It Matches**

Command	Matches
`rm libby1?.jpg`	`libby10.jpg` through `libby12.jpg`, but not `libby1.jpg`
`rm libby?.jpg`	`libby1.jpg` through `libby9.jpg`, but not `libby10.jpg`
`rm libby?.*`	`libby1.jpg` though `libby9.jpg`, as well as `libby1.txt`

The [ ] matches either a set of single characters ([12], for instance, which would match 1 or 2 but not 12, or [abc], which would match a or b or c but not ab or bc or abc) or a range of characters separated by a hyphen (such as [1-3], which would match 1, 2, or 3). Table 1.4 lists some uses of the [ ] and what they would match.

Table 1.4   **The Wildcard [] and What It Matches**

Command	Matches
`rm libby1[12].jpg`	`libby11.jpg` and `libby12.jpg`, but not `libby10.jpg`
`rm libby1[0-2].jpg`	`libby10.jpg` through `libby12.jpg`, but not `libby1.jpg`
`rm libby[6-8].jpg`	`libby6.jpg` through `libby8.jpg`, but nothing else

The { } also does two kinds of matches: strings and ranges. If you want to use brace expansion for strings, you must separate your list with commas, and then bash lists out all possible combinations, as you can see:

```
$ ls
huan.jpg  libby.gif  libby.jpg  libby.png
➥libby.tiff
$ ls libby.{jpg,png}
libby.jpg  libby.png
$ ls {libby,huan}.jpg
huan.jpg  libby.jpg
```

Your list of strings does need to be an actual list, though, so you can't just use {jpg} or it won't work.

In my note earlier in this section, I mentioned that brace expansion can also be used to generate files as well as match them. In Chapter 3, I'll cover the mkdir command, which creates directories. Here's an example in which I use brace expansion to create several directories quickly:

```
$ mkdir {dogs,cats,wombats}
$ ls
cats  dots  wombats
```

In that case, I didn't match existing files or directories (which the *, ?, and [ ] are limited to); instead, I used the curly braces to tell mkdir the names of new directories to create.

It's important to keep in mind that while [ ] matches single characters, the { } is used to match strings—but just remember that a string can be a single character! This can lead to some confusion, as you can see in the results of the fourth command:

```
$ ls
testa  testab  testb  testbc  testc
```

```
$ ls test[a,b]
testa    testb
$ ls test{a,b}
testa    testb
$ ls test[ab,bc]
testa    testb    testc
$ ls test{ab,bc}
testab    testbc
```

The second and third commands, matching test[a,b]
and test{a,b}, produce the same results because they're
both looking for single characters. But as soon as you
forget that [ ] *only* works with single characters, you
get unexpected results. The test[ab,bc] command does
not display testab and testbc, but instead returns testa,
testb, and testc because, given how it works, you
told it to look for testa, then testb, then test, (test
followed by a comma!), then testb again, and then
testc. It found three of those (it ignored your duplicate
request) and showed them to you. On the other hand,
since the { } works with strings, it knows you want
to see testab and testbc, so it outputs those to you.
And that hopefully makes the differences between the
square and curly brackets a bit more clear.

As for ranges, that feature allows you to specify a start
and end point within the { and }. These can be either
numbers or letters, but not both, and they must be
separated by two periods. Let's look at examples using
the touch command (covered in Chapter 3):

```
$ touch finny{1..3}
$ ls
finny1    finny2    finny3
$ touch finny{a..c}
$ ls
finny1    finny2    finny3    finnya    finnyb    finnyc
```

Interestingly, you can combine two instances of brace expansion, and all possible combinations will be matched or created, like this:

```
$ touch finny{1..3}{a..c}
finny1a  finny1b  finny1c  finny2a  finny2b
➥finny2c  finny3a  finny3b  finny3c
```

To wrap up our look at wildcards, it's good to know that you can combine any and all of them as needed. Want to match libby1.jpg, libby2.jpg, and libby1.txt, but not libby3.jpg or libby.jpg? Use libby[1-2].* and it's done! How about Libby1.jpg, libby1.jpg (note the uppercase L and lowercase l—to Linux, those are different files, remember?), libby2.jpg, and Libby3.txt but not libby4.jpg? Use ?ibby[1-3].{jpg,txt}. And so on.

You'll be using wildcards all through this book, so it's good to introduce them now. They make dealing with files on the command line that much easier, and you're going to find them extremely helpful.

Special Files That Affect Your Command Line

Throughout this book, I'm going to reference some hidden startup scripts in your home directory (hidden because they start with a dot, so that they're often colloquially referred to as *dotfiles*) that can greatly influence how your shell works. I'm never going to go into great detail about them, because I just don't have the space, but I do want to encourage you to learn as much as you can about them. Everyone has different needs from their shell, and you should customize these files to meet your specific needs.

NOTE: If you want to see my dotfiles, check out my blog at http://ChainsawOnATireSwing.com or https://github.com/rsgranne/syno-dotfiles. GitHub makes it really easy to view other folks' dotfiles—just go to http://dotfiles.github.io for more info. With just a little effort and learning, you can store your own dotfile at GitHub, too!

Before I can tell you about the startup scripts, I first need to distinguish between two ways to classify shells: *login* and *nonlogin*, and *interactive* and *noninteractive* mode.

A login shell is—surprise!—started by your OS when you log in, either locally or via SSH (discussed in Chapter 16, "Working on the Network"). When you start a login shell, bash configures your shell by reading /etc/profile, which applies to everyone. Then bash looks for the following files in order, stopping at the first one it finds:

- ~/.bash_profile: Like .profile below, but for bash only.

- ~/.bash_login

- ~/.profile: Compatible with the original Bourne shell, sh, so any Bourne-compatible shell will use it.

These files set things like environment variables, and those environment variables are then passed along to any processes that are spawned by the login shell, including *subshells* (subshells are created when a shell starts another shell, as with a shell script). Besides environment variables, these files can also refer to shell-based programs that you want to automatically configure or run at log in, like ssh-agent (see Chapter 16) and bash-completion (check out http://chnsa.ws/7d).

A nonlogin shell is a shell that you don't log in to (again, surprise!). A subshell is a nonlogin shell, for instance, and so is a shell that you open from within GNOME, KDE, Unity, or any other Linux Desktop Environment or Window Manager.

NOTE: Interestingly, Mac OS X treats all shells like login shells, so you should just use `.profile` in lieu of anything else.

So, shells are either login or nonlogin. But they can also be either interactive or noninteractive.

An interactive shell is one that responds to your typed commands—to your interactions, in other words—and sends output to STDOUT and STDERR (see Chapter 5, "Building Blocks," for more on those). A noninteractive shell would be like that used by a shell script, during which you're not really typing commands and getting output back directly.

NOTE: Yes, it is entirely possible for a shell script to work with an interactive shell, just as it is possible for a noninteractive shell to respond to commands, but that's rare and I'm trying to generalize here.

When you start an interactive, nonlogin shell, bash reads and executes `/etc/bash.bashrc` if it's there (some distros include it and some don't), which applies to everyone using bash. After that, bash sources each user's `.bashrc` in his home directory. You should use that file for your bash-specific settings, such as options (see http://chnsa.ws/7c) and prompts (see http://chnsa.ws/7b).

You can also put aliases and functions (both covered in Chapter 12, "Your Shell") in .bashrc, but once you get more than a few, it's a good idea to offload them into .bash_aliases (and perhaps .bash_functions, which I'll discuss later). To call .bash_aliases, put the following in .bashrc:

```
if [ -f ~/.bash_aliases ]; then
   source ~/.bash_aliases
fi
```

If .bash_aliases exists, it will be sourced; if it doesn't exist, it will be skipped. This is a great file to create and use, as you'll see throughout this book.

When a login shell finally exits, bash reads and executes ~/.bash_logout, if it exists. This isn't used a lot, but among those who do use it, one of the most popular commands to put in there is clear, discussed in the next section.

TIP: If you want to customize your bash environment even more, look into the various options for ~/.inputrc. Technically, when you edit ~/.inputrc, you're not customizing bash; you're customizing the Readline library that bash uses for editing command lines. Either way, you can do some awesomely cool things with that file. For some of them, see my blog post at www.chainsawonatireswing.com/2012/05/13/fun-with-inputrc-part-1/, or Brett Terpstra's excellent ideas at http://brettterpstra.com/2015/07/09/shell-tricks-inputrc-binding-fun/.

If There's Too Much Stuff on Screen, Reset

```
clear
```

Here's your first command, one that you may want to use as you make your way through this book: `clear`. Let's say you've been testing out several commands, some successfully, others less so. Your terminal is now full of commands, output, errors, and garbage. To make it all go away, just type `clear` and all that stuff is gone, to be replaced with a prompt at the top left, just like you'd just started from scratch.

That's all there is to it. The `clear` command is one of the few Linux commands that has no arguments or options. It's just a quick and simple way to go right back to square one.

NOTE: In Chapter 12, you're going to learn about the `history` command, which allows you to view and re-run previous commands. Keep in mind that using `clear` doesn't affect your history; instead, it just clears your screen.

Conclusion

You've learned the stuff about Linux that might not be obvious to the new user, but that will come in handy as you begin using your shell and its commands. The details in this chapter will save you headaches as you start applying the materials in later chapters. Wondering why you can't copy a directory with a space in it, how to delete 1,000 files at one time, or why you can't run RM `bookstobuy.txt`? Those are not fun questions. With a little up-front knowledge, you can avoid the common mistakes that have plagued so many others.

With that out of the way, it's time to jump in and start learning commands. Turn the page, and let's go!

## 2

Navigating Your File System

This chapter introduces the basic commands you'll find yourself using several times every day. Think of these as the hammer, screwdriver, and pliers that a carpenter keeps in the top of his toolbox. After you learn these commands, you can start controlling your shell and finding out all sorts of interesting things about your files, folders, data, and environment. In particular, you'll be learning about some of the metadata—the data describing your data—that Linux has to keep track of, and it may just surprise you how much there is.

NOTE: When I updated this book for its second edition, I removed the section about `mkdir -v` (which shows you what `mkdir` is doing as it does it) and `rm -v` (which does the same thing, but for `rm`). You can find the original text on my website, www.granneman.com/linux-redactions.

Also, I took the sections on `touch`, `mkdir`, `cp`, `mv`, `rm`, and `rmdir` and used them to create a new Chapter 3 titled "Creation and Destruction" (which of course renumbered everything after it!). Finally, the section on `su` was moved to Chapter 8, "Ownership and Permissions," which makes a lot more sense.

List Files and Folders

```
ls
```

The `ls` command is probably the one that people find themselves using the most. After all, before you can manipulate and use files in a directory (remember, *file* and *directory* are interchangeable), you first have to know what files are available. That's where `ls` comes in, as it lists the files and subdirectories found in a directory.

NOTE: The `ls` command might sound simple—just show me the files!—but there are a surprising number of permutations to this amazingly pliable command, as you'll see.

Typing `ls` lists the contents of the directory in which you're currently working. When you first log in to your shell, you'll find yourself in your home directory. Enter `ls`, and you might see something like the following:

```
$ ls
alias Desktop    iso    pictures program_files todo
bin   documents  music  podcasts  src            videos
```

List the Contents of Other Folders

```
ls [folder]
```

You don't have to be in a directory to find out what's in it. Let's say that you're in your home directory, but you want to find out what's in the `music` directory.

Simply type the `ls` command, followed by the folder whose contents you want to view, and you'll see this:

```
$ ls music
Buddy_Holly   Clash   Donald_Fagen   new
```

In the previous example, a relative path is used, but absolute paths work just as well.

```
$ ls /home/scott/music
Buddy_Holly   Clash   Donald_Fagen   new
```

The ability to specify relative or absolute paths can be incredibly handy when you don't feel like moving all over your file system every time you want to view a list of the contents of a directory. Not sure if you still have that video of a Bengal Tiger your brother took at the zoo? Try this (~ represents your home directory):

```
$ ls ~/videos
airhorn_surprise.wmv
apple_knowledge_navigator.mov
b-ball-e-mail.mov
carwreck.mpg
nerdtv_1_andy_hertzfeld
nerdtv_2_max_levchin_paypal
nerdtv_3_bill_joy
tiger.wmv
Ubuntu_Talk-Mark_Shuttleworth.mpeg
```

Yes, there it is: `tiger.wmv`.

List Folder Contents Using Wildcards

```
ls *
```

You just learned how to find a file by listing out its entire directory; but there's a faster method, especially for really long directory listings. If you know that the video of the Bengal Tiger you're looking for is in Windows Media format (Boo! Hiss!), and therefore ends with .wmv, you can use a wildcard to show just the files ending with that particular extension.

```
$ ls ~/videos
airhorn_surprise.wmv
apple_knowledge_navigator.mov
b-ball-e-mail.mov
carwreck.mpg
nerdtv_1_andy_hertzfeld
nerdtv_2_max_levchin_paypal
nerdtv_3_bill_joy
tiger.wmv
Ubuntu_Talk-Mark_Shuttleworth.mpeg
$ ls ~/videos/*.wmv
airhorn_surprise.wmv    tiger.wmv
```

There's another faster method, also involving wildcards: Look just for files that contain the word *tiger*.

```
$ ls ~/videos/*tiger*
tiger.wmv
```

NOTE: If your wildcard results in a match with a directory, the contents of that directory will be listed as well. If you want to omit that match and avoid showing the contents of subdirectories, add the -d option.

View a List of Files in Subfolders

```
ls -R
```

You can also view the contents of several subdirectories with one command. Say you're at a Linux Users Group (LUG) meeting and installations are occurring around you fast and furious. "Hey," someone hollers out, "does anyone have an ISO image of the new Kubuntu that I can use?" You think you downloaded that recently, so to be sure, you run the following command (instead of `ls -R`, you could have also used `ls --recursive`):

```
$ ls -R ~/iso
/home/scott/iso:
debian-6.0.4-i386-CD-1.iso  knoppix  ubuntu

/home/scott/iso/knoppix:
KNOPPIX_V7.2.0CD-2013-06-16-EN.iso
➡ KNOPPIX_V7.4.2DVD-2014-09-28-EN.iso

/home/scott/iso/ubuntu:
kubuntu-15.04-desktop-amd64.iso
➡ ubuntu-15.04-desktop-amd64.iso
ubuntu-14.04.3-server-amd64.iso
```

There it is, in `~/iso/ubuntu`: `kubuntu-15.04-desktop-amd64.iso`. The `-R` option traverses the `iso` directory recursively, showing you the contents of the main `iso` directory and every subdirectory as well. Each folder is introduced with its path—relative to the directory in which you started—followed by a colon, and then the items in that folder are listed. Keep in mind that the recursive option becomes less useful when you have many items in many subdirectories, as the listing goes on for screen after screen, making it hard to find the particular item for which you're looking. Of course, if all you want to do is verify that there are many files and folders in a directory, it's useful just to see everything stream by, but that won't happen very often.

View a List of Contents in a Single Column

```
ls -1
```

So far, you've just been working with the default outputs of ls. Notice that ls prints the contents of the directory in alphabetical columns, with a minimum of two spaces between each column for readability. But what if you want to see the contents in a different manner?

If multiple columns aren't your thing, you can instead view the results of the ls command as a single column using, logically enough, ls -1 (or ls --format=single-column).

```
$ ls -1 ~/bin
Desktop
documents
iso
music
pictures
podcaststodo
videos
```

This listing can get out of hand if you have an enormous number of items in a directory, and more so if you use the recursive option as well, as in ls -1R ~/. Be prepared to press Ctrl+C to cancel the command if a list is streaming down your terminal with no end in sight.

View Contents As a Comma-Separated List

```
ls -m
```

Another option for those who can't stand columns of any form, whether it's one or many, is the -m option (or --format=commas).

```
$ ls -m ~/
alias, bin, Desktop, documents, iso, music, pictures,
➥ podcasts, program_files, src, todo, videos
```

Think of the *m* in -m as a mnemonic for *comma*, and it is easier to remember the option. Of course, this option is also useful if you're writing a script and need the contents of a directory in a comma-separated list, but that's a more advanced use of a valuable option.

View Hidden Files and Folders

```
ls -a
```

Up to this point, you've been viewing the visible files in directories, but don't forget that many directories contain hidden files in them as well. Your home directory, for instance, is just bursting with hidden files and folders, all made invisible by the placement of a . at the beginning of their names. If you want to view these hidden elements, just use the -a option (or --all).

```
$ ls -a ~/
.                .gimp-2.2         .openoffice.org1.9.95
..               .gksu.lock        .openoffice.org1.9
.3ddesktop       .glade2           .openoffice.org2
.abbrev_defs     .gnome            .opera
.acrorc          .gnome2           .padminrc
.adobe           .gnome2_private   pictures
alias            .gnome_private    podcasts
[List condensed due to length]
```

You should know several things about this listing. First, ls -a displays both hidden and unhidden items, so you see both .gnome and pictures. Second, you'll always see the . and .. because . refers to the current directory, while .. points to the directory above this one, the parent directory. These two hidden files exist in every single folder on your system, and you can't get rid of them. Expect to see them every time you use the -a option. Finally, depending on the directory, the -a option can reveal a great number of hidden items of which you weren't aware.

TIP: I just said that ls -a shows you everything beginning with a dot, including the folder references . and ..; but if you don't want to see those two, use ls -A instead.

Visually Display a File's Type

```
ls -F
```

The ls command doesn't tell you much about an item in a directory besides its name. By itself, it's hard to tell if an item is a file, a directory, or something else.

An easy way to solve this problem and make ls really informative is to use the -F option (or --classify).

```
$ ls -F ~/bin
adblock_filters.txt    fixm3u*              pix2tn.pl*
addext*                flash.xml*           pop_login*
address_book.csv       getip*               procmail/
address_book.sxc       homesize*            programs_usual*
address_book.xls       html2text.py*        quickrename*
backup_to_chaucer*     list-urls.py*
```

This tells you quite a bit. An * or asterisk after a file means that it is executable, while a / or forward slash indicates a directory. If the filename lacks any sort of appendage at all, it's just a regular ol' file. Other possible endings are shown in Table 2.1.

Table 2.1   **Symbols and File Types**

Character	Meaning
*	Executable
/	Directory
@	Symbolic link
|	FIFO (AKA a *named pipe*)
=	Socket

Display Contents in Color

`ls --color`

In addition to the symbols that are appended to files and folders when you use the -F option, you can also ask your shell to display things in color, which gives an additional way to classify items and tell them

apart. Many Linux installs come with colors already
enabled for shells, but if yours does not, just use the
--color option (I know you can't see the colors, so
just pretend).

```
$ ls --color
adblock_filters.txt    fixm3u          pix2tn.pl
addext                 flash.xml       pop_login
address_book.csv       getip           procmail
address_book.sxc       homesize        programs_kill
address_book.xls       html2text.py    programs_usual
backup_ssh_to_chaucer  list-urls.py    quickrename
```

In this setup, executable files are green, folders are
blue, and normal files are black (which is the default
color for text in my shell). Table 2.2 gives you the full
list of common color associations (but keep in mind
that these colors may vary on your particular distro).

Table 2.2   **Colors and File Types**

Color	Meaning
Default shell text color	Regular file
Green	Executable
Blue	Directory
Magenta	Symbolic link
Yellow	FIFO
Magenta	Socket
Red	Archive (.tar, .zip, .deb, .rpm)
Magenta	Images (.jpg, .gif, .png, .tiff)
Magenta	Audio (.mp3, .ogg, .wav)

TIP: Want to see what colors are mapped to the various kinds of files on your system? Enter `dircolors --print-database`, and then read the results carefully. You can also use the `dircolors` command to change those colors as well.

With the combination of `--color` and `-F`, you can see at a glance what kinds of files you're working with in a directory. Now we're cookin' with gas!

```
$ ls -F --color
adblock_filters.txt     fixm3u*          pix2tn.pl*
addext*                 flash.xml*       pop_login*
address_book.csv        getip*           procmail/
address_book.sxc        homesize*        programs_kill*
address_book.xls        html2text.py*    programs_usual*
backup_ssh_to_chaucer*  list-urls.py*    quickrename*
```

List Permissions, Ownership, and More

```
ls -l
```

You've now learned how to format the results of `ls` to tell you more about the contents of directories, but what about the actual contents themselves? How can you learn more about the files and folders, such as their size, their owners, and who can do what with them? For that information, you need to use the `-l` option (or `--format=long`).

```
$ ls -l ~/bin
total 2951
-rw-r--r--  1 scott scott  15058 2015-10-03 18:49
➥adblock_filters.txt
-rwxr-xr--  1 scott root       33 2015-04-19 09:45
➥addext
-rw-r--r--  1 scott scott  84480 2015-04-19 09:45
➥addressbook.xls
-rwxr--r--  1 scott scott      55 2015-04-19 09:45
➥batchprint_home
drwxr-xr-x  9 scott scott   1080 2015-09-22 14:42
➥bin_on_bacon
-rwxr-xr--  1 scott scott     173 2015-04-19 09:45
➥changeext
-rwxr-xr--  1 scott root      190 2015-04-19 09:45
➥convertsize
drwxr-xr-x  2 scott scott      48 2015-04-19 09:45
➥credentials
[List condensed and edited due to length]
```

The -l option stands for *long*, and as you can see, it
provides a wealth of data about the files found in a
directory. Let's move from right to left and discuss
what you see.

On the farthest right is the easiest item: the name of
the listed item. Want ls to display more about it?
Then add the -F option to -l, like this: ls -lF. Color
is easily available as well, with ls -lF --color.

Moving left, you next see a date and time. This is
when the file was last modified, including the date
(in year-month-day format) and then the time (in
24-hour military time).

Further left is a number that indicates the size of the
item, in bytes. This is a bit tricky with folders—for
instance, the previous readout says that bin_on_bacon
is 1080 bytes, or just a little more than one kilobyte,

yet it contains 887KB of content inside it. The
`credentials` directory, according to `ls -l`, is 48 bytes,
but contains nothing inside it whatsoever! What is
happening?

Remember in Chapter 1, "Things to Know About
Your Command Line," when you learned that
directories are just special files that contain a list of
their contents? In this case, the contents of `credentials`
consists of nothing more than the `..` that all directories
have in order to refer to their parent, so it's a paltry 48
bytes; while `bin_on_bacon` contains information about
more than 30 items, bringing its size up to 1080 bytes.

The next two columns to the left indicate,
respectively, the file's owner and its group. As you can
see in the previous listing, almost every file is owned
by the user `scott` and the group `scott`, except for
`addext` and `convertsize`, which are owned by the user
`scott` and the group `root`.

NOTE: Those permissions need to be changed, which
you'll learn how to do in Chapter 8 (hint: the commands are `chown` and `chgrp`).

The next to last column as you move left contains a
number. If you're examining a file, this number tells
you how many hard links exist for that file (for more,
see Chapter 3's "Create a Link Pointing to Another
File or Directory" section); if it's a directory, it refers
to the number of subdirectories it contains, including
the two hidden pointers `.` (the current directory) and
`..` (the parent directory), which means that even if
there are no subdirectories, you will still see a `2` there.

And now you reach the final item on the left: the actual permissions for each file and directory. This might seem like some arcane code, but it's actually very understandable with just a little knowledge. There are ten items, divided (although it doesn't look that way) into four groups. The first group consists of the first character; the second group contains characters 2 through 4; the third consists of characters 5 through 7; and the fourth and final group is made up of characters 8 through 10. For instance, here's how the permissions for the credentials directory would be split up: d|rwx|r-x|r-x.

That first group tells you what kind of item it is. You've already seen that -F and --color do this in different ways, but so does -l. A d indicates that credentials is a directory, while a - in that first position indicates a file. (Even if the file is executable, ls -l still uses just a -, which means that -F and --color here give you more information.) There are, of course, other options that you might see in that first position, as detailed in Table 2.3.

Table 2.3   **Permission Characters and File Types**

Character	Meaning
-	Regular file
-	Executable
d	Directory
l	Symbolic link
s	Socket
b	Block device
c	Character device
p	Named pipe (AKA FIFO)

TIP: To view a list of files that shows at least one of almost everything listed in Table 2.3, try `ls -l /dev`.

The next nine characters—making up groups two, three, and four—stand for, respectively, the permissions given to the file's owner, the file's group, and all the other users on the system. In the case of `addext`, shown previously, its permissions are `rwxr-xr--`, which means that the owner `scott` has `rwx`, the group (in this case, also `scott`) has `r-x`, and the other users on the box have `r--`. What's that mean?

In each case, `r` means "yes, read is allowed"; `w` means "yes, write is allowed" (with "write" meaning both changing and deleting); and `x` means "yes, execute is allowed." A `-` means "no, do not allow this action." If the `-` is located where an `r` would otherwise show itself, that means "no, read is not allowed." The same holds true for both `w` and `x`.

Looking at `addext` and its permissions of `rwxr-xr--`, it's suddenly clear that the owner (`scott`) can read, write, and execute the file; the members of the group (`root`) can read and execute the file, but not write to it; and everyone else on the machine (often called the "world") can read the file but cannot write to it or run it as a program.

Now that you understand what permissions mean, you'll start to notice that certain combinations seem to appear frequently. For instance, it's common to see `rw-r--r--` for many files, which means that the owner can both read and write to the file, but both the group and world can only read the file. For programs, you'll often see `rwxr-xr-x`, which allows everyone on the computer to read and run the program, but restricts changing the file to its owner.

Directories, however, are a bit different. The permissions of r, w, and x are pretty clear for a file: You can read the file, write (or change) it, or execute it. But how do you execute a directory?

Let's start with the easy one: r. In the case of a directory, r means that the user can list the contents of the directory with the ls command. A w indicates that users can add more files into the directory, rename files that are already there, or delete files that are no longer needed. That brings us to x, which corresponds to the capability to access a directory in order to run commands that access and use files in that directory, or to access subdirectories inside that directory.

As you can see, -l is incredibly powerful all by itself, but it becomes even more useful when combined with other options. You've already learned about -a, which shows all files in a directory, so now it should be obvious what -la would do (or --format=long --all).

```
$ la -la ~/
drwxr-xr-x    2 scott  scott     200 2015-07-28 01:31
➥alias
drwx------    2 root   root       72 2015-09-16 19:14
➥.aptitude
-rw-------    1 scott  scott    8800 2015-10-18 19:55
➥.bash_history
-rw-r--r--    1 scott  scott      69 2015-04-20 11:00
➥.bash_logout
-rw-r--r--    1 scott  scott     428 2015-04-20 11:00
➥.bash_profile
-rw-r--r--    1 scott  scott    4954 2015-09-13 19:46
➥.bashrc
[List condensed and edited due to length]
```

Reverse the Order Contents Are Listed

```
ls -r
```

If you don't like the default alphabetical order that -l uses, you can reverse it by adding -r (or --reverse).

```
$ ls -lar ~/
-rw-r--r--   1 scott  scott   4954 2015-09-13 19:46
➥.bashrc
-rw-r--r--   1 scott  scott    428 2015-04-20 11:00
➥.bash_profile
-rw-r--r--   1 scott  scott     69 2015-04-20 11:00
➥.bash_logout
-rw-------   1 scott  scott   8800 2015-10-18 19:55
➥.bash_history
drwx------   2 root   root     72 2015-09-16 19:14
➥.aptitude
drwxr-xr-x   2 scott  scott    200 2015-07-28 01:31
➥alias
[List condensed and edited due to length]
```

NOTE: Keep in mind that this is -r, not -R. -r means reverse, but -R means recursive. Yes, that is confusing.

When you use -l, the output is sorted alphabetically based on the name of the files and folders; the addition of -r reverses the output, but is still based on the filename. Keep in mind that you can add -r virtually any time you use ls if you want to reverse the default output of the command and options you're inputting.

Sort Contents by Date and Time

```
ls -t
```

Letters are great, but sometimes you need to sort
a directory's contents by date and time. To do so,
use -t (or --sort=time) along with -l; to reverse the
sort, use -tr (or --sort=time --reverse) along with
-l. Using the reverse sort can be pretty handy—the
newer stuff ends up at the bottom, which is easier to
see, because that's where your prompt will be when
the command finishes!

```
$ ls -latr ~/
-rw-------    1 scott scott  8800 2015-10-18 19:55
➥.bash_history
drwx------   15 scott scott  1280 2015-10-18 20:07
➥.opera
drwx------    2 scott scott    80 2015-10-18 20:07
➥.gconfd
drwxr-xr-x    2 scott scott   432 2015-10-18 23:11
➥.qt
drwxr-xr-x  116 scott scott  5680 2015-10-18 23:11 .
drwx------    3 scott scott   368 2015-10-18 23:12
➥.gnupg
drwxr-xr-x   12 scott scott  2760 2015-10-18 23:14
➥bin
drwx------    4 scott scott   168 2015-10-19 00:13
➥.Skype
[list condensed and edited due to length]
```

All of these items except the last one were modified
on the same day; the last one would have been first if
you weren't using the -r option and thereby reversing
the results.

NOTE: Notice that you're using four options at one time in the previous command: `-latr`. You could have instead used `-l -a -t -r`, but who wants to type all of those hyphens and spaces? It's quicker and easier to just combine them all into one giant option. The long version of the options (those that start with two hyphens and consist of a word or two), however, cannot be combined and have to be entered separately, as in `-la --sort=time --reverse`. Note that this technique works with many Linux commands and programs, but not all of them.

Sort Contents by Size

```
ls -S
```

You can also sort by size instead of alphabetically by filename or extension, or by date and time. To sort by size, use `-S` (or `--sort=size`).

```
$ ls -laS ~/
-rw-r--r--   1 scott  scott  109587 2015-10-19 11:53
➥.xsession-errors
-rw-------   1 scott  scott   40122 2015-04-20 11:00
➥.nessusrc
-rw-r--r--   1 scott  scott   24988 2015-04-20 11:00
➥.abbrev_defs
-rwxr--r--   1 scott  scott   15465 2015-10-12 15:45
➥.vimrc
-rw-------   1 scott  scott   11794 2015-10-19 10:59
➥.viminfo
-rw-------   1 scott  scott    8757 2015-10-19 08:43
➥.bash_history
[List condensed and edited due to length]
```

When you sort by size, the largest items come first.
To sort in reverse, with the smallest at the top, just
use -r.

Express File Sizes in Terms of K, M, and G

```
ls -h
```

In the previous section, the 15465 on .vimrc's line
means that the file is about 15KB, but it's not always
convenient to mentally translate bytes into the
equivalent kilobytes, megabytes, or gigabytes. Most
of the time, it's more convenient to use the -h option
(or --human-readable), which makes things easier to
understand.

```
$ ls -laSh ~/
-rw-r--r--    1 scott scott 100K 2015-10-19 11:44
➥.xsession-errors
-rw-------    1 scott scott  40K 2015-04-20 11:00
➥.nessusrc
-rw-r--r--    1 scott scott  25K 2015-04-20 11:00
➥.abbrev_defs
-rwxr--r--    1 scott scott  16K 2015-10-12 15:45
➥.vimrc
-rw-------    1 scott scott  12K 2015-10-19 10:59
➥.viminfo
-rw-------    1 scott scott 8.6K 2015-10-19 08:43
➥.bash_history
[List condensed and edited due to length]
```

In this example, you see k for kilobytes; if the files
were big enough, you'd see m for megabytes or even g
for gigabytes. Some of you might be wondering how
40122 bytes for .nessusrc became 40K when you used

-h. Remember that 1024 bytes make up a kilobyte, so when you divide 40122 by 1024, you get 39.1816406 kilobytes, which `ls -h` rounds up to 40K. A megabyte is actually 1,048,576 bytes, and a gigabyte is 1,073,741,824 bytes, so a similar sort of rounding takes place with those as well. If you want exact powers of ten in your divisions (that is, what are referred to as "kibibytes," "mebibytes," and so on—see Chapter 6, "Viewing (Mostly Text) Files," for more), try the `--si` option.

NOTE: In my `~/.bashrc` file, I have the following aliases defined, which have served me well for years. Use what you've learned in this section to extend these examples and create aliases that exactly meet your needs (for more on aliases, see Chapter 12, "Your Shell").

```
alias l='ls -F'
alias ll='ls -1F'
alias la='ls -aF'
alias ll='ls -laFh'
alias ls='ls -F'
```

Display the Path of Your Current Directory

```
pwd
```

Of course, while you're listing the contents of directories hither and yon, you might find yourself confused about just where you are in the file system. How can you tell in which directory you're currently working? The answer is the `pwd` command, which stands for *print working directory*.

NOTE: The word *print* in *print working directory* means
"print to the screen," not "send to printer."

The pwd command displays the full, absolute path of
the current, or working, directory. It's not something
you'll use all the time, but it can be incredibly handy
when you get a bit discombobulated.

```
$ pwd
/home/scott/music/new
```

There is one thing you should be aware of, however,
and this can really confuse people. In Chapter 3 you're
going to find out about the ln command ("Create
a Link Pointing to Another File or Directory"), so
you might want to skip ahead and read that to fully
understand what I'm about to show you. Assuming
you have, check out the following:

```
# ls -l
lrwxrwxrwx   scott scott   websites -> /var/www/
$ cd websites
$ pwd
/websites
$ pwd -P
/var/www
```

So there's a soft link with a source websites that points
at a target /var/www. I cd using the soft link and enter
pwd. Notice what comes back: the *logical* directory of
/websites, the *source* of the soft link, which isn't the
actual working target directory of /var/www. This is the
default behavior of pwd, equivalent to entering pwd -L
(or --logical).

On the other hand, if you enter pwd -P (or --physical), you instead get back the target of the soft link, which is /var/www.

I don't know about you, but when I use pwd, I usually want to get back the actual physical location (the target), not the logical location (the source). Since I actually prefer the -P option as the default, I like to use an alias in my .bash_aliases file (discussed in Chapter 12's "Create a New Permanent Alias" section) that looks like this:

```
alias pwd="pwd -P"
```

Now you understand not only how to use pwd, but also the gotchas you might run into when you use it.

Change to a Different Directory

`cd`

It's possible to list the contents of any directory simply by specifying its path, but often you actually want to move into a new directory. That's where the cd command comes in, another one that is almost constantly used by shell aficionados.

The cd command is simple to use: Just enter cd, followed by the directory into which you want to move. You can use a relative path, based on where you are currently—cd src or cd ../../—or you can use an absolute path, such as cd /tmp or cd /home/scott/bin.

Change to Your Home Directory

```
cd ~
```

You should know about a few nice shortcuts for cd. No matter where you are, just enter a simple cd, and you'll immediately be whisked back to your home directory. This is a fantastic timesaver, one that you'll use all the time. Or, if you'd like, you can use cd ~ because the ~ is like a shortcut meaning "my home directory."

```
$ pwd
/home/scott/music
$ cd ~
$ pwd
/home/scott
```

Change to Your Previous Directory

```
cd -
```

Another interesting possibility is cd -, which takes you back to your previous directory and then runs the pwd command for you, printing your new (or is it old?) location. It's the shell equivalent of the Back button in a GUI file navigator window. You can see it in action in this example:

```
$ pwd
/home/scott
$ cd music/new
$ pwd
/home/scott/music/new
$ cd -
/home/scott
```

Using cd - can be useful when you want to jump into a directory, perform some action there, and then jump back to your original directory. The additional printing to the screen of the information provided by pwd is just icing on the cake to make sure you're where you want to be.

Conclusion

If this was law school, you would have learned in this chapter what misdemeanors, torts, and felonies are. If this was a hardware repair class, it would have been RAM, hard drives, and motherboards. Since this is a book about the Linux shell, you've examined the most basic commands that a Linux user needs to know to effectively use the command line: ls, pwd, and cd. Now that you know how to get around the file system, it's time to learn about two things that govern the universe: creation and destruction. Now not only will you be observing your environment, you'll be modifying it to your whims. Read on!

## 3

Creation and Destruction

Every culture has stories it tells itself about how things came to be (*cosmogony*) and how things will eventually be destroyed (*eschatology*). For the Norse, this was *Muspellsheimr* and *Niflheimr* at the beginning of time, and *Ragnarok* at the end. For Zoroastrianism, you would read the *Bundahishn* and then read about *frashokereti*. Christians would start with *Genesis* and end with *Revelation*. Linux isn't a religion, but it too enables users to create and to destroy. Read on, and act wisely with your newfound power!

NOTE: When I updated this book for its second edition, I removed the sections about `mkdir -v` (which shows you what `mkdir` is doing as it does it) and `rm -v` (which does the same thing, but for `rm`). You can find the original text on my website, at www.granneman.com/linux-redactions.

Change a File to the Current Time

```
touch
```

The touch command isn't one you'll find yourself using constantly, but you'll need it as you proceed through this book, so it's a good one to cover now. Interestingly, the main reason for the existence of touch—to update the access and modification times of a file—isn't the main reason you'll be using the command. Instead, you're going to rely on its secondary purpose, which undoubtedly gets more use than the primary purpose!

NOTE: You can use the touch command on a file and change the times only if you have write permission for that file. Otherwise, touch fails.

To simultaneously update both the access and modification times for a file (or folder), just run the basic touch command.

```
$ ls -l ~/
drwxr-xr-x  scott scott 2015-10-18 12:07 todo
drwxr-xr-x  scott scott 2015-10-18 12:25 videos
-rw-r--r--  scott scott 2015-09-10 23:12
➥wireless.log
$ touch wireless.log
$ ls -l ~/
drwxr-xr-x  scott scott 2015-10-18 12:07 todo
drwxr-xr-x  scott scott 2015-10-18 12:25 videos
-rw-r--r--  scott scott 2015-10-19 14:00
➥wireless.log
```

Thanks to touch, both the modification time and the access time for the wireless.log file have changed, although ls -l only shows the modification time. The file hadn't been used in more than a month, but touch now updates it, making it look like it was just... touched.

You can be more specific, if you'd like. If you want to change just the access time, use the -a option (or --time=access); to alter the modification time only, use -m (or --time=modify).

Change a File to Any Desired Time

```
touch -t
```

Keep in mind that you aren't constrained to the current date and time. Instead, you can pick whatever date and time you'd like, as long as you use this option and pattern: -t [[CC]YY]MMDDhhmm[.ss]. The pattern is explained in Table 3.1.

Table 3.1   **Patterns for Changing a File's Times**

Characters	Meaning
CC	First two characters of a four-digit year
YY	Two-digit year:
	▪ If 00–68, assumes that first two digits are 20
	▪ If 69–99, assumes that first two digits are 19
	▪ If nothing, assumes current year

Characters	Meaning
MM	Month (01–12)
DD	Day (01–31)
hh	Hour (01–23)
mm	Minute (00–59)
ss	Second (00–59)

It's very important that you include the zeroes if the number you want to use isn't normally two digits or your pattern won't work. Here are a few examples of touch with the -t option in action to help get you started.

```
$ ls -l
-rw-r--r-- scott scott 2015-10-19 14:00 wireless.log
$ touch -t 197002160701 wireless.log
$ ls -l
-rw-r--r-- scott scott 1970-02-16 07:01 wireless.log
$ touch -t 9212310000 wireless.log
$ ls -l
-rw-r--r-- scott scott 1992-12-31 00:00 wireless.log
$ touch -t 3405170234 wireless.log
$ ls -l
-rw-r--r-- 1 scott scott 2034-05-17 02:34
➥wireless.log
$ touch -t 10191703 wireless.log
$ ls -l
-rw-r--r-- scott scott 2015-10-19 17:03 wireless.log
```

First you establish that the current date and time for wireless.log is 2015-10-19 14:00. Then you go back in time quite a ways, to 1970-02-16 07:01, and then forward a bit to 1992-12-31 00:00, and then leap way into the future to 2034-05-17 02:34, when Linux computers will rule the world and humans will live in peace and open-source prosperity, and then finish back in our day and time.

You should draw a couple of lessons from this demonstration. You go back decades in time by specifying the complete four-digit year (1970), the month (02), the day (16), the hour (07), and the minute (01). You don't need to specify seconds. After that, you never specify a four-digit year again. 92 in 9212310000 is within the range of 69–99, so touch assumes you mean 19 as the base century, while 34 in 3405170234 lies between 00 and 68, so 20 is used as the base. The last time touch is used, a year isn't specified at all, just a month (10), a day (19), an hour (17), and minutes (03), so touch knows you mean the current year, 2015. By understanding how to manipulate touch, you can change the date stamps of files when necessary.

Create a New, Empty File

`touch`

But that's not the main reason many people use touch. The touch command has an interesting effect if you try to use it on a file that doesn't exist: It creates an empty file using the name you specified.

```
$ ls -l ~/
drwxr-xr-x scott scott 2015-10-19 11:36 src
drwxr-xr-x scott scott 2015-10-18 12:25 videos
$ touch test.txt
$ ls -l ~/
drwxr-xr-x scott scott 2015-10-19 11:36 src
-rw-r--r-- scott scott 2015-10-19 23:41 test.txt
drwxr-xr-x scott scott 2015-10-18 12:25 videos
```

Why would you use `touch` in this way? Let's say you want to create a file now, and then fill it with content later. Or you need to create several files to perform tests on them as you're playing with a new command you've discovered. Both of those are great reasons, and you'll find others as you start learning more about your shell.

Create a New Directory

`mkdir`

The `touch` command creates empty files, but how do you bring a new folder into existence? With the `mkdir` command, that's how.

```
$ ls -l
drwxr-xr-x scott scott 2015-10-19 11:36 src
drwxr-xr-x scott scott 2015-10-18 12:25
➥videos
$ mkdir test
$ ls -l
drwxr-xr-x scott scott 2015-10-19 11:36 src
drwxr-xr-x scott scott 2015-10-19 23:50
➥test
drwxr-xr-x scott scott 2015-10-18 12:25
➥videos
```

NOTE: On most systems, new directories created by `mkdir` give the owner read, write, and execute permissions, while giving groups and the world read and execute permissions. Want to change those? Look in Chapter 7, "Manipulating Text Files with Filters," at the `chmod` command.

It should make you happy to know that your shell takes care of you: Attempts to create a directory that already exists fail and result in a warning message.

```
$ mkdir test
mkdir: cannot create directory 'test': File exists
```

Create a New Directory and Any Necessary Subdirectories

```
mkdir -p
```

If you want to create a new subdirectory inside a new subdirectory inside a new subdirectory, this seems like a rather tedious task at first: create the first subdirectory, cd into that one, create the second subdirectory, cd into that one, and finally create the third subdirectory. Yuck. Fortunately, mkdir has a wonderful option that makes this whole process much more streamlined: -p (or --parents).

```
$ ls -l
drwxr-xr-x scott scott 2015-10-19 11:36 src
drwxr-xr-x scott scott 2015-10-18 12:25
➥videos
$ mkdir -p pictures/personal/family
$ ls -l
drwxr-xr-x scott scott 2015-10-20 00:12
➥pictures
drwxr-xr-x scott scott 2015-10-19 11:36 src
drwxr-xr-x   6 scott scott   632 2015-10-18 12:25
➥videos
$ cd pictures
$ ls -l
```

```
drwxr-xr-x scott scott 2015-10-20 00:12
➥personal
$ cd personal
$ ls -l
drwxr-xr-x scott scott 2015-10-20 00:12
➥family
```

Copy Files

```
cp
```

Making copies of files is one of those things that computer users, no matter the OS, find themselves doing all the time. One of the most venerable commands used by the Linux shell is cp, which duplicates files and directories. The easiest way to use cp is simply to type in the command, followed by the file you want to copy, and then the copied file's new name; think of the command's structure as cp file-you're-copying-from file-you're-copying-to. Another common way to express that relationship is cp source target.

```
$ pwd
/home/scott/libby
$ ls
libby.jpg
$ cp libby.jpg libby_bak.jpg
$ ls
libby_bak.jpg   libby.jpg
```

This example is pretty simple: The picture is copied into the same directory as the original file. You can also copy files to another directory, or even copy files from a directory in which you're not currently located to another directory located somewhere else on your filesystem.

```
$ ls ~/libby
libby_bak.jpg  libby.jpg
$ cp pictures/dogs/libby_arrowrock.jpg
➥~/libby/libby_arrowrock.jpg
$ ls ~/libby
libby_arrowrock.jpg  libby_bak.jpg  libby.jpg
```

The same filename, libby_arrowrock.jpg, is used in
this example, which is okay because the file is being
copied into another directory entirely. In the first
example for cp, however, you had to use a new name,
libby_bak.jpg instead of libby.jpg, because you were
copying the file into the same directory.

If you want to copy a file from another directory
into your working directory (the one in which
you currently find yourself), simply use . (dot).
(Remember how you learned earlier in this chapter
that . means "the current directory"? Now you see
how that information can come in handy.) Of course,
you can't change the name when you use . because
it's a shortcut for the original filename.

```
$ ls
libby_bak.jpg  libby.jpg
$ cp pictures/dogs/libby_arrowrock.jpg .
$ ls
libby_arrowrock.jpg  libby_bak.jpg  libby.jpg
```

You don't need to specify a filename for the target if
that target file is going to reside in a specific directory;
instead, you can just provide the directory's name.

```
$ ls -l
drwxr-xr-x scott scott 2015-10-18 12:35 iso
drwxr-xr-x scott scott 2015-10-20 12:34 libby
drwxr-xr-x scott scott 2015-09-29 23:17 music
drwxr-xr-x scott scott 2015-10-16 12:34 pictures
$ ls libby
libby_arrowrock.jpg   libby_bak.jpg   libby.jpg
$ cp pictures/dogs/libby_on_couch.jpg libby
$ ls libby
libby_arrowrock.jpg   libby_bak.jpg   libby.jpg
➥libby_on_couch.jpg
```

In the previous example, you need to be certain that a directory named libby already exists for libby_on_couch.jpg to be copied into, or you would have ended up with a file named libby in your home directory.

Copy Files Using Wildcards

cp *

It's time for more laziness, namely, the capability to copy several files at one time into a directory using wildcards. If you've been careful naming your files, this can be a really handy timesaver because you can exactly specify a group of files.

```
$ pwd
/home/scott/libby
$ ls ~/pictures/dogs
libby_arrowrock.jpg   libby_by_pool_03.jpg
➥libby_on_floor_03.jpg
libby_by_pool_01.jpg   libby_on_floor_01.jpg
➥libby_on_floor_04.jpg
libby_by_pool_02.jpg   libby_on_floor_02.jpg
$ ls
```

```
libby_arrowrock.jpg  libby_bak.jpg  libby.jpg
➥libby_on_couch.jpg
$ cp ~/pictures/dogs/libby_by_pool*.jpg .
$ ls
libby_arrowrock.jpg      libby_by_pool_02.jpg
➥libby_on_couch.jpg
libby_bak.jpg            libby_by_pool_03.jpg
libby_by_pool_01.jpg     libby.jpg
```

You aren't limited to the * wildcard; instead, you can
more precisely identify which files you want to copy
using a bracket that matches any characters named
between the [and] characters. If you want to copy
the first three libby_on_floor pictures but not the
fourth, that's easily done.

```
$ pwd
/home/scott/libby
$ ls ~/pictures/dogs
libby_arrowrock.jpg      libby_by_pool_03.jpg
➥libby_on_floor_03.jpg
libby_by_pool_01.jpg     libby_on_floor_01.jpg
➥libby_on_floor_04.jpg
libby_by_pool_02.jpg     libby_on_floor_02.jpg
$ ls
libby_arrowrock.jpg  libby_bak.jpg  libby.jpg
➥libby_on_couch.jpg
$ cp ~/pictures/dogs/libby_on_floor_0[1-3].jpg .
$ ls
libby_arrowrock.jpg      libby_on_couch.jpg
➥libby_on_floor_03.jpg
libby_bak.jpg            libby_on_floor_01.jpg
libby.jpg                libby_on_floor_02.jpg
```

Copy Files Verbosely

`cp -v`

Adding the -v option (or --verbose) shows you the progress of cp as it completes its work.

```
$ pwd
/home/scott/libby
$ ls ~/pictures/dogs
libby_arrowrock.jpg    libby_by_pool_03.jpg
➥libby_on_floor_03.jpg
libby_by_pool_01.jpg   libby_on_floor_01.jpg
➥libby_on_floor_04.jpg
libby_by_pool_02.jpg   libby_on_floor_02.jpg
$ ls
libby_arrowrock.jpg    libby_bak.jpg    libby.jpg
➥libby_on_couch.jpg
$ cp -v ~/pictures/dogs/libby_on_floor_0[1-3].jpg .
'/home/scott/pictures/dogs/libby_on_floor_01.jpg' ->
➥'./libby_on_floor_01.jpg'
'/home/ scott /pictures/dogs/libby_on_floor_02.jpg'
➥-> './libby_on_floor_02.jpg'
'/home/ scott /pictures/dogs/libby_on_floor_03.jpg'
➥-> './libby_on_floor_03.jpg'
$ ls
libby_arrowrock.jpg   libby_on_couch.jpg
➥libby_on_floor_03.jpg
libby_bak.jpg         libby_on_floor_01.jpg
libby.jpg             libby_on_floor_02.jpg
```

The -v option does a nice job of keeping you abreast of the cp command's progress. It does such a good job that you really don't need to run that last ls command because the -v option assures you that the files you wanted were in fact copied.

NOTE: As you start to get more experienced with the Linux command line, you'll find that `-v` is often used with programs to mean *verbose*. In fact, the more you use commands, the more you'll start to notice a similar consistency with other options. See, memorizing commands isn't *that* hard!

Stop Yourself from Copying over Important Files

```
cp -i
```

The previous example demonstrates something important about `cp` that you need to know. In the "Copy Files Using Wildcards" example, you copied three `libby_on_floor` pictures into the `libby` directory; in the previous example, you copied the same three `libby_on_floor` images into the `libby` directory again. You copied over files that already existed, but `cp` didn't warn you, which is how Linux works: It assumes you know what you're doing, so it doesn't warn you about things like overwriting your files...unless you ask it to do so. If you want to be forewarned before overwriting a file using the `cp` command, use the `-i` option (or `--interactive`). If you tried once again to copy the same files but used the `-i` option this time, you'd get a different result.

```
$ pwd
/home/scott/libby
$ ls ~/pictures/dogs
libby_arrowrock.jpg    libby_by_pool_03.jpg
➥libby_on_floor_03.jpg
libby_by_pool_01.jpg   libby_on_floor_01.jpg
```

```
➥libby_on_floor_04.jpg
libby_by_pool_02.jpg    libby_on_floor_02.jpg
$ ls
libby_arrowrock.jpg    libby_bak.jpg    libby.jpg
➥libby_on_couch.jpg
$ cp -i ~/pictures/dogs/libby_on_floor_0[1-3].jpg .
cp: overwrite './libby_on_floor_01.jpg'?
```

Bam! The cp command stops in its tracks to ask you if you want to overwrite the first file it's trying to copy, libby_on_floor_01.jpg. If you want to go ahead and copy the file, enter y; otherwise, enter n. If you do choose n, that doesn't mean the cp stops completely; instead, you're asked about the next file, and the next, and so on. The only way to give an n to the whole process is to cancel it by pressing Ctrl+C. Similarly, there's no way to say yes to every question ahead of time, so if you want to copy 1,000 files over 1,000 other files with the same names and also intend to use the -i option, make sure you have plenty of time to sit and interact with your shell, because you're going to get asked identical questions 1,000 times. It'll be like you're talking to your 3-year-old!

CAUTION: For normal users, -i usually isn't necessary. For root users, however, it's darn near essential, as a root user can errantly copy over a key system file, causing a disaster. For that reason, it's a good idea to create an alias in the root user's .bashrc file, making sure that cp is really cp -i instead.

```
alias cp='cp -i'
```

Copy Directories

`cp -r`

So far you've looked at copying files, but there are
times you'll want to copy directories as well. You
can't just enter cp source-directory target-directory,
though, because that won't work as you expected; the
directory will copy, but not the files inside it.

```
$ pwd
/home/scott
$ cp libby libby_bak
cp: omitting directory 'libby'
```

If you want to copy directories, you need to include
the -r option (or -R or --recursive), which you should
recall from the ls command. The addition of -r means
that the directory, as well as its contents, are copied.

```
$ pwd
/home/scott
$ ls -l
drwxr-xr-x scott scott 2015-10-17 14:42
➥documents
drwxr-xr-x scott scott 2015-10-18 12:35 iso
drwxr-xr-x scott scott 2015-10-20 17:16
➥libby
$ ls libby
libby_arrowrock.jpg  libby_on_couch.jpg
➥libby_on_floor_03.jpg
libby_bak.jpg         libby_on_floor_01.jpg
libby.jpg             libby_on_floor_02.jpg
$ cp -R libby libby_bak
$ ls -l
drwxr-xr-x scott scott 2015-10-17 14:42
➥documents
```

```
drwxr-xr-x  scott  scott  2015-10-18  12:35  iso
drwxr-xr-x  scott  scott  2015-10-20  17:16
➥libby
drwxr-xr-x  scott  scott  2015-10-20  17:17
➥libby_bak
```

Copy Files As Perfect Backups in Another Directory

```
cp -a
```

You might be thinking right now that cp would be useful for backing up files, and that is certainly true (although better programs exist, and we'll take a look at one of them—rsync—in Chapter 16, "Working on the Network"). With a few lines in a bash shell script, however, cp can be an effective way to back up various files and directories. The most useful option in this case would be the -a option (or --archive), which is also equivalent to combining several options: -dpr (or --no-dereference --preserve --recursive). Another way of thinking about it is that -a ensures that cp doesn't follow soft links (which could grossly balloon your copy), preserves key file attributes such as owner and timestamp, and recursively follows subdirectories.

```
$ pwd
/home/scott
$ ls -l
drwxr-xr-x  scott  scott  2015-10-21  11:31  libby
drwxr-xr-x  scott  scott  2015-09-29  23:17  music
$ ls -lR libby
libby:
total 312
```

```
-rw-r--r-- scott scott 2015-10-20 12:12
➥libby_arrowrock.jpg
-rw-r--r-- scott scott 2015-04-19 00:57 libby.jpg
drwxr-xr-x scott scott 2015-10-21 11:31 on_floor

libby/on_floor:
total 764
-rw-r--r-- scott scott 2015-10-20 16:11
➥libby_on_floor_01.jpg
-rw-r--r-- scott scott 2015-10-20 16:11
➥libby_on_floor_02.jpg
$ cp -a libby libby_bak
$ ls -l
drwxr-xr-x scott scott 2015-10-21 11:31 libby/
drwxr-xr-x scott scott 2015-10-21 11:31 libby_bak/
drwxr-xr-x scott scott 2015-09-29 23:17 music/
$ ls -lR libby_bak
libby_bak/:
total 312
-rw-r--r-- scott scott 2015-10-20 12:12
➥libby_arrowrock.jpg
-rw-r--r-- scott scott 2015-04-19 00:57 libby.jpg
drwxr-xr-x scott scott 2015-10-21 11:31 on_floor

libby_bak/on_floor:
total 764
-rw-r--r-- scott scott 218849 2015-10-20 16:11
➥libby_on_floor_01.jpg
-rw-r--r-- scott scott 200024 2015-10-20 16:11
➥libby_on_floor_02.jpg
```

NOTE: Yes, you've probably figured it out already, but let me confirm: Libby was my dog, a cute lil' shih-tzu who eventually ended up in some way or another in almost everything I wrote. She shuffled off this mortal coil in August of 2015.

Move Files and Folders

`mv`

So cp copies files. That seems simple enough, but what about moving files (or folders)? In the similar vein of removing unnecessary vowels in commands, we have the mv command, short for *move*.

At its simplest, mv moves a file from one location to another on your filesystem.

```
$ pwd
/home/scott/libby
$ ls
libby_arrowrock.jpg  libby_bak.jpg  libby.jpg
libby_on_couch.jpg  on_floor
$ ls ~/pictures/dogs
libby_on_floor_01.jpg  libby_on_floor_03.jpg
libby_on_floor_02.jpg  libby_on_floor_04.jpg
$ mv ~/pictures/dogs/libby_on_floor_04.jpg
libby_on_floor_04.jpg
$ ls
libby_arrowrock.jpg libby.jpg
libby_on_floor_04.jpg
libby_bak.jpg        libby_on_couch.jpg on_floor
$ ls ~/pictures/dogs
libby_on_floor_01.jpg  libby_on_floor_02.jpg
libby_on_floor_03.jpg
```

Just as you did with cp, you can use a dot to represent the current directory if you don't feel like typing out the filename again.

```
$ pwd
/home/scott/libby
$ ls
libby_arrowrock.jpg  libby_bak.jpg  libby.jpg
➥libby_on_couch.jpg  on_floor
$ ls ~/pictures/dogs
libby_on_floor_01.jpg  libby_on_floor_03.jpg
libby_on_floor_02.jpg  libby_on_floor_04.jpg
$ mv ~/pictures/dogs/libby_on_floor_04.jpg .
$ ls
libby_arrowrock.jpg libby.jpg
➥libby_on_floor_04.jpg
libby_bak.jpg        libby_on_couch.jpg on_floor
$ ls ~/pictures/dogs
libby_on_floor_01.jpg  libby_on_floor_02.jpg
➥libby_on_floor_03.jpg
```

If you're moving a file into a directory and you want
to keep the same filename, you just need to specify
the directory. The filename stays the same.

```
$ pwd
/home/scott/libby
$ ls
libby_arrowrock.jpg libby.jpg
➥libby_on_floor_04.jpg
libby_bak.jpg        libby_on_couch.jpg on_floor
$ ls on_floor
libby_on_floor_01.jpg libby_on_floor_02.jpg
➥libby_on_floor_03.jpg
$ mv libby_on_floor_04.jpg on_floor
$ ls
libby_arrowrock.jpg libby_bak.jpg libby.jpg
➥libby_on_couch.jpg on_floor
$ ls on_floor
libby_on_floor_01.jpg  libby_on_floor_03.jpg
libby_on_floor_02.jpg  libby_on_floor_04.jpg
```

To visually communicate that on_floor is in fact a directory, it's a good idea to use a / at the end of the directory into which you're moving files, like this: mv libby_on_floor_04.jpg on_floor/. If on_floor is not a directory, your mv won't work, thus preventing you from accidentally writing over a file.

NOTE: The cp and mv commands use many of the same options, which work the same way for either command. For instance, -v copies and moves verbosely, and -i copies and moves interactively.

Rename Files and Folders

```
mv
```

As you'll soon see, however, mv does something more than move, something that might seem a bit counterintuitive, but which makes perfect sense after you think about it a moment.

At this point, it's a good idea to introduce the other cool feature of mv. Yes, mv moves files—that's its name, after all—but it also renames files. If you move a file, you have to give it a target name. There's no rule that the target name has to be the same as the source name, so shell users since time immemorial have relied on the mv command to rename files and directories.

```
$ pwd
/home/scott/libby/by_pool
$ ls -F
libby_by_pool_02.jpg  liebermans/
$ mv liebermans/ lieberman_pool/
$ ls -F
libby_by_pool_02.jpg  lieberman_pool/
```

When moving a directory using `cp`, you had to specify the `-r` option in order to copy the actual directory itself. Not so with `mv`, which, as you can see in the previous example, happily moves or renames directories without the need for any extra option at all, a nice change from `cp`. This is because `mv` is fundamentally a much more lightweight command than `cp`; it isn't creating any new files or rearranging them to a new location on disk (unless you're actually moving from one filesystem or partition to another); all it does is change the name of the single file or directory you specify.

CAUTION: You need to know a very important, and unfortunately easy to overlook, detail about `mv`. If you are moving a soft link that points to a directory, you need to be extremely careful about what you type. Let's say you have a soft link named dogs in your home directory that points to `/home/scott/pictures/dogs`, and you want to move the link into the `/home/scott/libby` subdirectory. This command moves just the soft link:

```
$ mv dogs ~/libby
```

This command, however, moves the directory to which the soft link points:

```
$ mv dogs/ ~/libby
```

What was the difference? A simple forward slash at the end of the soft link. No forward slash and you're moving the soft link itself, and just the link; include a forward slash and you're moving the directory to which the soft link is designed to point, not the soft link. Be careful!

Understand How Linux Stores Files

The next section introduces the `ln`, or *link*, command. Before we can look at how links work, however, we first need a short detour into how Linux stores files on a computer. Back in Chapter 1, "Things to Know About Your Command Line," there was a section titled "Everything Is a File," and that's still true. But let's complicate that just a bit.

Everything is a file, but what makes a file a file? I realize this is starting to get ontological, but hang in there with me. It turns out that what you see as a file is really a pointer to an *inode*: a data structure that stores information about where the physical data is actually located on your computer, and also metadata about that data, such as file type, size, modification time, ownership, permissions, and more (see Chapters 2, "Navigating Your File System," and 8, "Ownerships and Permissions," for more on those). When you create a file, it is assigned a unique inode number by your filesystem and a name by you, both of which are stored in a table of inodes on your drive. Refer to a file by its name, and Linux uses that name to look up the inode associated with it; once Linux has the info stored in the inode, it can act on the file.

If you want to see the inode number associated with a file, use the `ls -i` command:

```
$ ls -i
49889 backup_daily.sh
49796 dotfiles/
49795 dotfiles.sh
49886 extra/
49291 wp_upgrade.sh
```

See the numbers to the left of the files and directories? Those are the inode numbers. Notice that directories also have inode numbers. Why? Back in Chapter 1, I told you: "But what about a directory? It's a file, too—a special kind of file that contains information about other files." Now you know what that really means: A directory or folder is a file (with its own inode) that associates the files inside with their inodes.

Most filesystems create a fixed number of inodes, so theoretically you could have plenty of drive space but be prevented from creating any more files because you're out of inodes (it's extremely rare, but yes, I managed to do this one time). If you want to know more about how many inodes your filesystem has and how many you have left, use the df command from Chapter 13, "Monitoring System Resources," but use the -h (for human readable) and -i (or --inodes) options, and you'll see something like this:

```
# df -h
Filesystem   Size  Used Avail Use% Mounted on
/dev/sda     4.9G  742M  4.1G  16% /
none         396M  308K  395M   1% /run
/dev/sdb      42G   33G  8.8G  79% /var
$ df -i
Filesystem    Inodes   IUsed   IFree IUse% Mounted on
/dev/sda      327680   40627  287053   13% /
none          505701     826  504875    1% /run
/dev/sdb     2785280  706754 2078526   26% /var
```

So, for instance, you can see that /var has used 79% of its space, but only 26% of its available inodes. Need to create a bunch of small files? Go right ahead!

Now that you know what inodes are, let's continue to the ln command.

Create a Link Pointing to Another File or Directory

```
ln
```

Sometimes it would be nice to have the same file in two or more places at the same time, or have more than one way to refer to a file or directory. When you want to do that, you want to use the `ln` command, which is short for *link*.

There are two kinds of links: *hard* (which is the default) and *soft* (which is the one you will probably find yourself using most often). They are actually quite different from each other, as you will see.

If you haven't already, go read the previous section, because you're going to need to know what an inode is in order to understand this section. I'll wait... oh, you're back? Now that we know about inodes and why they're important, let's take a look at some of the characteristics of hard links. To create a hard link, you use `ln original-file link-name`, but that's just a start.

```
$ ls -l
drwxr-xr-x 2 root root 4096 melville/
-rw-r--r-- 1 root root   16 moby_dick.txt
$ cat moby_dick.txt
Call my Ishmael
$ ln moby_dick.txt white_whale.txt
$ ls -l
drwxr-xr-x 2 root root 4096 melville/
-rw-r--r-- 2 root root   16 moby_dick.txt
-rw-r--r-- 2 root root   16 white_whale.txt
$ ls -i
40966 melville/
25689 moby_dick.txt
```

```
25689 white_whale.txt
$ cat white_whale.txt
Call my Ishmael
```

To start with, we have a directory named melville and a text file named moby_dick.txt with the words "Call my Ishmael" in it (I know, I know... calm down, *Moby-Dick* readers). I next use the ln command with the file we're linking from first, and then the hard link name after that. Notice that when I run ls -l again, both the file and the hard link are exactly the same size, and also notice that the number 1 in the results for moby_dick.txt in the first ls changes to the number 2 in the second ls. Why? Because that number shows how many hard links there are for the file (that number has nothing to with directories and inodes because, as I mentioned in Chapter 2, that number in the case of a directory tells you how many subdirectories there are). 1 means that the file exists, since there has to be at least *one* link between the file and its inode. When you create a new hard link, the number increments by 1, and when you delete a link, it decrements by 1. In fact, that's what using rm, introduced in the next section, really does: It severs the link between the file and its inode; when you're down to 1 and you rm the file, it's finally gone.

NOTE: Another way to remove a link is via the unlink command: unlink moby_dick.txt. If you're paying attention, you might notice that I've just used unlink to remove the original file. That's perfectly okay, because white_whale.txt will still work just fine, since it's pointing to the exact same inode and therefore the same data.

Getting back to the previous example, when I run `ls -i` to see the inode numbers of the files, `moby_dick.txt` (the original file) and `white_whale.txt` (the hard link) have the same inode number: `25689`. Finally, when I run `cat white_whale.txt`, it has the same text as in `moby_dick.txt`. From all of this, you can see that `moby_dick.txt` and `white_whale.txt` are in reality the same file! But wait—there's more!

```
$ echo "Call me Ishmael" > white_whale.txt
$ cat white_whale.txt
Call me Ishmael
$ cat moby_dick.txt
Call me Ishmael
$ mv moby_dick.txt moby-dick.txt
$ cat while_whale.txt
Call me Ishmael
$ mv moby-dick.txt melville/
$ cat white_whale.txt
Call me Ishmael
```

Now I realize that the first line of *Moby-Dick* is "Call me Ishmael," not "Call my Ishmael." I use the `echo` command (which spits back what I enter) and then redirect the output (see Chapter 5's "Redirect a Command's Output to a File") to the hard link, `white_whale.txt`. When I `cat` both files, they have the same content, proving again that they're really the same file, and that it doesn't matter which one you alter now, because you're really only working with the same data.

And one more interesting thing—if you rename the original file using the `mv` command (see earlier in this chapter), the link still works. Why? Because it's the same inode, pointing to the same data on disk. And if you use mv to actually move the file to a new location, again, the link still works and shows the same content. Why? See the previous answer!

Still, as powerful as hard links are, they have a few limitations. The biggie is that you cannot make a hard link to a directory, no way, no how (for that, use a soft link, explained next). Another is that the hard link and the original file have to both be on the same filesystem, so you can't have a file on one partition and a hard link on a different partition (remember, each partition has its own inodes!). If you try that, you get the "Invalid cross-device link" error message.

You now know about how a hard link works, so what about its cousin, the soft link? To create a soft link (also known as a *symbolic link* or *symlink*), you use the same syntax as before, but you add the -s option, like this: ln -s original-file link-name. Let's take a look at one of my servers, and then I'll explain what you see:

```
$ ls -l /
drwxr-xr-x 98 4096 etc/
drwxr-xr-x  2 4096 home/
lrwxrwxrwx  1   28 mb -> /var/shared/multiblog/
lrwxrwxrwx  1   18 shared -> /var/shared/
drwxr-xr-x 17 4096 var/
lrwxrwxrwx  1   12 webconf -> /etc/apache2/
lrwxrwxrwx  1    8 www -> /var/www/
[Listing truncated due to length]
```

This is a partial listing of that server's root directory, which happens to contain four soft links: mb, shared, webconf, and www. My partners and I got tired of SSH-ing into the server and then typing, for instance, cd /var/www, so we created a soft link called www that points there (yes, I know that seems silly, but if you had to do it repeatedly, you'd get tired of it, too!). We could have done that in several ways. Here's the first:

```
$ sudo ln -s /var/www /www
```

In the previous example, I'm using absolute paths to create a soft link at /www that points to /var/www (I'm using sudo because a normal user can't create links, or anything else, in /). The advantage to this method is that I can be anywhere on the system and create the link, since I'm using absolute paths. But what if I'm feeling a bit lazier?

```
$ cd /
$ sudo ln -s /var/www .
```

In the previous example, I cd to the directory in which I want to create the soft link, and then I create it, but instead of a link name, I just put a . (dot), which tells ln that I want the link name to be the same as the file or folder to which I'm linking. In this example, then, the name of the soft link will be www, because that's the last thing in the original path. That's lazy (which, remember, is good!). But what if I'm feeling a bit lazier?

```
$ cd /
$ sudo ln -s /var/www
```

In the previous example, I cd to the directory in which I want to create the soft link, and then I create it, but instead of a link name, I don't put anything at all. This actually tells ln that I want the link name to be the same as the file or folder to which I'm linking.

In this example, just like the previous one, the name of the soft link will be www, because that's the last component of the original path. Now *that* is lazy!

No matter how you created it, a soft link works like the file or folder it links to (pwd and pwd -P are discussed in Chapter 2's "Display the Path of Your Current Directory").

```
$ pwd
/home/scott
$ ln -s /var/www
$ ls -l
lrwxrwxrwx  1  8  www -> /var/www/
$ cd www
$ pwd -P
/var/www
$ ls -l
lrwxrwxrwx  1  8  notes -> /home/scott/notes.txt
$ cat notes
Notes about websites go here.
```

The first soft link I create points to a directory, and when I cd into that soft link, I am actually ending up in the directory to which I was pointing. After that, I cat a soft link that points to a file, and I see the contents of the file to which I was pointing. If I were to open the soft link in an editor, I would actually be changing the content of the original file.

So now you know how to create soft links and how they work, but how are soft links different from hard links? Oh, in many ways! Let's start by looking at the results of some ls commands, and please assume that the directory in which we're looking has both hard and soft links in it.

```
$ ls -l
-rw-r--r--  2 moby_dick.txt
lrwxrwxrwx 12 webconf -> /etc/apache2/
-rw-r--r--  2 white_whale.txt
$ ls -i
25689 moby_dick.txt
25372 webconf
25689 white_whale.txt
$ ls -i /etc
59948 apache2/
```

Let's start with what we can see using ls -l. The first column shows l (short for *link*) if it's a soft link, but a - (representing a "normal" file) if it's a hard link. Why? Because to your filesystem, hard links are just normal files that share inodes. The other thing you should see is that ls -l shows a pointer to the file or folder to which the soft link is directed, which is really handy. This doesn't make sense for a hard link, because both the original file and any hard links to it are really the same thing. They're identical as far as the operating system is concerned, and there is no distinction between the "original" and any additional links to it. Further, while a soft link can only point to one file or folder, you can have lots of hard links for the same file, so to which one would it point? That's right—it would be a mess, so it doesn't even try.

The second command—ls -i—also shows some key differences between hard and soft links. Hard links have the same inode numbers, of course, but soft links and the files to which they point have different numbers, because they are completely different files. Unlike hard links, which are really the exact same files, soft links use a name to point to files and directories, and the file with that name has its own inode. In other words, a soft link has its own inode that points to the inode of the original file, which then points at the actual data on your drive!

A few more differences: A biggie is that soft links can point to files or folders, while hard links can only point to files. Unlike a hard link, a soft link and the file to which it points do not have to be on the same filesystem. If you delete or move the original file, the soft link breaks, but you can always change the name of the soft link without any problem. Table 3.2 compares and contrasts hard and soft links to help bring out what makes each one special.

Table 3.2 **Hard and Soft Links**

Type	Hard	Soft
Link points to	Inode	Name
Link to directory	No	Yes
Link across filesystems	No	Yes
Source file moved	Link works	Link broken
Target's name changed	Link works	Link broken
Link deleted	Target still exists*	Target still exists
Link's inode	Same as target's	Different from target's
Storage space	Nil	~4 KB

* Unless it was the last link deleted, or a running process has the file open.

Hard links and soft links both have their purpose, and they can be wonderfully useful when you need them. Link away!

Delete Files

`rm`

The `rm` command (short for *remove*) deletes files. It really, really removes them. They're gone. There's no trash can or recycle bin on the Linux command line. You're walking a tightrope, baby, and if you fall, you go splat!

Okay, that's a little extreme. It's true that the shell lacks an undelete command, but you're not completely hosed if you delete a file. *If* you stop working on your machine the second you realize your mistake, *if* the operating system hasn't overwritten the erased file's sectors, and *if* you can successfully use some rather complicated file recovery software, yes, it's possible to recover files. But it's no fun, and you'll be cursing the whole time. Better to just be careful in the first place.

TIP: Many folks have tried to provide some sort of safety net for `rm`, ranging from remapping or replacing the `rm` command to a temporary trash can (http://blogs.adobe.com/cantrell/archives/2012/03/stop-using-rm-on-the-command-line-before-its-too-late.html) to creating a new command, `trash`, to replace `rm` (https://github.com/andreafrancia/trash-cli).

If, on the other hand, you want to make positively sure that no one can possibly recover your deleted files, even men in black working for shadowy U.S. government agencies, use the `shred` command instead of `rm`. The `shred` command overwrites the file 25 times (which is adjustable by using the `-n #` option) so it is impossible to re-create it. Before using `shred`, however, read its `man` page, as its success rate is highly dependent on the type of filesystem you're using.

Using rm is easy. Some would say almost too easy.

```
$ pwd
/home/scott/libby/by_pool/lieberman_pool
$ ls
libby_by_pool_01.jpg        libby_by_pool_03.jpg
libby_by_pool_01.jpg_bak    libby_by_pool_03.jpg_bak
$ rm libby_by_pool_01.jpg_bak
$ ls
libby_by_pool_01.jpg  libby_by_pool_03.jpg
➥libby_by_pool_03.jpg_bak
```

Remove Several Files at Once with Wildcards

```
rm *
```

Wildcards such as * help to delete several files with one keystroke. But be careful—you could obliterate a lot of important stuff very easily!

```
$ pwd
/home/scott/libby/by_pool/lieberman_pool
$ ls
libby_by_pool_01.jpg        libby_by_pool_03.jpg
libby_by_pool_01.jpg_bak    libby_by_pool_03.jpg_bak
$ rm *_bak
$ ls
libby_by_pool_01.jpg  libby_by_pool_03.jpg
```

CAUTION: Be very, very, very careful when removing files using wildcards, or you may delete far more than you intended! A classic example is typing `rm * txt` instead of typing `rm *txt` (see the errant space in the first one?). Instead of deleting all text files (which the second one does), the star means that all files were deleted, and then `rm` tries to delete a file named `txt`. Oops!

Prevent Yourself from Deleting Key Files

```
rm -i
```

The `-i` option (or `--interactive`) provides a kind of safety net. It asks you for confirmation before deleting every file. This is a good thing to use while you're running as `root`! If fact, many sysadmins alias `rm` to `rm -i` for this very reason, and it's a darn good—and safe—idea.

```
$ pwd
/home/scott/libby/by_pool/lieberman_pool
$ ls
libby_by_pool_01.jpg       libby_by_pool_03.jpg
libby_by_pool_01.jpg_bak   libby_by_pool_03.jpg_bak
$ rm -i *_bak
rm: remove regular file 'libby_by_pool_01.jpg_bak'?
➥y
rm: remove regular file 'libby_by_pool_03.jpg_bak'?
➥y
$ ls
libby_by_pool_01.jpg   libby_by_pool_03.jpg
```

When rm asks you what to do, a y is an agreement to nuke the file, and an n is an order to spare the file and continue onward to the next file.

Delete an Empty Directory

```
rmdir
```

Removing files isn't hard at all, but what about directories?

```
$ pwd
/home/scott/libby/by_pool
$ ls
libby_by_pool_02.jpg  lieberman_pool
➥lieberman_pool_bak
$ ls lieberman_pool_bak
libby_by_pool_01.jpg      libby_by_pool_03.jpg
libby_by_pool_01.jpg_bak  libby_by_pool_03.jpg_bak
$ rm lieberman_pool_bak
rm: cannot remove 'lieberman_pool_bak/':
➥Is a directory
```

After a few moments of looking around, you might find the rmdir command, which is specifically designed for deleting directories. So you try it.

```
$ rmdir lieberman_pool_bak
rmdir: 'lieberman_pool_bak/': Directory not empty
```

Dang it! That doesn't work either. The rmdir command only deletes empty directories. In this case, the lieberman_pool_bak folder only contains four items, so it wouldn't be too hard to get rid of them with rm lieberman_pool_bak/* and then use rmdir. But what if you want to delete a directory that

contains 10 subdirectories that each contain 10 more
subdirectories, and every single subdirectory contains
25 files? You're going to be deleting forever. There
has to be an easier way! For that, see the next section.

Remove Files and Directories
That Aren't Empty

```
rm -rf
```

There is an easier way to remove directories with files.
Use the combination of the -r (or -R or --recursive)
and -f (or --force) options. The -r tells rm to go
down into every subdirectory it finds and delete
everything, while the -f tells rm to just do it without
bothering you with the niceties, such as folders that
aren't empty.

```
$ pwd
/home/scott/libby/by_pool
$ ls
libby_by_pool_02.jpg   lieberman_pool
➥lieberman_pool_bak
$ ls lieberman_pool_bak
libby_by_pool_01.jpg       libby_by_pool_03.jpg
libby_by_pool_01.jpg_bak   libby_by_pool_03.jpg_bak
$ rm -rf lieberman_pool_bak
$ ls
libby_by_pool_02.jpg   lieberman_pool
```

Pow! That's a sure-fire way to get rid of a directory
and all the files and subdirectories inside it.

CAUTION: The `rm -rf` command can destroy your important files and your system. Double-check what you're deleting before you use `rm -rf`!

The classic Linux warning is not to type `rm -rf /*` as `root`. Yes, you will erase your system. No, it will not be pretty. Yes, you will feel stupid.

In general, be careful when using wildcards with `rm -rf`. There's a huge difference between `rm -rf libby*` and `rm -rf libby *`. The former deletes everything in the working directory that begins with `libby`; the latter deletes any file or folder named exactly `libby`, and then deletes *everything else* in the directory.

You can also inadvertently create a disaster if you mean to enter `rm -rf ~/libby/*` and instead fat finger your command and tell the shell `rm -rf ~/libby /*`. First the `~/libby` directory leaves, and then it starts in on the filesystem root, `/`—upon which your system begins its rapid journey toward nonexistence.

Here's one that's bitten a few folks trying to be clever: Never type `rm -rf .*/*` to delete a directory that begins with . (dot) because you'll also match .. and end up deleting everything above your current working folder as well. Oops!

Once again: Be careful using `rm -rf` when you're a normal user. Be hypervigilant and paranoid when using `rm -rf` as `root`!

Deleting Troublesome Files

Before leaving `rm`, you should know a couple of things about its relationship to certain files on your system. First, no matter how hard you try, you will not be able to remove the . or .. directories because they are required to keep your filesystem hierarchy in place. Besides, why would you want to remove them? Leave 'em alone!

How do you remove a file with a space in it? The normal way of invoking rm—the command, followed by the filename—won't work because rm thinks you're talking about two different files. Actually, removing Cousin Harold's picture isn't too hard. Just put the name of the file in quotation marks.

```
$ ls
cousin harold.jpg  -cousin_roy.jpg  cousin_beth.jpg
$ rm cousin harold.jpg
rm: cannot remove 'cousin': No such file or
➥directory
rm: cannot remove 'harold.jpg': No such file or
➥directory
$ rm "cousin harold.jpg"
$ ls
-cousin_roy.jpg  cousin_beth.jpg
```

Here's more of a head-scratcher: How do you remove a file whose name starts with -?

```
$ ls
-cousin_roy.jpg  cousin_beth.jpg
$ rm -cousin_roy.jpg
rm: invalid option -- c
Try 'rm --help' for more information.
```

D'oh! The rm command sees the - and thinks it's the start of an option, but it doesn't recognize an option that starts with c. It continues with ousin_roy.jpg and doesn't know what to do.

You have two solutions. You can preface the problematic filename with --, which indicates to the command that anything coming afterward should not be taken as an option, and is instead a file or folder.

```
$ ls
-cousin_roy.jpg  cousin_beth.jpg
$ rm -- -cousin_roy.jpg
$ ls
cousin_beth.jpg
```

Otherwise, you can use the . as part of your pathname, thus bypassing the space before the - that confuses the rm command and leads it into thinking the filename is actually an option.

```
$ ls
-cousin_roy.jpg  cousin_beth.jpg
$ rm ./-cousin_roy.jpg
$ ls
cousin_beth.jpg
```

It just goes to show that the ingenuity of Linux users runs deep. That, and try not to put a hyphen at the beginning of your filename!

Conclusion

This chapter reminds me of my 6-year-old son: He loves to build fantastic creatures out of his Legos and give them all crazy names, but soon enough, he demolishes them while laughing in glee. Likewise, we learned how to create files and directories (touch, mkdir, and cp), change their location or name (mv), create links to them (ln), and finally destroy them (rm and rmdir). With these vital commands under your belt, you're ready to move ahead to learning about how to learn about commands. Sound twisty? You ain't seen nothin' yet.

## 4

Learning About Commands

In Chapter 2, "Navigating Your File System," you started learning about some basic system commands. You covered a lot, but even so, much was left out. The ls command is an incredibly rich, powerful tool, with far more options than were provided in Chapter 2. So how can you learn more about that command or others that pique your interest? And how can you discover commands if you don't even know their names? That's where this chapter comes in. Here you will find out how to learn more about the commands you already know, those you know you don't know, and even those that you don't know that you don't know!

Let's start with the two 800-pound gorillas—man and info—and move from there to some smaller, more precise commands that actually use much of the data collected by man. By the time you're finished, you'll be ready to start learning about the huge variety of tools available to you in your shell environment.

NOTE: When I updated this book for its second edition, I removed info about `man -u` (which rebuilds `man`'s database of commands) and `man -t` (which prints `man` pages). In addition, `whatis` was moved into `man -f` and `apropos` was moved into `man -k`. You can find the original text on my website, at www.granneman.com/linux-redactions.

Find Out About Commands with `man`

`man`

Want to find out about a Linux command? Why, it's easy! Let's say you want to find out more about the `ls` command. Enter `man ls`, and the man (short for *manual*) page appears, chock full of info about the various facets of `ls`. Try the same thing for some of the other commands you've examined in this book. You'll find man pages for (almost) all of them.

However, as useful as man pages are, they still have problems. You have to know the name of a command to really use them (although there are ways around that particular issue), and they're sometimes out of date and missing the latest features of a command. They don't always exist for every command, which can be annoying. But worst of all, even if you find one that describes a command in which you're interested and it's up to date, you might still have a big problem: It might be next to useless.

The same developers who write the programs often write the man pages. Most of the developers who write applications included with a Linux distribution are excellent programmers, but not always effective writers or explainers of their own work. They know how things work, but they too often forget that users don't know the things that developers find obvious and intuitive.

With all of those problems, however, man pages are still a good resource for Linux users at all levels of experience. If you're going to use Linux on the command line, you need to learn how to use and read man pages.

As stated before, using this command isn't hard. Just enter man, followed by the command about which you want to learn more.

```
$ man ls
LS(1)               User Commands              LS(1)
NAME
       ls - list directory contents
SYNOPSIS
       ls [OPTION]... [FILE]...
DESCRIPTION
       List  information  about  the FILEs (the
➥current directory by default).
       Sort entries alphabetically if none of -
➥cftuSUX nor --sort.
       Mandatory arguments to long options are
➥mandatory for short options too.
       -a, --all
               do not hide entries starting with .
       -A, --almost-all
               do not list implied . and ..
```

The list of data man provides in this case is quite extensive—over 200 lines, in fact. Of course, not all commands provide that much, and some provide far more. Your job is to read the various sections provided in a man page, which usually (but not always) consist of the following:

- NAME—The name of the command and a brief description
- SYNOPSIS—The basic format of the command
- DESCRIPTION—A longer overview of the command's purpose
- OPTIONS—The real meat and potatoes: the various options for the command, along with short explanations of each one
- FILES—Other files used by the command
- AUTHOR—Who wrote the command, along with contact information
- BUGS—Known bugs and how to report new ones
- COPYRIGHT—This one's obvious: information about copyright
- SEE ALSO—Other related commands

Moving around in a man page isn't that hard. To move down a line at a time, use the down arrow; to move up a line at a time, use the up arrow. To jump down a page, press the space bar or f (for *forward*); to jump up a page, press b (for *backward*). When you reach the end of a man page, man might quit itself, depositing you back on the shell; it might, however, simply stop at the end without quitting, in which case you should press q to quit the program. In fact, you can press q at any time to exit man if you're not finding the information you want.

It can be hard to find a particular item in a man page, so sometimes you need to do a little searching. To search on a man page after it's open, type /, followed

by your search term, and then press Enter. If your
term exists, you'll jump to it; to jump to the next
occurrence of the term, press Enter again (or n), and
keep pressing Enter (or n) to jump down the screen to
each occurrence; to go backward, press Shift+n.

NOTE: By default, man uses less (discussed in Chapter
6) as its *pager*—the software that actually displays the
man pages. These key commands for navigating are
really coming from less; for more on those key commands, run man less. If you don't want to use less
for some reason, you'll need to change the MANPAGER
or PAGER environment variables. To find out how to do
that, do some searching!

Quickly Find Out What a Command Does Based on Its Name

```
man -f
whatis
```

If you know a command's name but don't know
what it does, there's a quick and dirty way to find out
without requiring you to actually open the man page
for that command. Use man with the -f or --whatis
options, or use the whatis command (yep, just like man
--whatis), and the command's synopsis appears.

```
$ man -f ls
ls (1)                  - list directory contents
$ whatis ls
ls (1)                  - list directory contents
```

Which one should you use? Personally, I like whatis, as I can remember it easier; friends of mine prefer man -f, on the other hand, because it's shorter to type.

Another big advantage of the whatis command is that it supports regular expressions and wildcards. To search the man database using wildcards, use the -w option (or --wildcard).

```
$ whatis -w ls*
ls (1)     - list directory contents
lsb (8)    - Linux Standard Base support for Debian
lshal (1)  - List devices and their properties
lshw (1)   - list hardware
lskat (6)  - Lieutnant Skat card game for KDE
```

Using wildcards might result in a slightly slower search than whatis without options, but it's virtually negligible on today's fast machines, so you probably don't have to worry about it.

Regular expressions can be used with the -r (or --regex) option.

```
$ whatis -r ^rm.*
rm (1)     - remove files or directories
rmail (8)  - handle remote mail received via uucp
rmdir (1)  - remove empty directories
rmt (8)    - remote magtape protocol module
```

TIP: There's not enough room in this book to cover regular expressions, but you can read more in *Sams Teach Yourself Regular Expressions in 10 Minutes* (ISBN: 0672325667) by Ben Forta. Learn as much as you can—they're awesomely useful. Even cool, as you can see at http://xkcd.com/208/!

Search for a Command Based on What It Does

```
man -k
apropos
```

With just a little training, you find that you can zoom around man pages and find exactly what you need... assuming you know which man page to read. What if you know a little about what a command does, but you don't know the actual name of the command? Try using the -k option (or --apropos) with man, or just use the apropos command, and search for a word or phrase that describes the kind of command you want to discover. You'll get back a list of all commands whose name or synopsis matches your search term.

```
$ man list
No manual entry for list
$ man -k list
last (1)   - show listing of last logged
➥in users
ls (1)     - list directory contents
lshw (1)   - list hardware
lsof (8)   - list open files
[Listing condensed due to length]
```

Be careful with the -k option, as it can produce a long list of results, and you might miss what you were looking for. Don't be afraid to try a different search term if you think it might help you find the command you need.

TIP: If your results are particularly long and you can't easily find what you want, try piping `man -k` to `grep`. (The pipe is coming up in the next chapter, while `grep` is discussed at length in Chapter 10, "Finding Files, Directories, Words, and Phrases.") For now, here's a sample command you'd type: `man -k list | grep hardware`. Or just try `apropos`, discussed right here!

The `apropos` command is the same thing as `man -k`, with one big exception: Like `whatis` (discussed in the previous section), you can use the `-w` (or `--wildcard`) or the `-r` (or `--regex`) options for searches. More interestingly, though, you can use the `-e` option (or `--exact`) when you want to tightly focus on a word or phrase, without any exception. For instance, in the previous listing, searching for *list* turned up the `last` command because it had the word *listing* in its description. Let's try that same search, but with the `-e` option.

```
$ apropos -e list
ls (1)    - list directory contents
lshw (1) - list hardware
lsof (8) - list open files
```

This time, `last` doesn't show up because you wanted only results with the exact word *list*, not *listing*. In fact, the list of results for *list* went from 80 results without the `-e` option to 55 results with the `-e` option, which makes it far easier to precisely target your command searches and find exactly the command you want.

NOTE: The word *apropos* isn't exactly in common usage, but it is a real word, and it means, essentially, "relevant" or "pertinent." The word *appropriate* has a somewhat similar meaning, but it's based on a different Latin root than *apropos*. Check the words out at www.dictionary.com for yourself if you don't believe me.

Read a Command's Specific Man Page

```
man [1-8]
```

You might notice in the previous listing that the first line of man's page on `ls` references `LS(1)`, while earlier, when you used the `-k` option, all the names of commands were also followed by numbers in parentheses. Most of them are 1, but one, `lsof`, is 8. So what's up with all these numbers?

The answer is that man pages are categorized into various sections, numbered from 1 to 8, which break down as follows (and don't worry if you don't recognize some of the examples, as many of them are pretty arcane and specialized):

1. General commands. Examples are `cd`, `chmod`, `lp`, `mkdir`, and `passwd`.

2. Low-level system calls provided by the kernel. Examples are `gettimeofday`, `fork`, and `chmod`.

3. C library functions. Examples are `beep`, `HTML::Parser`, and `Mail::Internet`.

4. Special files, such as devices found in /dev. Examples are `console`, `lp`, and `mouse`.

5. File formats and conventions. Examples are
   `apt.conf`, `dpkg.cfg`, `hosts`, and `passwd`.

6. Games. Examples are `atlantik`, `bouncingcow`,
   `kmahjongg`, and `rubik`.

7. Miscellanea, including macro packages. Examples
   are `ascii`, `samba`, and `utf-8`.

8. System administration commands used by `root`.
   Examples are `mount` and `shutdown`.

Almost every command we've looked at so far in this
book falls into section 1, which isn't surprising because
we're focused on general use of your Linux system.
But notice how some commands fall into more than
one section: `chmod`, for instance, is in both 1 and 2,
while `passwd` can be found in 1 and 5. By default, if
you enter `man passwd` in your shell, `man` defaults to the
lower number, so you'll get the section 1 man page
for `passwd`, which isn't very helpful if you want to
learn about the file `passwd`. To see the man page for
the file `passwd`, follow `man` with the section number for
the data you want to examine.

```
$ man passwd
PASSWD(1)                                    PASSWD(1)
NAME
       passwd - change user password
SYNOPSIS
       passwd [-f|-s] [name]
       passwd [-g] [-r|-R] group
       passwd [-x max] [-n min] [-w warn] [-i inact]
➥login
       passwd {-l|-u|-d|-S|-e} login
DESCRIPTION
       passwd changes passwords for user and group
➥accounts. A normal user...
```

```
[Listing condensed due to length]
$ man 5 passwd
PASSWD(5)                                    PASSWD(5)
NAME
       passwd - The password file
DESCRIPTION
       passwd contains various pieces of information
➡for each user account.
[Listing condensed due to length]
```

Learn About Commands with info

```
info
```

The man command, and the resulting man pages, are
simple to work with, even if the content isn't always
as user friendly as you might like. In response to that
and other perceived shortcomings with man pages, the
GNU Project, which is responsible in many ways for
a large number of the commands you're reading about
in this book, created its own format: info pages, which
use the info command for viewing.

While info pages tend to be better written, more
comprehensive, and more user friendly in terms of
content than man pages, man pages are far easier to
use. A man page is just one page, while info pages
almost always organize their contents into multiple
sections, called *nodes*, which might also contain
subsections, called *subnodes*. The trick is learning how
to navigate not just around an individual page, but
also between nodes and subnodes. It can be a bit
overwhelming to just move around and find what
you're seeking in info pages, which is rather ironic:

Something that was supposed to be nicer than man is actually far harder to learn and use.

NOTE: Personally, I dislike info pages so much that if I'm forced to use one (because no good man page exists), I just usually whip out the Google.

There are many facets to info (that's putting it mildly!). To learn how to use info, as well as read about info, enter the following command:

```
$ info info
```

This opens the info page for the info command (after that, try just info all by itself). Now you need to learn how to get around in this new Info world.

Navigate Within info

Within a particular section's screen, to move down, or forward, one line at a time, use the down arrow; to move up, or back, one line at a time, use the up arrow. When you reach the bottom, or end, of a particular section, your cursor stops and you are not able to proceed.

If you instead want to jump down a screen at a time, use your keyboard's PageDown button; to jump up a screen at a time, use the PageUp key instead. You are not able to leave the particular section you're in, however.

If you reach the end of the section and you want to jump back to the top, just press b, which stands for *beginning*. Likewise, e takes you to the *end*.

If, at any time, as you're jumping around from place to place, you notice that things look a little strange, such as the letters or words being distorted, press Ctrl+l to redraw the screen, and all should be well.

Now that you know how to navigate within a particular section or node, let's move on to navigating between nodes. If you don't want to use PageDown and PageUp to move forward and backward within a section, you can instead use the spacebar to move down and the Backspace or Delete keys to move up. These keys offer one big advantage over PageDown and PageUp, besides being easier to reach: When you hit the end of a node, you automatically proceed onward to the next node, through subnodes if they exist. Likewise, going up moves you back to the previous node, through any subnodes. Using the spacebar, or the Backspace or Delete buttons, you can quickly run through an entire set of info pages about a particular command.

If you want to engage in fewer key presses, you can use n (for *next*) to move on to the next node at the same level. If you are reading a node that has subnodes and you press n, you skip those subnodes and move to the next node that's a peer of the one you're currently reading. If you're reading a subnode and press n, however, you jump to the next subnode. If n moves you to the next node at the current level, then p moves you to the previous one (p for *previous*, get it?), again at the same level.

If you instead want to move forward to a node or subnode, use the], or right square brace, key. If you're reading a node and you press], you'll jump to that node's first subnode, if one exists. Otherwise, you'll move to that node's next peer node. To move backward in the same fashion, use the [, or left square brace, key.

If you want to move up a node, to the parent of the node you're currently reading, use the u (for *up*) key. Be careful, though—it's easy to jump up past the home page of the command you're reading about in info to what is termed the Directory node, the root node that leads to all other info nodes (another way to reach the Directory node is to type d, for *directory*, at any time).

The Directory node is a particularly large example of a type of page you find all throughout info: a Menu page, which lists all subnodes or nodes. If you ever find yourself on a Menu page, you can quickly navigate to one of the subnodes listed in that menu in one of two ways. First, type an m (for *menu*) and then start typing the name of the subnode to which you want to jump. For instance, here's the first page you see when you enter info on the command line:

```
File: dir,  Node: Top  This is the top of the INFO
➥tree

This (the Directory node) gives a menu of major
➥topics.
Typing "q" exits, "?" lists all Info commands,
➥"d" returns here,
"h" gives a primer for first-timers,
➥"mEmacs<Return>" visits the Emacs manual, etc.

* Menu:

Basics
* Common options: (coreutils)Common options.
```

```
* Coreutils: (coreutils). Core GNU (file, text,
➥shell) utilities.
* Date input formats: (coreutils)Date input
➥formats.
* Ed: (ed). The GNU line editor
```

To jump to Coreutils, you could type m, followed by
Core. At this point, you could finish typing utils, or
you could just press the Tab key and info fills in the
rest of the menu name that matches the characters
you've already entered. If info complains, you have
entered a typo, or more than one menu choice
matches the characters you've typed. Fix your typo, or
enter more characters until it is obvious to info which
menu choice is the one in which you're interested.
If you realize that you don't want to go to a Menu
choice at this time, press Ctrl+G to cancel your
command, and go back to reading the node on which
you find yourself.

Alternatively, you could just use your up or down
arrow key to position the cursor over the menu choice
you want, and then press Enter. Either method works.

If you don't want to navigate info pages and instead
want to search, you can do that as well, in two ways:
by searching just the titles of all nodes for the info
pages about a particular command, or by searching in
the actual text of all nodes associated with a particular
command. To search the titles, enter i (for *index*
because this search uses the node index created by
info), followed by your search term, and press Enter.
If your term exists somewhere in a node's title, you'll
jump to it. If you want to repeat your search and go
to the next result, press the comma key.

If you want to search text instead of titles, enter s
(for *search*), followed by your search term or phrase,

and then press Enter. To repeat that search, enter s, followed immediately by Enter. That's not as easy as just pressing the comma key like you do when you're searching titles, but it does work.

If at any time you get lost inside info and need help, just press the ? key and the bottom half of your window displays all of the various options for Info. Move up and down in that section using the keys you've already learned. When you want to get out of Help, press l.

Finally, and perhaps most importantly, to get out of info altogether, just press q, for *quit*, which dumps you back into your shell. Whew!

Locate the Paths for a Command's Executable, Source Files, and Man Pages

`whereis`

The whereis command performs an incredibly useful function: It tells you the paths for a command's executable program, its source files (if they exist), and its man pages. For instance, here's what you might get for KWord, the word processor in the KOffice set of programs (assuming, of course, that the binary, source, and man files are all installed):

```
$ whereis kword
kword: /usr/src/koffice-1.4.1/kword /usr/bin/kword
➥/usr/bin/X11/kword usr/share/man/man1/kword.1.gz
```

The `whereis` command first reports where the
source files are: `/usr/src/koffice-1.4.1/kword`.
Then it informs you as to the location of any binary
executables: `/usr/bin/kword` and `/usr/bin/X11/kword`.
KWord is found in two places on this machine, which
is a bit unusual but not bizarre. Finally, you find
out where the man pages are: `/usr/share/man/man1/`
`kword.1.gz`. Armed with this information, you can
now verify that the program is in fact installed on this
computer, and you know now how to run it.

If you want to search only for binaries, use the `-b`
option.

```
$ whereis -b kword
kword: /usr/bin/kword /usr/bin/X11/kword
```

If you want to search only for man pages, the `-m`
option is your ticket.

```
$ whereis -m kword
kword: /usr/share/man/man1/kword.1.gz
```

Finally, if you want to limit your search only to
sources, try the `-s` option.

```
$ whereis -s kword
kword: /usr/src/koffice-1.4.1/kword
```

The `whereis` command is a good, quick way to find
vital information about programs on the computer
you're using. You'll find yourself using it more than
you think.

Find Out Which Version of a Command Will Run

```
which
```

Think back to the `whereis` command and what happened when you ran it against KWord using the `-b` option, for *show binaries only*.

```
$ whereis -b kword
kword: /usr/bin/kword /usr/bin/X11/kword
```

The executable for KWord is in two places. But which one will run first? You can tell that by running the `which` command.

```
$ which kword
/usr/bin/kword
```

The `which` command tells you which version of a command will run if you just type its name. In other words, if you type in `kword` and then press Enter, your shell executes the one found inside `/usr/bin`. If you want to run the version found in `/usr/bin/X11`, you have to change directories using the `cd` command and then enter `./kword`, or use the absolute path for the command and type out `/usr/bin/X11/kword`.

The `which` command is also a speedy way to tell if a command is on your system. If the command is on your system and in your PATH, you'll be told where to find it; if the command doesn't exist, you're back on the command line with nothing.

```
$ which arglebargle
$
```

If you want to find all the locations of a command (just like you would if you used `whereis -b`), try the `-a` (for *all*) option.

```
$ which -a kword
/usr/bin/kword
/usr/bin/X11/kword
```

Discover How a Command Will Be Interpreted

```
type
```

The `type` command shows you how bash will interpret the commands you run. This will make more sense with a few examples.

To start with, let's see what happens when we use `type`:

```
$ type ls
ls is aliased to '/bin/ls -F --color'
$ type cd
cd is a shell builtin
$ type whereis
whereis is /usr/bin/whereis
$ type mark
mark is a function
mark ()
{
  mkdir -p "$MARKPATH";
  ln -s "$(pwd)" "$MARKPATH/$1"
}
$ type do
do is a shell keyword
```

The output of the `type` command tells how bash sees each of those commands. There are five possible answers:

- `alias`: A soft link that you have created, including the target of the alias. This doesn't work with a hard link, which won't display anything. (For more on links, see Chapter 3, "Creation and Destruction.")

- `builtin`: A command built in to bash that it runs directly in itself, as opposed to calling an external program. Examples of builtins are `alias`, `cd`, `echo`, `history`, `source`, and `type`.

- `file`: A command that is not built into the shell, and so is called externally. Examples are `whereis` and `whatis` from this chapter.

- `function`: A function (covered in Chapter 12, "Your Shell") created by Linux, software, or you. Just as with `alias`, `type` also outputs the actual content of the function.

- `keyword`: A reserved word used only by bash, such as `do`, `for`, `if`, `then`, `while`, and `!`.

If you just want to see which of the five applies to a command and nothing else, use the `-t` option.

```
$ type -t ls
alias
$ type -t cd
builtin
$ type -t mark
function
```

That's short and sweet. The `-a` option is a bit longer, because it provides not only the kind of command it

is but also a list of all locations in which you can find
the command.

```
$ type -a ls
ls is aliased to '/bin/ls -F --color'
ls is /bin/ls
```

So now we know that ls is an alias, as well as
the target of that alias and the path of the original
command.

The type command is not something you'll be
whipping out everyday, but if you're wondering why
a command isn't acting the way you expected, type
will help you figure that out.

Conclusion

The title of this chapter is "Learning About
Commands," and that's what we've covered. By now,
you've seen that there are a variety of ways to find out
more about your options on the command line. The
two big dogs are man and info, with their volumes of
data and descriptions about virtually all the commands
found on your Linux computer. Remember that
whereis, which, and type all have their places as well,
especially if your goal is to avoid having to wade
through the sometimes overwhelming verbiage of man
and info, an understandable but often impossible goal.
Sometimes you just have to roll up your sleeves and
start reading a man page. Think of it like broccoli:
You might not enjoy it, but it's good for you.

It's true that many of the commands in this chapter
overlap to a degree. For instance, man -k is the
same as apropos and man -f is just like whatis, while

whereis -b is functionally equivalent to which -a. The choice of which one to use in a given situation is up to you. It's still a good idea, however, to know the various similarities, so you'll be able to read shell scripts or instructions given by others and understand exactly what's happening. Linux is all about variety and choice, even in such seemingly small matters as commands run in the shell.

## 5

Building Blocks

When you're young, you learn numbers, and then later you learn how to combine and work with those numbers using symbols such as +, −, ×, and =. So far in this book, you've learned several commands, but each one has been run one at a time. Commands can actually be combined in more complex and interesting ways, however, using various symbols such as |, >, >>, <, and even < and > together. In fact, the ability to join commands using those symbols goes a long way to explaining the power of UNIX, as you'll see. This chapter takes a look at those building blocks that enable you to do some awesomely useful things with the commands you've learned and the commands you'll be examining in greater detail in subsequent chapters.

Run Several Commands Sequentially

```
;
```

What if you have several commands you need to run consecutively, but some of them are going to take a long time, and you don't feel like babysitting your computer? For instance, what if you have a huge number of John Coltrane MP3s in a zipped archive file, and you want to unzip them, place them in a new subdirectory, and then delete the archive file? Normally you'd have to run those commands one at a time, like this:

```
$ ls -l /home/scott/music
-rw-r--r--  1 scott scott 1437931 2005-11-07 17:19
➡John_Coltrane.zip
$ unzip /home/scott/music/John_Coltrane.zip
$ mkdir -p /home/scott/music/coltrane
$ mv /home/scott/music/John_Coltrane*.mp3
➡/home/scott/music/coltrane/
$ rm /home/scott/music/John_Coltrane.zip
```

John_Coltrane.zip is a 1.4GB file, and even on a fast machine, unzipping that monster is going to take some time, and you probably have better things to do than sit there and wait. Command stacking to the rescue!

Command stacking puts all the commands you want to run on one line in your shell, with each specific command separated by a semicolon (;). Each command is then executed in sequential order and each must terminate—successfully or unsuccessfully—before the next one runs. It's easy to do, and it can really save you some time.

With command stacking, the previous series of commands now looks like this:

```
$ ls -l /home/scott/music
-rw-r--r--  1 scott scott 1437931 2005-11-07 17:19
➡John_Coltrane.zip
$ unzip /home/scott/music/John_Coltrane.zip ;
➡mkdir -p /home/scott/music/coltrane ;
➡mv /home/scott/music/John_Coltrane*.mp3
➡/home/scott/music/coltrane/ ;
➡rm /home/scott/music/John_Coltrane.zip
```

This technique can be especially handy if each step in a sequence itself takes a long time to run. If you don't want to hang around babysitting your computer just to enter the next command each time, you can stack the commands with semicolons and then let the computer run all afternoon, moving from one command to the next automatically as each completes. You're free to enjoy a movie or a meal or otherwise do something productive while the computer lives up to its billing as a labor-saving device.

Of course, you can also use this method to introduce short delays as commands run. If you want to take a screenshot of everything you see in your monitor, just run the following command (this assumes you have the ImageMagick package installed, which virtually all Linux distributions do):

```
$ sleep 3 ; import -frame window.tif
```

The sleep command in this case waits three seconds, and then the screenshot is taken using import. The delay gives you time to minimize your terminal application and bring to the foreground any windows you want to appear in the screenshot. The ; makes it easy to separate the commands logically so you get maximum use out of them.

CAUTION: Be very careful when command stacking, especially when deleting or moving files! Make sure what you typed is what you want because the commands will run, one right after another, even if the previous one fails, and you might end up with unexpected surprises. Read the next section for an example.

Run Commands Only If the Previous Ones Succeed

```
&&
```

In the previous section, you saw that ; separates commands, as in this example:

```
$ unzip /home/scott/music/John_Coltrane.zip ;
➥mkdir -p /home/scott/music/coltrane ;
➥mv /home/scott/music/John_Coltrane*mp3
➥/home/scott/music/coltrane/ ;
➥rm /home/scott/music/John_Coltrane.zip
```

What if you fat finger your command, and instead type this:

```
$ unzip /home/scott/John_Coltrane.zip ;
➥mkdir -p /home/scott/music/coltrane ;
➥mv /home/scott/music/John_Coltrane*mp3
➥/home/scott/music/coltrane/ ;
➥rm /home/scott/music/John_Coltrane.zip
```

Instead of `unzip /home/scott/music/John_Coltrane.zip`, you accidentally enter `unzip /home/scott/John_Coltrane.zip`. You fail to notice this, so you go ahead and press Enter, and then get up and walk away. Your computer can't unzip `/home/scott/John_Coltrane.zip` because that file doesn't exist, so it blithely continues onward to the next command (`mkdir`), which it performs without a problem. However, the third command can't be performed (`mv`) because there aren't any MP3 files to move because `unzip` didn't work. Finally, the fourth command runs, deleting the zip file (notice that you provided the correct path this time) and leaving you with no way to recover and start over. Oops!

NOTE: Don't believe that this chain of events can happen? I did something very similar once. Yes, I felt like an idiot.

That's the problem with using `;` for command stacking—commands run in sequence, regardless of their successful completion. A better method is to separate the commands with `&&`, which also runs each command one after the other, but only if the previous one completes successfully (technically, each command must return an exit status of `0` for the next one to run). If a command fails, the entire chain of commands stops.

If you'd used `&&` instead of `;` in the sequence of previous commands, it would have looked like this:

```
$ unzip /home/scott/John_Coltrane.zip &&
➥mkdir -p /home/scott/music/coltrane &&
➥mv /home/scott/music/John_Coltrane*mp3
➥/home/scott/music/coltrane/ &&
➥rm /home/scott/music/John_Coltrane.zip
```

Because the first `unzip` command couldn't complete successfully, the entire process stops. You walk back later to find that your series of commands failed, but `John_Coltrane.zip` still exists, so you can try once again. Much better!

Here are two more examples that show you just how useful `&&` can be. In Chapter 14, "Installing Software," you're going to learn about `apt`, a fantastic way to upgrade your Debian-based Linux box. When you use `apt`, you first update the list of available software, and then find out if there are any upgrades available. If the list of software can't be updated, you obviously don't want to bother looking for upgrades. To make sure the second process doesn't (uselessly) occur, separate the commands with `&&`:

```
# apt-get update && apt-get upgrade
```

Example two: You want to convert a PostScript file to a PDF using the `ps2pdf` command, print the PDF, and then delete the PostScript file. The best way to set up these commands is with `&&`:

```
$ ps2pdf foobar.ps && lpr foobar.pdf && rm foobar.ps
```

If you had instead used `;` and `ps2pdf` failed, the PostScript file would still end up in nowheresville, leaving you without a way to start over.

Now are you convinced that `&&` is often the better way to go? If there's no danger that you might delete a file, `;` might be just fine, but if one of your commands involves `rm` or something else perilous, you'd better use `&&` and be safe.

Run a Command Only If the Previous One Fails

```
||
```

The && runs each command in sequence only if the previous one completes successfully. The || does the opposite: If the first command fails (technically, it returns an exit status that is not 0), only then does the second one run. Think of it like the words *either*/*or*— either run the first command or the second one.

The || is often used to send an alert to an administrator when a process stops. For instance, to ensure that a particular computer is up and running, an administrator might constantly query it with the ping command (you'll find out more about ping in Chapter 15, "Connectivity"); if ping fails, an email is sent to the administrator to let him know.

```
ping -c 1 -w 15 -n 8.8.8.8 ||
{
  echo "Server down" | mail -s 'Server down'
➥admin@website.com
}
```

NOTE: Wondering what the | is? Look ahead in this chapter to the "Use the Output of One Command As Input for Another" section to find out what it is and how to use it.

With just a bit of thought, you'll start to find many places where || can help you.

Plug the Output of a Command into Another Command

```
$()
```

Command substitution takes the output of a command and plugs it in to another command as though you had typed that output in directly. Surround the initial command that's run—the one that's going to produce the output that's plugged in—with $(). An example makes this much clearer.

Let's say you just arrived home from a family dinner, connected your digital camera to your Linux box, pulled the new photos off of it, and now you want to put them in a folder named today's date.

```
$ pwd
/home/scott/photos/family
$ ls -1F
2015-11-01/
2015-11-09/
2015-11-15/
$ date "+%Y-%m-%d"
2015-11-24
$ mkdir $(date "+%Y-%m-%d")
$ ls -1F
2015-11-01/
2015-11-09/
2015-11-15/
2015-11-24/
```

In this example, date "+%Y-%m-%d" is run first, and then the output of that command, 2015-11-24, is used by mkdir as the name of the new directory. It's just as though you had typed mkdir 2015-11-24. This is powerful stuff, and as you look at the shell scripts written by others (which you can easily find all over the Web), you'll find that command substitution is used all over the place.

NOTE: In the past, you were supposed to surround the initial command with backticks, the ` character at the upper left of your keyboard. Now, however, you're better advised to use the characters used in this section: `$()`. `$()` is nestable, so you can have a `$()` inside another `$()`, while it's much more difficult to use backticks within other backticks. And on top of that, `$()` is a lot easier to see!

Understand Input/Output Streams

To take advantage of the information in this chapter, you need to understand that there are three input/output streams for a Linux shell: *standard input*, *standard output*, and *standard error*. Each of these streams has a file descriptor (or numeric identifier), a common abbreviation, and a usual default.

For instance, when you're typing on your keyboard, you're sending input to standard input, abbreviated as *stdin* and identified as 0. When your computer presents output on the terminal, that's standard output, abbreviated as *stdout* and identified as 1. Finally, if your machine needs to let you know about an error and displays that error on the terminal, that's standard error, abbreviated as *stderr* and identified as 2.

Let's look at these three streams using a common command, `ls`. When you enter `ls` on your keyboard, that's using stdin. After typing `ls` and pressing Enter, the list of files and folders in a directory appears as stdout. If you try to run `ls` against a folder that doesn't exist, the error message that appears on your terminal is courtesy of stderr.

Table 4.1 can help you keep these three streams straight.

Table 4.1   **The Three Input/Output Streams**

File Descriptor (Identifier)	Name	Common Abbreviation	Typical Default
0	Standard input	stdin	Keyboard
1	Standard output	stdout	Terminal
2	Standard error	stderr	Terminal

In this chapter, we're going to learn how to redirect input and output. Instead of having output appear on the terminal, for instance, you can redirect it to another program. Or instead of acquiring input from your typing, a program can get it from a file. There are many cool things you can do after you understand the tricks you can play with stdin and stdout.

Use the Output of One Command As Input for Another

It's a maxim that UNIX is made up of small pieces, loosely joined. Nothing embodies that principle more than the concept of pipes. A pipe is the | symbol on your keyboard, and when placed between two commands, it takes the output from the first and uses it as input for the second. In other words, | redirects stdout so it is sent to be stdin for the next command.

Here's a simple example that helps to make this concept clear. You already know about ls, and you're going to find out about the less command in Chapter 6, "Viewing (Mostly Text) Files." For now, know that less allows you to page through text files one screen at a time. If you run ls on a directory that has many files, such as /usr/bin, things just zoom by too fast to read. If you pipe the output of ls to less, however, you can page through the output one screen at a time.

```
$ pwd
/usr/bin
$ ls -1
zipinfo
zipnote
zipsplit
zsoelim
zxpdf
[Listing truncated due to length - 2318 lines!]
$ ls -1 | less
7z
a2p
acidrip
aconnect
```

You see one screen of results at a time when you pipe the results of ls -1 through to less, which makes it much easier to work with.

Here's a more advanced example that uses two commands discussed later: ps and grep. You'll learn in Chapter 10, "Finding Files, Directories, Words,

and Phrases," that ps lists running processes and in
Chapter 13, "Monitoring System Resources," that
grep helps find lines in files that match a pattern. Let's
say that Firefox is acting strange, and you suspect that
multiple copies are still running in the background.
The ps command lists every process running on your
computer, but the output tends to be lengthy and
flashes by in an instant. If you pipe the output of ps
to grep and search for *firefox*, you'll be able to tell
immediately if Firefox in fact is still running.

```
$ ps ux
1504  0.8  4.4  75164 46124 ? S Nov20 1:19 kontact
19003  0.0  0.1  3376 1812 pts/4 S+ 00:02 0:00 ssh
➥admin@davidhart.com
21176  0.0  0.0  0 0 ? Z 00:14 0:00
➥[wine-preloader] <defunct>
24953  0.4  3.3 51856 34140 ? S 00:33 0:08 08
➥kdeinit: kword /home/scott/documents/clientele/
➥current
[Listing truncated for length]
$ ps ux | grep firefox
8272  4.7  10.9 184072 112704 ? Sl Nov19 76:45
➥/opt/firefox/firefox-bin
```

From 58 lines of output to one—now that's much
easier to read!

NOTE: Keep in mind that many programs can work with
pipes, but not all. The text editor vim (or pico, nano, or
emacs), for instance, takes over the entire shell so that
all input from the keyboard is assumed to be directed
at vim, while all output is displayed somewhere in the
program. Because vim has total control of the shell,
you can't pipe output using the program. You'll learn
to recognize non-pipable programs as you use the shell
over time.

Redirect a Command's Output to a File

>

Normally, output goes to your screen, otherwise known as stdout. If you don't want output to go to the screen and instead want it to be placed into a file, use the > (greater than) character.

```
$ pwd
/home/scott/music
$ ls -1F
Hank_Mobley/
Horace_Silver/
John_Coltrane/
$ ls -1F Hank_Mobley/ > hank_mobley.txt
$ cat hank_mobley.txt
1958_Peckin'_Time/
1960_Roll_Call/
1960_Soul_Station/
1961_Workout/
1963_No_Room_For_Squares/
$ ls -1F
Hank_Mobley/
hank_mobley.txt
Horace_Silver/
John_Coltrane/
```

Notice that before you used the >, the file hank_mobley.txt didn't exist. When you use > and redirect to a file that doesn't already exist, that file is created. Here's the big warning: If hank_mobley.txt had already existed, it would have been completely overwritten.

CAUTION: Once again: Be careful when using redirection, as you could potentially destroy the contents of a file that contains important stuff!

Prevent Overwriting Files When Using Redirection

```
set -o noclobber
```

There's a way to prevent overwriting files when redirecting, however—the noclobber option. If you set noclobber to on, bash won't allow redirection to overwrite existing files without your explicit permission. To turn on noclobber, use this command:

$ **set -o noclobber**

At that point, if you want to use redirection and overwrite a file, use >| instead of just >, like this:

```
$ pwd
/home/scott/music
$ ls -1F
Hank_Mobley/
hank_mobley.txt
Horace_Silver/
John_Coltrane/
$ ls -1F Hank_Mobley/ > hank_mobley.txt
ERROR
$ ls -1F Hank_Mobley/ >| hank_mobley.txt
$ cat hank_mobley.txt
1958_Peckin'_Time/
1960_Roll_Call/
1960_Soul_Station/
1961_Workout/
1963_No_Room_For_Squares/
```

If you decide you don't like or need `noclobber`, you can turn it off again:

```
$ set +o noclobber
```

(That's right: `-o` is on, and `+o` is off. Don't worry, you're not going crazy. In this case, it's `bash` that's to blame.)

To permanently turn on `noclobber`, you need to add `set -o noclobber` to your `.bashrc` file.

Append a Command's Output to a File

```
>>
```

As you learned previously, the `>` character redirects output from stdout to a file. For instance, you can redirect the output of the `date` command to a file easily enough:

```
$ date
Mon Nov 21 21:33:58 CST 2015
$ date > hank_mobley.txt
$ cat hank_mobley.txt
Mon Nov 21 21:33:58 CST 2015
```

Remember that `>` creates a new file if it doesn't already exist and overwrites a file that already exists. If you use `>>` instead of `>`, however, your output is *appended* to the end of the named file (and yes, if the file doesn't exist, it's created).

```
$ cat hank_mobley.txt
Mon Nov 21 21:33:58 CST 2015
$ ls -1F Hank_Mobley/ >> hank_mobley.txt
$ cat hank_mobley.txt
Mon Nov 21 21:33:58 CST 2015
1958_Peckin'_Time/
1960_Roll_Call/
1960_Soul_Station/
1961_Workout/
1963_No_Room_For_Squares/
```

CAUTION: Be careful with >>. If you accidentally type >
instead, you won't append, you'll overwrite!

Use a File As Input for a Command

`<`

Normally your keyboard provides input to commands,
so it is termed stdin. In the same way that you can
redirect stdout to a file, you can redirect stdin so it
comes from a file instead of a keyboard. Why is this
handy? Some commands can't use files as arguments,
and in those cases, the < (lesser than) is just what you
need. And often you'll find that it's necessary for
scripting, but that's a whole other book.

For instance, the `tr` command (which we'll cover later
in Chapter 7's "Substitute Selected Characters with
Others" section) doesn't take files as inputs; instead,
`tr` only reads from stdin. But what if you have a file
that you want to use with `tr`? The good news is, you
can—as long as you redirect stdin.

Let's say my editor sends me a text file with a list
of commands he wants me to cover for this book.
I take a look at it, only to find, to my utter horror,
that he typed them in all-caps! Let's correct that mess,
courtesy of `tr` & a redirected stdin:

```
$ cat commands.txt
CP
LS
MKDIR
RM
TR
$ tr 'A-Z' 'a-z' < commands.txt
cp
ls
mkdir
rm
tr
```

The file `commands.txt` is used for input, and `tr` does its
job. Notice, however, how `tr` outputs the results to
stdout, and not to a file. That's to be expected, but in
my case, it's not super useful. I really want to take that
output and put it in a file. To find out how to do that,
keep reading.

Combine Input and Output
Redirection

`[command] < [file] > [output]`

In the previous section, we used the `tr` command
to change the contents of a file from all uppercase
to all lowercase. By default, though, when you use
`tr`, it spits the results back onto stdout. But what if

you want to save the results into a new, correctly-capitalized file? A command like this will do the job:

```
tr 'A-Z' 'a-z' < commands.txt > commands_lower.txt
```

Let's see how this works, using a very short file.

```
$ ls
commands.txt
$ cat commands.txt
CP
LS
MKDIR
RM
TR
$ tr 'A-Z' 'a-z' < commands.txt > commands_lower.txt
$ ls
commands_lower.txt   commands.txt
$ cat commands_lower.txt
cp
ls
mkdir
rm
tr
```

Of course, you can immediately use `mv` to rename that new file so that it has the same name as the old file. If you're really clever, you could use `&&` to chain that `mv` command onto what you've done with `tr`. Just make sure that the new file contains the right output before you blow the old one away!

Now I need to call that editor. Uppercase commands! In UNIX?! Oh, my stars and garters!

NOTE: You might think you could do this:

```
tr 'A-Z' 'a-z' < commands.txt > commands.txt
```

But alas, due to the way that `bash` orders redirections, that command will result in a completely blank file (for a very detailed explanation, see "Illustrated Redirection Tutorial" at http://wiki.bash-hackers.org/howto/redirection_tutorial). That's why you have to output to a different file.

Send Output to a File and to stdout at the Same Time

`tee`

In this chapter, we've seen all sorts of methods to write to standard output. In prior chapters, we saw many different ways to write command output to a file (we'll see more ways to do so in coming chapters, too). But golly, what if we wanted to write to stdout *and* write to a file at the same time? Is such a crazy thing possible?

It sure is! Hello, `tee` command!

The `tee` command splits output into two streams: one goes to stdout and the other simultaneously goes to a file (hence the name: the output splits in two, like a plumber's tee; for an example, see http://en.wikipedia.org/wiki/Piping_and_plumbing_fittings#Tee).

Here's a simple example: You want to both see the contents of a folder *and* write those contents to a file.

```
$ ls -1 ~/music/Hank_Mobley/ | tee hank_mobley.txt
1958_Peckin'_Time
1960_Roll_Call
1960_Soul_Station
1961_Workout
1963_No_Room_For_Squares
$ ls
hank_mobley.txt
$ cat hank_mobley.txt
1958_Peckin'_Time
1960_Roll_Call
1960_Soul_Station
1961_Workout
1963_No_Room_For_Squares
```

As the `ls` command does its job, you see the results on stdout; at the same time, `tee` ensures that those same results are written to a file.

Keep in mind that if the file to which you're writing already exists, it will be overwritten with the new data provided by `tee`. If you want to instead append the output to the file, use the `-a` option:

```
ls -1 ~/music/Hank_Mobley/ | tee -a hank_mobley.txt
```

You can even pipe the results of `tee` to yet another command! You'll be learning about the `sort` command in Chapter 7 ("Sort the Contents of a File"); the `-r` option reverses the sorted results.

```
$ ls -1 ~/music/Hank_Mobley/ | tee hank_mobley.txt |
➥sort -r > hank_mobley_reverse.txt
1958_Peckin'_Time
1960_Roll_Call
1960_Soul_Station
1961_Workout
1963_No_Room_For_Squares
```

```
$ ls
hank_mobley_reverse.txt   hank_mobley.txt
$ cat hank_mobley_reverse.txt
1963_No_Room_For_Squares
1961_Workout
1960_Soul_Station
1960_Roll_Call
1958_Peckin'_Time
```

Once you get this down, the possibilities are endless.

Conclusion

This book started with some simple commands, but now you've learned the building blocks that allow you to combine those commands in new and interesting ways. Going forward, it's going to get more complicated, but it's going to get more powerful as well. The things covered in this chapter are key factors in gaining that power. Now, onward!

## 6

Viewing (Mostly Text) Files

One of the great things about most Linux boxes is that virtually all important system configurations, logs, and information files are in text files. Nowadays, these text files are almost always encoded as the all-encompassing, Unicode-compliant UTF-8, taking over from the ancient (in computer terms, 45 years and counting is ancient!) ASCII standard. Because text files have been the basis of UNIX since its beginnings, there's a wealth of software commands you can use to view their contents (and even if they're not text files, you can still find out some necessary information about them). This chapter looks at commands you'll use when working with text—and other—files.

Figure Out a File's Type

```
file
```

Most of the time, it's pretty obvious what kind of file is in front of you. If it ends with txt, it's a text file; jpg, an image; html, a webpage. But things aren't always as clear as they should be. Filename suffixes (extensions) in UNIX are not required for files to work; they're only there as a courtesy and as a vestigial effect of other operating systems. What if a file doesn't have an extension? What if the extension is wrong (I've seen that more times than I'd like)? What if it has an extension that you've never seen? In all these cases, it would be nice if you knew what kind of file you were dealing with. Enter the file command.

The file command performs various tests on the files you feed it in order to determine what those files are (you can read about those tests at man file). It then prints its best determination (which is almost always correct) to stdout. Here's an example with a motley collection of files that I would hope you never actually place into the same directory!

```
$ ls -1F
838005x.docx
event.h
Lovecraft/
mtr*
Outline.md
Paper.doc
test
test.sh*
tix.jpg
www@
Yeats.txt
```

```
$ file *
838005x.docx: Zip archive data, at least v2.0 to
➡extract
event.h:      ASCII C program text
Lovecraft:    directory
mtr:          ELF 64-bit LSB executable, x86-64,
➡version 1 (SYSV), dynamically linked (uses shared
➡libs), for GNU/Linux 2.6.8, stripped
Outline.md:   UTF-8 Unicode English text
Paper.doc:    CDF V2 Document, Little Endian, Os:
➡Windows, Version 5.1, Code page: 1252, Author:
➡JohnDoe, Template: Normal, Last Saved By: John,
➡Revision Number: 14, Name of Creating Application:
➡Microsoft Office Word, Total Editing Time: 30:00,
➡Create Time/Date: Mon Mar 26 11:35:00 2012, Last
➡Saved Time/Date: Tue Mar 27 11:54:00 2012, Number
➡of Pages: 9, Number of Words: 2101, Number of
➡Characters: 11978, Security: 0
test:         HTML document text
test.sh:      Bourne-Again shell script text
➡executable
tix.jpg:      JPEG image data, JFIF standard 1.01
www:          symbolic link to '/var/www'
Yeats.txt:    ASCII English text
```

There are several interesting things going on in these results.

First, consider the text files, which are all created with a simple text editor: event.h, Outline.md, test, test.sh, and Yeats.txt. But notice how file differentiates between them as different *kinds* of text files, and is even able to delineate the nature of the more specialized files: event.h as a C header file, test as an HTML file (even though the extension is missing; generally, you can leave off an extension, and file will figure things out), and test.sh as a bash shell script.

NOTE: I wish that Outline.md was identified as a Markdown file, but alas, it is not. That said, Markdown files are just text files with Markdown in them, so it's not wrong, just not as precise as I'd have liked. For more on Markdown, which I cannot praise highly enough, see the overview at Wikipedia (http://en.wikipedia.org/wiki/Markdown); Pandoc, a universal document converter that speaks Markdown (http://johnmacfarlane.net/pandoc/index.html); and my own blog's posts on the subject (www.chainsawonatireswing.com/?s=markdown).

Second, Linux executables are identified as such, whether they are compiled (mtr) or shell scripts (test.sh). The file command can tell that it's a bash shell script; the same is true for scripts written in Perl, Python, and pretty much every other language.

Third, directories and symbolic links (and the other kinds of "special" files that show up when you use ls -F) are sussed out easily by file. And images are also presented with extra info, like the version of the image standard (if that was a GIF, for instance, it might have said something like GIF image data, version 89a, 500 x 500).

Finally, both 838005x.docx and Paper.doc were generated by Word (I know, I know), but look at the different results file gives! Paper.doc, which was saved using the "old" Word format by a student of mine and mailed to me, provides a crazily detailed amount of information to file, including the author, the Windows version, the template, the number of words, and dates. 838005x.docx was saved using the "new" Word format, which is actually a zipped collection of XML documents. In fact, if you use the -z option with `file`, it attempts to peek inside a zipped archive to figure out its contents:

```
$ file -z 838005x.docx
838005x.docx: XML document text (Zip archive data,
➥at least v2.0 to extract)
```

Got questions about what a file *is*? Run `file` against that file!

View Files on stdout

`cat`

DOS users have the `type` command that displays the contents of text files on a screen. Linux users can use `cat`, which does the same thing.

```
$ cat Yeats_-_When_You_Are_Old.txt
WHEN you are old and grey and full of sleep,
And nodding by the fire, take down this book,
And slowly read, and dream of the soft look
Your eyes had once, and of their shadows deep;

How many loved your moments of glad grace,
And loved your beauty with love false or true,
But one man loved the pilgrim soul in you,
And loved the sorrows of your changing face;

And bending down beside the glowing bars,
Murmur, a little sadly, how Love fled
And paced upon the mountains overhead
And hid his face amid a crowd of stars.
$
```

The `cat` command prints the file to the screen, and then deposits you back at the command prompt. If the file is longer than your screen, you need to scroll up to see what flashed by.

That's the big problem with `cat`: If the document you're viewing is long, it zooms by, maybe for quite a while, making it hard to read (can you imagine what this would produce: `cat Melville_-_Moby_Dick.txt`?). The solution to that is the `less` command, discussed in "View Text Files a Screen at a Time" later in this chapter.

Concatenate Files to stdout

```
cat file1 file2
```

`cat` is short for *concatenate*, which means "to join together." The original purpose of `cat` was to take two or more files and concatenate them into one file; the fact that you can use the `cat` command on just one file and print it on the screen—now its primary use case— was a bonus. For instance, let's say you have two short poems by A. E. Housman (an excellent poet, by the way), and you want to view them at the same time.

```
$ cat With_rue.txt Oh_when_I_was_in_love.txt
WITH rue my heart is laden
   For golden friends I had,
For many a rose-lipt maiden
   And many a lightfoot lad.

By brooks too broad for leaping
   The lightfoot boys are laid;
The rose-lipt girls are sleeping
   In fields where roses fade.
OH, when I was in love with you
   Then I was clean and brave,
```

```
And miles around the wonder grew
  How well did I behave.

And now the fancy passes by
  And nothing will remain,
And miles around they'll say that I
  Am quite myself again.
```

Notice that cat doesn't separate the two files with a horizontal rule, a dash, or anything else. Instead, cat mashes the two files together and spits them out. If you want more of a separation—having the last line of "With rue my heart is laden" jammed up right next to the first line of "Oh, when I was in love with you" makes them hard to read, for instance—make sure there's a blank line at the end of each file you're going to concatenate together. Edit them if necessary.

Concatenate Files to Another File

```
cat file1 file2 > file3
```

In the previous example, you concatenated two files and printed them on the screen to stdout. This might not be what you want, though. If you're concatenating two files, it might be nice to save the newly joined creation as another file you can use. To do this, redirect your output from stdout to a file, as you learned in Chapter 5, "Building Blocks."

```
$ ls
Oh_when_I_was_in_love.txt  With_rue.txt
$ cat With_rue.txt Oh_when_I_was_in_love.txt >
➥Housman.txt
$ ls
Housman.txt   Oh_when_I_was_in_love.txt   With_rue.txt
```

Now you can do whatever you want with Housman.txt. If you want to add more poems to it, that's easy enough to do:

```
$ cat Loveliest_of_trees.txt >> Housman.txt
```

Notice that the >> was used to append the new poem to Housman.txt this time. The following command would *not* have worked:

```
$ cat Loveliest_of_trees.txt Housman.txt >
➥Housman.txt
```

If you tried concatenating a file to itself, you'd see this error message, helpfully explaining that it is impossible to fulfill your request:

```
cat: Housman.txt: input file is output file
```

Concatenate Files and Number the Lines

cat -n

When working with poems and source code, it's really nice to have numbered lines so that references are clear. If you want to generate line numbers when you use cat, add the -n option (or --number).

```
$ cat -n With_rue.txt Oh_when_I_was_in_love.txt
     1    WITH rue my heart is laden
     2      For golden friends I had,
     3    For many a rose-lipt maiden
     4      And many a lightfoot lad.
     5
     6    By brooks too broad for leaping
     7      The lightfoot boys are laid;
```

```
 8    The rose-lipt girls are sleeping
 9       In fields where roses fade.
10
11    OH, when I was in love with you
12       Then I was clean and brave,
13    And miles around the wonder grew
14       How well did I behave.
15
16    And now the fancy passes by
17       And nothing will remain,
18    And miles around they'll say that I
19       Am quite myself again.
```

Line numbers can be incredibly useful, and cat provides a quick and dirty way to add them to a file.

NOTE: For an interesting alternative to cat, check out tac. Yes, that's cat backward. And that's what tac does: It concatenates files backward. Cute!

View Text Files a Screen at a Time

`less`

The cat command is useful, but if you're trying to read a long file, it's not useful at all because text just flows past in an unending, unreadable stream. If you're interested in viewing a long file on the command line (and by "long," think more than a page or two), you don't want cat; you want less.

The less command is an example of a *pager*, a program that displays text files one page at a time. Others are more, pg, and most; in fact, less was released back in 1985 as an improved `more`, proving once again that less is more!

Opening a file with `less` couldn't be easier:

```
$ less Milton_-_Paradise_Lost.txt
```

The `less` command takes over your entire screen, so you have to navigate within `less` using your keyboard, and you have to quit `less` to get back to the command line. To navigate inside `less`, use the keys in Table 6.1.

Table 6.1   **Key Commands for** `less`

Key Command	Action
PgDn, e, or spacebar	Forward one page
PgUp or b	Back one page
Return, e, j, or down arrow	Forward one line
y, k, or up arrow	Back one line
G or p	Forward to end of file
1G	Back to beginning of file
Esc-), or right arrow	Scroll right
Esc-(, or left arrow	Scroll left
q	Quit less

As you can see, you have many options for most commands. Probably the two you'll use most often are those used to move down a page at a time and quit the program.

To view information about the file while you're in `less`, press = (or open `less` with the -M option), which displays some data at the very bottom of your screen similar to the following:

```
Paradise_Lost.txt lines 7521-7560/10762 byte 166743
➥/237306 70%  (press RETURN)
```

As you can see, you're helpfully told to press Enter to get rid of the data and go back to using `less`.

In the same way that you could tell `cat` to stick in line numbers for a file, you can also order `less` to display line numbers. Those numbers only appear, of course, while you're using `less`. After you press q, the numbers are gone. To view the file, but with numbers at the start of each line, start `less` with the `-N` (or `--LINE-NUMBERS`) option, and yes, you must use all caps:

```
$ less -N Milton_-_Paradise_Lost.txt
```

TIP: This may cause you problems: you use `ls` `--color` (discussed in Chapter 2's "Display Contents in Color") and pipe it to `less`. This is what you'll get:

```
$ ls
Burroughs   Howard   Lovecraft
$ ls --color | less
ESC[0mESC[01;34mBurroughsESC[0m
ESC[01;34mHowardESC[0m
ESC[01;34mLovecraftESC[0m
```

What the heck is all that? The problem is that `bash` uses invisible control characters to display colors, and when you pipe your `ls` to `less`, it gets very confused by those control characters. The fix is to use `-R` (or `--RAW-CONTROL-CHARS`) with `less`:

```
$ ls --color | less -R
Burroughs
Howard
Lovecraft
```

By the way, I know some of you are thinking that this doesn't apply to you, since you don't use `ls --color`.

Well, neither do I...directly. Instead, my alias (see Chapters 5 and 15, "Connectivity") for `ls` contains `--color`, so it's easy to forget that I'm *always* using that option! If you use `ls --color` directly or in an alias, don't forget to add the `-R` to `less` when needed.

Search Within Your Pager

If you're using `less` to view a large file or an especially dense one, it can be difficult to find the text in which you're particularly interested. For instance, what if you want to know if Milton uses the word *apple* in *Paradise Lost* to describe the fruit that Adam and Eve ate? While in `less`, press / and then type in the pattern for which you'd like to search—and you can even use regular expressions if you'd like. After your pattern is in place, press Enter and `less` jumps to the first instance of your search pattern, if it exists. If your pattern isn't in the file, `less` tells you that:

```
Pattern not found  (press RETURN)
```

Repeating your search is also easy and can be done either forward or backward in your file. Table 6.2 covers the main commands you need for searching within `less`.

Table 6.2 **Search Commands for** `less`

Key Command	Action
/pattern	Search forward for pattern using regex
n	Repeat search forward
N	Repeat search backward

NOTE: No, Milton never explicitly refers to the fruit as an apple; instead, it's just a "fruit." Yes, I worked on a doctorate in Seventeenth Century British Literature for a number of years. No, I didn't finish it, which explains why I'm writing this book and not one devoted to John Milton.

Edit Files Viewed with a Pager

It's true that `less` itself is not an editor, just a viewer, but you can pass the file you're viewing with `less` to a text editor such as `vim` or `nano` for editing by pressing v. Try it. View a file with `less`, and then press v. Within a second or two, `less` disappears and a full-screen text editor takes its place. Make your edits, quit your editor, and you're back in `less` with your new changes in place.

If you aren't happy with the editor that you find yourself in when you press v, you can change it to one of your choice. For instance, if you want to use `vim`, run the following command before using `less`:

```
$ export EDITOR=vim
```

You only need to run that command once per session, and every time you open `less` after that, `vim` will be your editor. If you end the session, however, you'll need to enter the `export` command again, which can quickly grow tedious. Better to add the following line to your `.bashrc` file, so that it's automatically applied:

```
export EDITOR=vim
```

NOTE: I love `vim`, and it—or its progenitor `vi`—is found on almost every UNIX everywhere, so why aren't I covering it in this book? Because it deserves books of its own! For starters, check out *Learning the vi and Vim Editors* and then head over to http://zzapper.co.uk/vimtips.html for further mastery.

View the First 10 Lines of a File

`head`

If you just need to see the first 10 lines of a file, there's no need to use either `cat` or `less`. Instead, use the `head` command, which prints out exactly the first 10 lines of a file and then deposits you back on the command line. Let's try it with Chaucer:

```
$ head Canterbury_Tales.txt
Here bygynneth the Book of the Tales of Caunterbury

General Prologue

Whan that Aprill, with his shoures soote
The droghte of March hath perced to the roote
And bathed every veyne in swich licour,
Of which vertu engendred is the flour;
Whan Zephirus eek with his sweete breeth
Inspired hath in every holt and heeth
$
```

The `head` command is great for quick glances at a text file, even if that file is enormous. In just a second, you see enough to know if it's the file you need or not.

View the First 10 Lines of Several Files

```
head file1 file2
```

You can use head to view the first 10 lines of several files at one time. This sounds a bit similar to cat, and it is, except that head helpfully provides a header that separates the files so it's clear which one is which.

```
$ head Canterbury_Tales.txt Paradise_Lost.txt
==> Canterbury_Tales.txt <==
Here bygynneth the Book of the Tales of Caunterbury

General Prologue

Whan that Aprill, with his shoures soote
The droghte of March hath perced to the roote
And bathed every veyne in swich licour,
Of which vertu engendred is the flour;
Whan Zephirus eek with his sweete breeth
Inspired hath in every holt and heeth

==> Paradise_Lost.txt <==
Book I

Of Man's first disobedience, and the fruit
Of that forbidden tree whose mortal taste
Brought death into the World, and all our woe,
With loss of Eden, till one greater Man
Restore us, and regain the blissful seat,
Sing, Heavenly Muse, that, on the secret top
Of Oreb, or of Sinai, didst inspire
That shepherd who first taught the chosen seed,
```

The head command automatically separates the two excerpts with a space and then a header, which really makes it easy to see the different files clearly.

View the First Several Lines of a File or Files

```
head -n
```

If you don't want to see the first 10 lines of a file, you can tell head to show you a different number of lines by using the -n option followed by a number such as 5 (or --lines=5). If you specify two or more files, the results include all the files and show the number specified for each file, as you can see in the example.

```
$ head -n 5 Canterbury_Tales.txt Paradise_Lost.txt
==> Canterbury_Tales.txt <==
Here bygynneth the Book of the Tales of Caunterbury

General Prologue

Whan that Aprill, with his shoures soote

==> Paradise_Lost.txt <==
Book I

Of Man's first disobedience, and the fruit
Of that forbidden tree whose mortal taste
Brought death into the World, and all our woe,
```

Notice that the five lines include blank lines as well as those with text. Five lines are five lines, no matter what those lines contain.

Note that you can just as easily specify --lines=100 (for instance) to see more of a file's contents than the default 10.

View the First Several Bytes, Kilobytes, or Megabytes of a File

```
head -c
```

The -n option allows you to specify the number of lines you view at the top of a file, but what if you want to see a certain number of bytes? Or kilobytes? Or (and this is a bit silly because it would scroll on forever) megabytes? Or even (and this is *really* silly, unless you're piping or redirecting the output) gigabytes and terrabytes? Then use the -c (or --bytes=) option.

To see the first 100 bytes of Chaucer's *Canterbury Tales*, you'd use this:

```
$ head -c 100 Canterbury_Tales.txt
Here bygynneth the Book of the Tales of Caunterbury

General Prologue

Whan that Aprill, with his sh
```

100 bytes means 100 bytes, and if that means the display is cut off in the middle of a word, so be it.

To view the first 100 kilobytes of Chaucer's *Canterbury Tales*, you'd use this:

```
$ head -c 100KB Canterbury_Tales.txt
Here bygynneth the Book of the Tales of Caunterbury

General Prologue

Whan that Aprill, with his shoures soote
```

```
The droghte of March hath perced to the roote
And bathed every veyne in swich licour,
Of which vertu engendred is the flour;
Whan Zephirus eek with his sweete breeth
Inspired hath in every holt and heeth
```

And to view the first 100 megabytes of Chaucer's
Canterbury Tales, you'd use…no, that would take up the
rest of the book! But if you wanted to do it, try this:

```
$ head -c 100MB Chaucer_-_Canterbury_Tales.txt
```

The *MB* here means 1000000 bytes, or 1000 × 1000.
I can just hear many of you right now. "What?!"
you're saying, "A megabyte isn't 1000 kilobytes! It's
1024!"

I don't mean to sound like Inigo Montoya, but I do
not think the word *megabyte* means what you think
it means. Ever since 2000, a new set of prefixes is
supposed to be used (Wikipedia has a good article on
this subject at http://en.wikipedia.org/wiki/Mebibyte,
so go check that out for more details). Table 6.3
shows the old and the new prefixes and what they
indicate.

Table 6.3   **Prefixes and Multiples of Bytes**

Old Prefix	Value	Meaning	Meaning	Value	New Prefix
kilobyte (kB)	10^3	1000 bytes	1024 bytes	2^{10}	kibibyte (KiB or K)
megabyte (MB)	10^6	1000 kB	1024 KiB	2^{20}	mebibyte (MiB or M)
gigabyte (GB)	10^9	1000 MB	1024 MiB	2^{30}	gibibyte (GiB or G)
terabyte (TB)	10^{12}	1000 GB	1024 GiB	2^{40}	tebibyte (TiB or T)

Old Prefix	Value	Meaning	Meaning	Value	New Prefix
petabyte (PB)	10^{15}	1000 TB	1024 TiB	2^{50}	pebibyte (PiB or P)
exabyte (EB)	10^{18}	1000 PB	1024 PiB	2^{60}	exbibyte (EiB or E)

So what many of you (and I'm in this bunch, too!) thought was a megabyte—1024 kilobytes—is actually supposed to be called a *mebibyte*, and it's really 1024 *kibibytes*. That cool new three terabyte hard drive I bought? I'm actually supposed to say "Hey, check out my new three *tebibyte* drive!" which makes me sound like I'm stuttering, to my ears. It's too bad, really. Beyond the confusion of new terms, a *terabyte* always sounded like a cool, fierce dinosaur to me. A *tebibyte*? Like something you'd step on and keep walking.

With all that in mind, now you know the various values which you can use with head -c. If you want to see values in terms of 1000, use kB, MB, GB, and so on. If, on the other hand, you want to see values in terms of 1024, use K, M, G, and so on (don't use KiB, MiB, GiB, as those won't work). It might not be what you were expecting, but it's good to know nonetheless.

View the Last 10 Lines of a File

```
tail
```

The head command allows you to view the first 10 lines of a file, and in typical whimsical UNIX fashion, the tail command allows you to view the last 10 lines of a file. From head to tail, get it?

```
$ tail Paradise_Lost.txt
To the subjected plain—then disappeared
They, looking back, all the eastern side beheld
Of Paradise, so late their happy seat,
Waved over by that flaming brand; the gate
With dreadful faces thronged and fiery arms.
Some natural tears they dropped, but wiped them
➥soon;
The world was all before them, where to choose
Their place of rest, and Providence their guide.
They, hand in hand, with wandering steps and slow,
Through Eden took their solitary way.
```

Why use `tail`? Most often, to view the end of a log file to see what's going on with an application or your system. Of course, there's an important option you want to use in that case, as you'll learn in the upcoming "View the Constantly Updated Last Lines of a File or Files" section.

View the Last 10 Lines of Several Files

`tail file1 file2`

You can view the first 10 lines of several files at one time using `head`; unsurprisingly, you can do the same thing with `tail`.

```
$ tail Paradise_Lost.txt Miller's_Tale.txt
==> Paradise_Lost.txt <==
To the subjected plain—then disappeared
They, looking back, all the eastern side beheld
Of Paradise, so late their happy seat,
Waved over by that flaming brand; the gate
With dreadful faces thronged and fiery arms.
```

```
Some natural tears they dropped, but wiped them
➥soon;
The world was all before them, where to choose
Their place of rest, and Providence their guide.
They, hand in hand, with wandering steps and slow,
Through Eden took their solitary way.
==> Miller's_Tale.txt <==
With othes grete he was so sworn adoun
That he was holde wood in al the toun;
For every clerk anonright heeld with oother.
They seyde, "The man is wood, my leeve brother";
And every wight gan laughen at this stryf.
Thus swyved was this carpenteris wyf,
For al his kepyng and his jalousye;
And Absolon hath kist hir nether ye;
And Nicholas is scalded in the towte.
This tale is doon, and God save al the rowte!
```

Also like head, tail includes a header/separator
between the entries, which is helpful.

TIP: As nice as it is that tail lets you see multiple
files, multitail is even better at that task. Why?
Because instead of concatenating the results and
spewing them all out in one big lump like tail does,
multitail shows the last few lines of the files you
specify *at the same time*, each in its own little sub-
window in your terminal. You can download it from
your distro's software repository (see Chapter 14,
"Installing Software," for info) or grab it from
www.vanheusden.com/multitail/. Learn more about
this cool little program from William von Hagen's
"Monitoring logs and command output" (www.ibm.com/
developerworks/aix/library/au-monitorlogs/).

View the Last Several Lines of a File or Files

`tail -n`

Continuing the similarities between head and tail, you can specify the number of a file's lines you want to see instead of accepting the default of 10 by utilizing the -n (or --lines=#) option. Want to see more than one file? Just add it to your command.

```
$ tail -n 4 Paradise_Lost.txt Miller's_Tale.txt
==> Paradise_Lost.txt <==
The world was all before them, where to choose
Their place of rest, and Providence their guide.
They, hand in hand, with wandering steps and slow,
Through Eden took their solitary way.
==> Miller's_Tale.txt <==
For al his kepyng and his jalousye;
And Absolon hath kist hir nether ye;
And Nicholas is scalded in the towte.
This tale is doon, and God save al the rowte!
```

Do you have more than one log file that you want to view? Then this is a useful command. But it's still not perfect. For the perfect command, read the next section.

View the Constantly Updated Last Lines of a File or Files

`tail -f`

The great thing about log files is that they constantly change as things happen on your system. To view them, why not use tail? The problem is that the tail command just shows you a snapshot of a file, and then you are once again at the command line. Want to see the log file again? Then run `tail` again…and again… and again. Blech!

With the `-f` (or `--follow`) option, `tail` doesn't close. Instead, it shows you the last 10 lines of the file (or a different number if you add `-n` to the mix) as the file changes, giving you a way to watch all the changes to a log file as they happen. This is wonderfully useful if you're trying to figure out just what is happening to a system or program in real time.

For instance, a web server's logs might look like this:

```
$ tail -f /var/log/httpd/ d20srd_org _log_20151201
"GET /srd/skills/bluff.htm HTTP/1.1"...
"GET /srd/skills/senseMotive.htm HTTP/1.1"...
"GET /srd/skills/concentration.htm HTTP/1.1"...
"GET /srd/classes/monk.htm HTTP/1.1"...
"GET /srd/skills/escapeArtist.htm HTTP/1.1"...
```

It's hard to represent in a book, but this file doesn't close. Instead, `tail` keeps it open, and makes sure that it shows any new changes. The file continues to scroll up, apparently forever or until you press Ctrl+C, which cancels the command and places you back at your command prompt.

Try it with one of your log files, such as `/var/log/syslog`. Add in the `-n` option to see only a certain number of lines to begin with, and then try it with two files, such as `/var/log/syslog` and `/var/log/messages`, and see what happens. (Hint: It's remarkably similar to what you saw in "View the First 10 Lines of Several Files," but with constant updates.)

One more cool option you can use is `--retry`, which is useful in cases where the file may disappear or become temporarily inaccessible. Think a `/tmp` file, for instance, or a file you're writing to and then destroying in a shell script. With the combination of `-f` and `--retry`, you can keep an eye on almost any file, even if the file might disappear and then come back!

TIP: If you know the PID of the process that is generating the file you're watching with `tail`, you can use `tail -f --pid=PID#`. The cool thing about that is that when the process identified by the PID dies, `tail` will stop its monitoring. For example, say that `apache` has a PID of 2112. Use this command to watch the file generated by that process:

```
$ tail -f --pid=2112 /var/log/apache2/error.log
```

When the `apache` process dies, `tail` will stop monitoring the `error.log` file. Keep in mind that you have to know the file *and* the PID that's generating that file for this to work (`ps` comes in handy here for figuring that out!).

Conclusion

You've looked at five commands in this chapter: `file`, `cat`, `less`, `head`, and `tail`. The first one tells you what kind of file you're dealing with, so you know if the other commands will work with it. The other four all show you text files in read-only mode, but they do so in different ways. The `cat` command shows you the whole file all at once, while `less` allows you to page through a file one screen at a time. The `head` and `tail` commands are two sides of the same coin—or, rather, the same file—as the former enables you to view the beginning of a file and the latter displays the end. Together, these commands make it easy to view just about any part of a text file that you might need to see.

Manipulating Text Files with Filters

The commands in this chapter are all *filters*. A filter takes in input, often via standard input, processes it, and then writes the results to standard output. You will often find pipes in the midst to help move the input and output along, from filter to filter, forming a pipeline (see Chapter 5, "Building Blocks," for stdin, stdout, and pipes).

This chapter looks at wc, nl, cut, sort, uniq, tr, sed, and awk. For a longer list of UNIX filters, check out Wikipedia's article at https://en.wikipedia.org/wiki/Filter_(software). Most of the commands in that list are discussed in this book. Besides this chapter, you can find tee in Chapter 5; cat, head, less, more, tac, and tail in Chapter 6, "Viewing (Mostly Text) Files"; compress mentioned in Chapter 9, "Archiving and Compression"; and grep (extensively!) in Chapter 10, "Finding Files, Directories, Words, and Phrases."

You will find as you are reading this chapter, especially if you've read about the filters in other chapters, that there is a lot of crossover between what these commands can do. The `sort` command can do some things `uniq` can do, and while `sed` and `awk` can do what a lot of other commands can do, `tr` can often perform a job that `sed` and `awk` could do, but faster. And so on.

That's OK! There's often more than one way to do something, and there's nothing wrong with that. The more you learn about these filters, the better you will be at choosing the tool that's best for the task at hand. More knowledge is always a good thing, especially when it comes to Linux and its commands.

Count the Number of Words, Lines, and Characters in a File

`wc`

The `wc` command is a dinosaur, dating all the way back to the First Edition of UNIX in 1971. But it's one that's still useful today; in fact, I ran `wc` earlier today before I started working on this section of the book you're reading! Here we have a command that's 44 years old but is still one you should know and utilize: That is one of the great things about UNIX (and Linux, of course) in a nutshell!

So what does `wc` do? Sometimes I need to count the number of words in a document. Far more often, I need to count the number of lines in a document, and every once in a long while I need to count the number of characters. Fortunately, there's a way to do all three with the same command: `wc`.

```
$ wc "The Call of Cthulhu.txt"
192   11863   70246 The Call of Cthulhu.txt
```

In order, that's the number of lines, words, and characters in H.P. Lovecraft's famous short story. What if I only want the number of words?

```
$ wc -w "The Call of Cthulhu.txt"
11863 The Call of Cthulhu.txt
```

It's pretty easy to remember: -l (or --lines) gives you lines (duh!), -w (or --words) gives you words (double duh!), and -m (or --chars) gives you characters (what?!). Why not -c for characters? Because -c (or --bytes) is used for the *count* of bytes in the document. Ah, well. Everything can't be as simple as we'd like.

What if you have two documents? It gets even more nifty!

```
$ wc "Beyond the Walls of Sleep.txt" "The Call of
➥Cthulhu.txt"
 62  4307 24953 Beyond the Walls of Sleep.txt
192 11863 70246 The Call of Cthulhu.txt
254 16170 95199 total
```

So now you get the number of lines, words, and characters for each Lovecraft tale, but you also get a total. Very nice!

That's pretty useful, but you can do more than just count the lines, words, and characters in a document. You can also count any of those in text that is piped in from another command (it's a filter, remember?).

For instance, I recently wanted to find out how many times a web crawler called JerkyJerks was pounding my server before I blocked it (I'm being nice and not actually naming who it was). I used grep (from Chapter 10) to look for JerkyJerks in a log file, and

then used `wc -l` to count how many times those
morons had been beating on my machine.

```
$ grep JerkyJerks server_access.log | wc -l
15428
```

Ridiculous! Blocked!

Here's another example you're going to see later in
Chapter 13's "End a Running Process":

```
$ ps aux | grep [/]usr/bin/cronolog | wc -l
83
```

I want to know how many instances of `cronolog`
are running, so I first get a list of all processes
with `ps aux` (see Chapter 13, "Monitoring System
Resources") and then `grep` that list for the path to the
`cronolog` command. Finally, I use `wc -l` to find out
how many times `cronolog` is being run on my server:
83. Totally fine.

NOTE: Wondering why I put square brackets around
the first / like this: `[/]usr/bin/cronolog`? Go read
"Search the Output of Other Commands for Specific
Words" in Chapter 10 and find out why!

And now, one final example that also tells you
something important about `wc`. When `wc` counts lines,
that also includes blank lines as well, because what
`wc` is really doing is counting the number of newline
characters in the document.

If you do not want to include the number of blank
lines in the output you get from `wc`, use `sed` (discussed
later in this chapter) to delete all blank lines from the
document and then pipe the results to `wc -l`.

```
$ sed '/^$/d' "The Call of Cthulhu.txt" | wc -l
103
```

The `'/^$/d'` is sed-speak for "search for all lines that begin (represented by the `^`) and end (the `$`) with nothing in between them and delete them (the `d`)." When we first counted the number of lines in "The Call of Cthulhu," we got 192; without the empty lines, we get 103. Big difference!

NOTE: For another example piping output to `wc`, see Chapter 8's "Set and Then Clear `suid`."

Number Lines in a File

`nl`

When you're working with code, it's imperative that you see line numbers so you can orient yourself and others. For that reason, virtually every developer's editor displays line numbers.

But what if you have a story like "The Call of Cthulhu" and you want to insert line numbers in it so your H.P. Lovecraft discussion group can all focus on the same hideous plot points at the same time? In that case, the `nl` command is your friend (in the following example, I've used an ellipsis—the ...) to indicate where I've truncated the lines that were too long).

```
$ nl "The Call of Cthulhu.txt"
1  The Call of Cthulhu by H.P. Lovecraft

2  (Found Among the Papers of the Late Francis...

3  "Of such great powers or beings there may be...
```

```
4   —Algernon Blackwood.

5   I.
6   The Horror in Clay.
[Listing truncated—it's 192 lines long!]
```

If you look carefully at the output, you'll notice that
the blank lines aren't numbered. This is the default
with nl. It is also equivalent to using the -b t option.
The -b lets you tell nl which body lines (hence the -b)
you want numbered, but you then must immediately
follow it up with a type of t (non-empty) or a (all
lines). Yes, there are others, but you're probably not
going to need them; if you do, check the man page.

So, if you wanted to count *all* lines, and not just the
non-empty ones, you'd do this:

```
$ nl -b a "The Call of Cthulhu.txt"
1   The Call of Cthulhu by H.P. Lovecraft
2
3   (Found Among the Papers of the Late Francis…
4
5   "Of such great powers or beings there may be…
6   —Algernon Blackwood.
7
8   I.
9   The Horror in Clay.
```

If I wanted to save the resulting output, I would use
redirection (examined back in Chapter 5) to create a
new file:

```
$ nl "The Call of Cthulhu.txt" > "Cthulhu
➥numbered.txt"
```

I don't know about you, but I'm willing to nominate `nl -b a` as one of the most cryptic command options I've seen. There are worse, but that one is pretty abstruse and not exactly easy to remember.

Select an Entire Column of Data in a Delimited File

```
cut
```

This is also a pretty old command, and it was designed back in the days when tab-delimited files were everywhere. Sure, we still see them now, but now we have lots of other ways to present data in files. That said, even if we're not using tabs to delimit data in files, we're often using something else: commas, semicolons, colons, and periods, for example. The `cut` command lets you select specified columns from a delimited-by-something file and then output them.

Let's start with tabs, since that's what `cut` looks for by default. You have a tab-delimited file named `cool_movies.txt` that contains the following (it's OK that columns don't line up perfectly, because the important thing is that they're still separated by tabs):

```
Movie     Genre   Hero    Year
Die Hard     Action  John McClane   1988
Star Wars    Sci-Fi  Luke Skywalker 1977
John Wick    Action  John Wick      2014
Aliens   Sci-Fi  Ellen Ripley   1986
The Thing    Horror  MacReady       1982
```

To extract the first and third columns of that data, you'd use the following:

```
$ cut -f 1,3 cool_movies.txt
Movie    Hero
Die Hard    John McClane
Star Wars    Luke Skywalker
John Wick    John Wick
Aliens  Ellen Ripley
The Thing    MacReady
```

The -f (or --fields) option tells cut which columns to retrieve. In my example, I told it to get columns 1 and 3 with -f 1,3. If I wanted columns one through three, I'd use -f 1-3. If I wanted all of the columns except the second, I'd use -f 1,3-4.

Here's something that might bite you unless you know what to expect. One server's hostname is wu.images.granneman.com and I want the top-level domain (com), the second-level domain (granneman), and the third-level domain (images), but not the fourth-level domain (wu). To get that, I use this:

```
$ echo wu.images.granneman.com | cut -d '.' -f 2-4
images.granneman.com
```

Did you see that? I got back the third-level, second-level, and top-level domain, but they were separated by a . instead of a tab or something else. Why? Because I indicated that the delimiter was a ., so when I get the fields back, they're separated by the same delimiter.

What if want something else, like a comma? Just use the --output-delimiter option and tell cut what you want.

```
$ cut -f 1,3 --output-delimiter=',' cool_movies.txt
Movie,Hero
Die Hard,John McClane
Star Wars,Luke Skywalker
John Wick,John Wick
Aliens,Ellen Ripley
The Thing,MacReady
```

In the cool_movies.txt example, a tab acted as the
delimiter. But what if it's something else? In that case,
you use the -d (or --delimiter) option to specify that
character.

Here's a simple example. On Linux boxes, $HOSTNAME
is an environment variable that contains the hostname
(surprise!) of the computer, something like
perseus.websanity.com. In some scripts, however, I just
want the actual name of the computer (perseus, in this
case) and not the domain name (websanity.com). The
parts of the domain name are separated by periods, so
those act as my delimiters, giving me this:

```
$ echo $HOSTNAME
perseus.websanity.com
$ echo $HOSTNAME | cut -d '.' -f 1
perseus
```

NOTE: I'm actually being pretty slangy when I use the
words "actual name of the computer" and "domain
name," but I figured it'd be OK here. For more on DNS
and what the various aspects of it are called, see
https://en.wikipedia.org/wiki/Domain_name.

What if I have a URL like http://www.granneman.com/
writing/books/ and I just want the fully qualified
domain name (such as www.granneman.com) out of it?

My delimiters in this case are forward slashes (/).
Here's how I'd use `cut` in this situation:

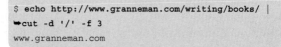

```
$ echo http://www.granneman.com/writing/books/ |
➥cut -d '/' -f 3
www.granneman.com
```

I told `cut` that my delimiter was a / by using `-d '/'`,
and I told it that I wanted the third field with `-f 3`.
However, if you look at the URL, asking for the
third field that was delimited by a / might be slightly
confusing, so let's walk through it. The first field is the
one before the first /, so that's `http:`. The second field
is in front of the second /, which immediately follows
the first / (`//`, in other words), so in essence, the
second field is null with nothing in it. And the third
field is found before the third /, which gives us
`www.granneman.com`. It worked!

Sort the Contents of a File

`sort`

The `sort` command does just what it says—it sorts the
contents of files. Let's say I have a tab-delimited file
named `cool_movies.txt` that contains the following:

```
Movie   Genre   Hero    Year
Die Hard    Action  John McClane    1988
Star Wars   Sci-Fi  Luke Skywalker  1977
John Wick   Action  John Wick   2014
Aliens  Sci-Fi  Ellen Ripley    1986
The Thing   Horror  MacReady    1982
```

Now I want to sort it by movie, so I use the
appropriate command:

```
$ sort cool_movies.txt
Aliens   Sci-Fi  Ellen Ripley    1986
Die Hard    Action  John McClane    1988
John Wick   Action  John Wick   2014
Movie    Genre   Hero    Year
Star Wars   Sci-Fi  Luke Skywalker  1977
The Thing   Horror  MacReady    1982
```

Hmmm. That mostly worked, but it also included the header column in the results, and I don't want that. Fortunately, I can use the sed command (discussed later in this chapter) to delete the first line with the 1d option and then pipe the results to sort.

```
$ sed 1d cool_movies.txt | sort
Aliens   Sci-Fi  Ellen Ripley    1986
Die Hard    Action  John McClane    1988
John Wick   Action  John Wick   2014
Star Wars   Sci-Fi  Luke Skywalker  1977
The Thing   Horror  MacReady    1982
```

What if want to sort not on the names of the movies, but on the years the films were released? Then I use the -k (or --key) option to select a different column for the sort operation, which in this case is the fourth tab-selected field. However, by default, sort uses a space as a delimiter, so you need to tell it to look for a tab as a delimiter.

```
$ sed 1d cool_movies.txt | sort -t '    ' -k 4
Star Wars   Sci-Fi  Luke Skywalker  1977
The Thing   Horror  MacReady    1982
Aliens   Sci-Fi  Ellen Ripley    1986
Die Hard    Action  John McClane    1988
John Wick   Action  John Wick   2014
```

The easiest way to specify a tab after the -t is to type a single quote, press Ctrl-v and then Tab, and finish with another single quote.

What if I want to sort by the year, but in reverse order? Time to use -r (or --reverse).

```
$ sed 1d cool_movies.txt | sort -t '    ' -k 4 -r
John Wick    Action  John Wick    2014
Die Hard     Action  John McClane    1988
Aliens   Sci-Fi  Ellen Ripley    1986
The Thing    Horror  MacReady    1982
Star Wars    Sci-Fi  Luke Skywalker  1977
```

From 2014 all the way back to 1977—and all films that are definitely fun to watch.

Sort the Contents of a File Numerically

```
sort -n
sort -h
```

One last cool feature of sort: numeric sorting. You might be thinking that when we sorted on years in the previous section, it was happening numerically, but in fact, sort saw those years as strings.

Here's an example from my server the other day that shows more clearly how numeric sorting works. I wanted to find out what was taking all the space up in /var, so I started with the du command (which will be discussed in Chapter 13), which reports the disk usage of a file system or folder. The -d 1 option for du specifies the depth to which du should report; -d 1 means to report back the size of the directories

immediately inside /var (hence, at a depth of 1).
Here's the command I used, in which I got the sizes
in bytes of the subdirectories of /var and then piped
the results to sort.

```
$ cd /var
$ du -d 1 | sort
154272    ./cache
1724      ./backups
200976    ./lib
21624     ./mysql_import
2263216   ./log
34479828  ./www
[Listing truncated for length]
```

That didn't really work, did it? Notice that the bytes
were sorted as a string: the 1s came first, and then
the 2s, and then the 3s. But those bytes sure weren't
sorted numerically! Let's try that again, but this time
we'll use the -n (or --numeric-sort) option with sort.

```
$ du -d 1 | sort -n
1724      ./backups
21624     ./mysql_import
154272    ./cache
200976    ./lib
324204    ./shared_assets
2264292   ./log
34434904  ./www
[Listing truncated for length]
```

That worked—the bytes are now in fact sorted
numerically—but it can be a bit hard to understand
what those bytes mean. If we would instead use the
-h (or --human-readable) option with du, we'll get
the sizes reported back in kibibytes, mebibytes, or
gibibytes, for instance. (Not sure what those words

mean? Take a look at "Find Files by File Size" in Chapter 11, "The find Command.") Here's what would happen:

```
$ du -d 1 -h | sort -n
1.7M ./backups
2.2G ./log
22M ./mysql_import
33G ./www
151M ./cache
197M ./lib
317M ./shared_assets
[Listing truncated for length]
```

That's not what we wanted either! The *numbers* are getting sorted numerically, but it doesn't really understand the values those numbers have. It turns out, if you use -h with du, you have to use -h with sort also, so that it knows how to do its job correctly, but you cannot also include -n, as that is incompatible.

```
$ du -d 1 -h | sort -h
1.7M ./backups
22M ./mysql_import
151M ./cache
197M ./lib
317M ./shared_assets
2.2G ./log
33G ./www
[Listing truncated for length]
```

And there we have it! Sometimes it's really helpful to see mistakes and how to fix them instead of just the correct way to do things, so that's why I walked through this step by step. As I always tell my students, making mistakes is the best way to learn—and that's why I've learned so much.

Remove Duplicate Lines in a File

`uniq`

I think everyone reading this is a special little snowflake, different from every other snowflake in the whole wide world. In other words, you're all unique (and yes, I am purposely laying it on a little thick). Now for a segue that's really stretching it... it turns out that Linux can combine duplicate lines in a file down to one unique line for each set of duplicates. In other words, three lines with the words Linux Phrasebook (and only Linux Phrasebook) on them would become one line of Linux Phrasebook. Sorcery! No, it's just a command called uniq.

A few weeks ago I wanted to find out which commands we're running on a server, and how often we're running those commands. Let me walk you through what I did and how uniq played a part. (All of the following examples are truncated; otherwise they'd go on for thousands of lines!)

```
$ history
12291 man rsync
12293 ps aux | grep agent
12294 ps aux | grep ssh
12296 apt-cache search keychain
12297 cat ~/.ssh/authorized_keys
12300 cd /var/www
12302 ln -s /var/shared_assets ~/
12303 cd bin
12314 man dig
```

The history command, as you'll find out in Chapter 12, "Your Shell," spits out a numbered list of the

commands you've entered in to bash. The first column
is a list of numbers, which I don't care about for this
task. After the numbers I see a long list of commands,
options, and files (for example, cd /var/www/ or man
rsync), and I only want commands (for example, cd or
man). So I use awk (covered later in this chapter) to pull
out the second space-separated column of the output
from history:

```
$ history | awk '{print $2}'
man
ps
ps
apt-cache
cat
cd
ln
cd
man
```

OK, that's better in that I now know all the
commands we're running, but that great big long
list (trust me, it's long) isn't helpful since there are
duplicate commands: two each of man, ps, and cd, for
instance. Let's use uniq, since that should just give me
a list of commands, but only one of each.

```
$ history | awk '{print $2}' | uniq
man
ps
apt-cache
cat
cd
ln
cd
man
```

That doesn't seem to have worked. I still see two
entries for man and cd, but only one for ps. What
happened? It turns out that uniq omits repeated lines
only if they are next to each other. In the listing I'm
showing you, the two entries for man are far apart, and
the two for cd have ln between them, so those two
commands didn't get joined into one line. The two
entries for ps, however, are next to each other, so they
get concatenated into one.

To fix this, we first need to use sort, discussed in
the previous section, to order the list of commands
alphabetically, and then pipe the sorted results to uniq.

```
$ history | awk '{print $2}' | sort | uniq
apt-cache
cat
cd
ln
man
ps
```

OK, now we're getting somewhere. The sort
command put the two listings for cd together, as well
as man and ps. Since they were adjacent, uniq reduced
them down to one line in its output. That's better, but
I wanted to know *how many* of each command I was
running. Fortunately, if I use the -c (or --count) option
with uniq, I will get back a list of all the occurrences of
each command before the duplicates were tossed out.

```
$ history | awk '{print $2}' | sort | uniq -c
  14 apt-cache
  50 cat
 229 cd
 249 ln
  84 man
  17 ps
```

That's good—now I know how many times each command was used. But it's not exactly in an order that's useful to me. It's still in alphabetical order thanks to `sort`, but I want it to be in numeric order. Again, `sort`, with the `-n` option (for `numeric`), to the rescue!

```
$ history | awk '{print $2}' | sort | uniq -c |
➥sort -n
 14 apt-cache
 17 ps
 50 cat
 84 man
229 cd
249 ln
```

And there we have it—a sorted, numbered list of commands we've used on this server. You'll often find that you're piping `sort` and `uniq` back and forth, as they really do complement each other very well.

Substitute Selected Characters with Others

`tr`

The `tr` command is used to translate (actually, *substitute* would be a better word) one set of characters into another. For instance, you can use `tr` to convert words from lowercase to uppercase, like this:

```
$ echo "H.P. Lovecraft" | tr a-z A-Z
H.P. LOVECRAFT
```

After `tr`, you specify what you want to translate *from* and then what you want to translate *to*. In the previous example, `a-z` represents lowercase letters, while `A-Z` represents uppercase letters. Instead of using `a-z` or `A-Z`, however, which is the old school method, you should use newer and more portable character classes, like `[:lower:]` and `[:upper:]`. Character classes represent an entire set of characters, and there are many. Here are a few you might find useful, along with the kind of characters they represent:

- `[:alnum:]` Alphanumeric (A-Z, a-z, and 0-9)

- `[:alpha:]` Alphabetic (A-Z and a-z)

- `[:blank:]` White space (space and tab)

- `[:digit:]` Numeric (0-9)

- `[:lower:]` Lowercase alphabetic (a-z)

- `[:punct:]` Punctuation and symbols (what you'd expect)

- `[:space:]` Space (space, tab, newline, and vertical whitespace as well)

- `[:upper:]` Uppercase alphabetic (A-Z)

After looking at that list, you can see what I should have used:

```
$ echo "H.P. Lovecraft" | tr [:lower:] [:upper:]
H.P. LOVECRAFT
```

I sure hope H.P. is cool with that. Wouldn't want to get a shoggoth sicced on me!

Replace Repeated Characters with a Single Instance

```
tr -s
```

The `tr` command has many useful options, and one of them is `-s` (or `--squeeze-repeats`), which allows you to reduce every repeated instance of a particular character down to a single instance. Say you receive a text file from someone and you start reading it, only to find out to your horror that the writer has used two spaces after each period, a certain mark of a barbarian. With `-s`, you can reduce those down to one space each, the way all intelligent, kind, and good-looking people do (I am *clearly* not biased).

```
$ cat "Written by a barbarian.txt"
I clearly do not know how to compose a letter.
➥  Nope, I don't.  In general, Conan is my
➥ hero.  What is best in life?  Crush your
➥ enemies.  See them driven before you.
➥  Hear the lamentations of their women.
$ tr -s [:blank:] < "Written by a barbarian.txt"
I clearly do not know how to compose a letter.
➥ Nope, I don't. In general, Conan is my
➥ hero. What is best in life? Crush your
➥ enemies. See them driven before you. Hear
➥ the lamentations of their women.
```

You can see that the file went from two spaces after each period (*shudder*) to just one (*ahhhh!*). You might be wondering why I used `[:blank:]` instead of `[:space:]`, however. They sound similar, but remember that `[:blank:]` only represents spaces and tabs, while `[:space:]` gets those and also newlines (and some others). If that file had multiple paragraphs in it,

`[:space:]` would strip out the newlines, which would mean that all the paragraphs would be crammed against each other. Not even a barbarian would like that.

And here's one little gotcha about `tr` you should know: I used the `<` to redirect `stdin` so it comes from the file (discussed in Chapter 5's "Use a File As Input for a Command") because `tr` is one of the few commands that does not let you specify filenames as arguments. In other words, you cannot do this: `tr -s [:blank:] Barbarian.txt`. Instead, you must use redirection via `>`, `|`, `<`, and other methods (see Chapter 5 for details): `echo "Too    many    spaces" | tr -s [:blank:]`.

So what if I want to create a new, correctly-formatted file from the barbarian's original? Easy. I use redirection to a *new* file. (Remember, you can't redirect a file to itself, or a small black hole will form that sucks you and your computer into oblivion.)

```
$ tr -s [:blank:] < "Written by a barbarian
➥.txt" > Corrected.txt
```

Now at least you can send the file on, secure in the knowledge that your good name will not end up besmirched thanks to those hideous double spaces after a period!

Delete Matching Characters

`tr -d`

Finally, `tr` with the `-d` (or `--delete`) option deletes characters (bet you didn't see that one coming). I'm going to show you that as part of a function I use to make files Web-ready. (For more on what functions

are and how they work, see Chapter 12's "Create
a New Temporary Function" and "Create a New
Permanent Function"). The following function is
stored in ~/.bash_functions (I've formatted line 4 so
it's easier to read):

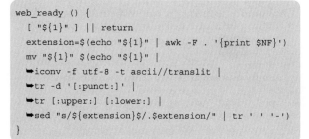

```
web_ready () {
  [ "${1}" ] || return
  extension=$(echo "${1}" | awk -F . '{print $NF}')
  mv "${1}" $(echo "${1}" |
  ➥iconv -f utf-8 -t ascii//translit |
  ➥tr -d '[:punct:]' |
  ➥tr [:upper:] [:lower:] |
  ➥sed "s/${extension}$/.$extension/" | tr ' ' '-')
}
```

Before I explain it, here it is in action:

```
$ ls
What They Know, What You Don't.pdf
$ web_ready "What They Know, What You Don't.pdf"
$ ls
what-they-know-what-you-dont.pdf
```

In order to make a file ready to post on the Web,
I need to remove punctuation, change all letters to
lowercase, and replace spaces with hyphens. Here's
how the function works.

The first line of the function—["${1}"] || return—
makes sure that an argument (the name of the file) is
submitted after the web_ready command, and if one
isn't, the function exits.

The second line—extension=$(echo "${1}" | awk
-F . '{print $NF}')—is a bit more complicated.
We're creating a variable named *extension*; the value

assigned to that variable is the result of the command substitution done inside `$(` and `)` (see Chapter 5). We're echoing the first and only argument to the `web_ready` command, which is the name of the file and represented by `"${1}"` (the double quotes are there in case the filename has spaces in it).

We then pipe that filename to `awk` (coming up at the end of this chapter), which knows that the `.` is a delimiter thanks to the `-F` option. The `'{print $NF}'` tells `awk` to print the last field in a delimited file, which in this case will always be the file's extension (`pdf` in this case, but it could be anything, such as `html`, `markdown`, or `jpg`).

Our extension variable now holds the value of the file's extension: `pdf`. That will be used very shortly.

The third line is long—`mv "${1}" $(echo "${1}" | iconv -f utf-8 -t ascii//translit | tr -d '[:punct:]' | tr [:upper:] [:lower:] | sed "s/$extension$/.$extension/" | tr ' ' '-')`—but it's really not that hard to figure out, with a few small exceptions. We're using `mv` to rename the file from it's original name, represented by that first argument again (`"${1}"`), to the Web-ready name, which uses command substitution to get the result of 5 pipes. That's the interesting part.

First, we state the name of the file with `echo "${1}"` and then we immediately pipe the result to `iconv -f utf-8 -t ascii//translit`. Whoa! What is that? Look carefully at the filename (`What They Know, What You Don't.pdf`), and you should notice that the apostrophe in `Don't` isn't straight; instead it's a *typographic*, or curly, apostrophe. In other words, instead of `Don't` (which uses ASCII encoding), it's `Don't` (which uses UTF-8 encoding).

NOTE: I briefly mentioned UTF-8 in the previous chapter, but I didn't really explain what it is and why it's important. I prepared a webpage and some slides for my students that cover ASCII and UTF-8 and a few other formats. If you want to learn more, check out the webpage at www.granneman.com/webdev/coding/characterencoding/ and the slides at http://files.granneman.com/presentations/webdev/Web-Dev-Intro.pdf.

The problem is that, as of 2015, `tr` doesn't understand UTF-8 yet (which is kinda nutty), which means that my function just won't work. You can run it, but `tr` will choke on that typographer's apostrophe. So we need to use the `iconv` command, which converts files and text from one encoding format (in this case, `-f utf-8`) to another (here, `-t ascii`).

The `//translit` at the end tells `iconv` that if it finds characters outside the target encoding (ASCII, thanks to `-t ascii`), it can substitute similar-looking characters automatically. In other words, when `iconv` hits that typographer's apostrophe, which is encoded as UTF-8 and certainly not part of the much older and simpler ASCII, it will substitute it with the ASCII equivalent, the straight apostrophe (actually the *typewriter* apostrophe). Without `//translit`, `iconv` will run into ʹ and immediately post an error and stop, which isn't good.

Once we get our ASCII apostrophe, the filename is now `What They Know, What You Don't.pdf`. We pipe that along to `tr -d '[:punct:]'`, which removes all punctuation from the name, which in this case includes the comma, the apostrophe, and the period in front of the extension. Uh oh. We need that dot!

Don't worry—it'll be back in just a moment.

At this point, the file's name is now What They Know What You Dontpdf (again, I know the dot is missing in front of pdf!). We pipe that to tr [:upper:] [:lower:], which substitutes uppercase letters for lowercase, so it's now what they know what you dontpdf.

Time to fix the extension problem (told you it would be in just a moment!) with sed "s/${extension}$/ .$extension/". We pipe the current name (what they know what you dontpdf) to sed (coming up at the end of this chapter) and finally utilize our extension variable ${extension}. We tell sed to substitute the value of the extension variable (pdf) with a period and then the value of the extension variable, giving us .pdf.

NOTE: What's the difference between ${extension} and $extension? Nothing—they mean the same thing. It's just that ${extension} is easier to read and see as a variable.

It's obvious that ${extension} is the variable, which stands for pdf, but what does ${extension}$ mean? Look at the following, where it is missing:

```
$ extension=pdf
$ echo "this pdf is ready for youpdf" |
➥sed "s/${extension}/.$extension/"
this .pdf is ready for youpdf
```

After sed finds its first substitution, it stops, so we end up with a dot before the *first* instance of pdf (This .pdf), leaving the filename without a real extension (youpdf). However, a $ in regular expressions always means the end of a string, so that second $ in

${extension}$ matches the extension, since it's always at the end of the filename. In essence, ${extension}$ tells sed to look for the value of ${extension} (pdf), but only when that value appears at the end of a string, represented by the $ (therefore, the youpdf, which becomes you.pdf).

Our filename is now what they know what you dont.pdf, and it's time for our final command: tr ' ' '-'. This uses tr to change every space in the filename into a hyphen, giving us what we've been seeking, a file with a Web-ready name: what-they-know-what-you-dont.pdf. Whew!

Transform Text in a File

```
sed
```

Let me be blunt right up front: The sed command is enormously powerful, complicated, and useful, and the idea that I could cover it effectively in one short section in this book is laughable. That said, I'm going to give it the old college try and focus only on a few major uses of sed that will give you an idea of some of the things you can do with it.

NOTE: The sed command has been showcased several times in this book, so you might want to read those sections too.

- This chapter's "Count the Number of Words, Lines, and Characters in a File," "Sort the Contents of a File," and "Delete Matching Characters" (especially that one)

- Chapter 12's "Create a New Permanent Function"

In addition to my own small contributions, I recommend the following:

- Bruce Barnett's "Sed - An Introduction and Tutorial" (www.grymoire.com/Unix/Sed.html)

- Peteris Krumins' "Article series 'Sed One-Liners Explained'" (www.catonmat.net/series/sed-one-liners-explained)

- Peteris Krumins' *Sed One-Liners Explained* (www.catonmat.net/blog/sed-book/)

- Eric Pement's "Useful One-Line Scripts for sed" (www.pement.org/sed/sed1line.txt)

- Dale Dougherty & Arnold Robbins' *sed & awk*

---

sed is short for *stream editor*, which means that it allows you to transform a stream of text provided either in a file or through redirection. To really use sed to the fullest, you need to understand regular expressions (AKA *regex* or *regexp*), which I cover in Chapter 10's "The Basics of Searching Inside Text Files for Patterns" and in several other sections in that chapter as well.

The first thing to find out about sed is that you can use it to make substitutions. Let's say you have an automatically-generated file that ends with .markdown. txt, and you want the extension to be .markdown without the .txt. The following would get you the proper extension:

```
$ ls
The Cats of Ulthar.markdown.txt
$ title="The Cats of Ulthar.markdown.txt"
$ mv "$title" "$(echo "$title" |
↪sed 's/markdown.txt/markdown/')"
$ ls
The Cats of Ulthar.markdown
```

I used sed in the fourth line to change markdown.txt to simply markdown. Of course, if this is a common task, it wouldn't be too hard to create a function that did the same thing a bit more cleanly. For an example of just that, see the previous section.

Note that the sed command in the previous code listing stops when it gets to its first match on every line. This isn't a problem in that example, as there will only be one double extension (.markdown.txt) in each filename (which is definitely just one line!). But what if we want to perform a substitution every single time the matched text is found, no matter the number of lines?

```
$ cat twisters.txt
1. How much wud would a wudchuck chuck if a
➥wudchuck could chuck wud?
2. How much myrtle would a wud turtle hurdle if a
➥wud turtle could hurdle myrtle?
$ sed 's/wud/wood/g' twisters.txt
1. How much wood would a woodchuck chuck if a
➥woodchuck could chuck wood?
2. How much myrtle would a wood turtle hurdle if a
➥wood turtle could hurdle myrtle?
$ cat twisters.txt
1. How much wud would a wudchuck chuck if a
➥wudchuck could chuck wud?
2. How much myrtle would a wud turtle hurdle if a
➥wud turtle could hurdle myrtle?
```

There are two things to note about that code sample. The first is the g in s/wud/wood/g, which stands for *global*. When you add the g flag, sed replaces every instance of the matched word or pattern on every line of the input. So in my example, every wud becomes wood, even those inside other words (which might be something you do not want in some situations).

The second thing to notice is the original file didn't change! We got the right output printed to the screen, but the file remains the same. To change the file, we could redirect to a new file, like this:

```
$ sed 's/wud/wood/g' twisters.txt >
➥twisters_fixed.txt
```

A better method, though, is to use the -i (or --in-place) option with sed. This actually changes the file to reflect our sed command's changes, so you obviously better be sure that sed is going to do what you want it to do. Look at the screen output of sed to make sure everything is A-OK, and then use -i.

```
$ sed -i 's/wud/wood/g' twisters.txt
$ cat twisters.txt
1. How much wood would a woodchuck chuck if a
➥woodchuck could chuck wood?
2. How much myrtle would a wood turtle hurdle if a
➥wood turtle could hurdle myrtle?
```

I mentioned earlier that you can—and *will*—use regular expressions with sed. They're useful in almost every aspect of sed (you'll end up using regex a *lot* with substitutions), but they can be a lifesaver when it comes to deletions.

Let's say you have a file containing a bash shell script that's filled with comments: lines that start with #. You want to remove those lines because you no longer need them, except for the first one, which is required in a shell script. That's easy with do with sed. You'll need to use the d command (short for *delete*) and a bit of regex. Don't worry about what the following script means; instead, focus on what sed does.

```
$ cat handconv.sh
#!/bin/sh
# Set IFS to split on newlines, not spaces, but 1st
➥save old IFS
SAVEIFS=$IFS
IFS=$'\n'
# Convert files in folder
for i in * ; do
  # Get the extension of the file, so we can get
  ➥$filename
  extension=${i##*.}
  # Get the name of the file, sans extension
  filename=$(basename "$i" $extension)
  # Encode files with HandBrakeCLI
  HandBrakeCLI -i "$i" -o ~/Desktop/"$filename"m4v
  ➥ --preset="Normal"
done
# Restore IFS so it's back to splitting on <space>,
➥<tab>, & <newline>
IFS=$SAVEIFS
$ sed -i '1n; /^[[:blank:]]*#/d' handconv.sh
$ cat handconv.sh
#!/bin/sh

SAVEIFS=$IFS
IFS=$'\n'

for i in * ; do
  extension=${i##*.}
  filename=$(basename "$i" $extension)
  HandBrakeCLI -i "$i" -o ~/Desktop/"$filename"m4v
  ➥ --preset="Normal"
done

IFS=$SAVEIFS
```

The part of the command that performed all the magic
is 1n; /^[[:blank:]]*#/d. The d at the end deletes, but

what about the rest? Remember I said that we do not
want to delete the first line with its # at the beginning
(#!/bin/sh), since it's required for a shell script. That
what 1n; does—it tells sed to skip the first line and
continue onwards. Then we get into pattern matching.

We want to delete the remaining lines that start with a
#; in that case, our pattern would be /^#/ (the ^ means
the beginning of the line). That would catch all the
lines that start with #, but be careful. Some lines that
you might assume would match that will not actually
match. Look at these two lines, both taken from the
shell script:

```
# Convert files in folder
  # Encode files with HandBrakeCLI
```

The first line starts with a # at the very beginning of
the line, which would match /^#/. The second line
appears to start with a #, but actually there are two
spaces before the octothorp, so it doesn't match.

The solution is /^[[:blank:]]*#/. The ^ is still the
beginning of the line, but then the [[:blank:]]
character class (that and others are discussed earlier in
"Substitute Selected Characters with Others") kicks
in and looks for a space or tab. However, we need to
look for more than one space, so we put the *, which
means to match the preceding character *zero or more
times*, after [[:blank:]]. So, to put it into English,
/^[[:blank:]]*#/ means to start at the beginning of the
line (^) and look for a space or tab [[:blank:]] that
may appear zero or more times (*), followed by an
octothorp (#).

And that's how it works with regex, and with sed.
I've barely scratched the surface of sed, but hopefully

I've left you wanting to learn more. And, if you're a computer nerd like I am, or even if you're not, the more regex you can learn, the better able you will be to do all sorts of amazing things on your computer. Learn `sed` and learn regular expressions—you will be very glad you did.

Print Specific Fields in a File

`awk`

I said this at the beginning of the previous section on `sed`, and I have to say it again now that we've moved on to `awk`: The `awk` command is enormously powerful, complicated, and useful, and the idea that I could cover it effectively in one short section in this book is crazypants. I'm going to do here what I did for `sed`— do my best to focus only on a few major uses of `awk`, in this case, primarily selecting columns and printing them. That should give you a glimpse of some of the things you can do with this amazing command.

NOTE: The awk command is also used in an example in Chapter 12's "Create a New Permanent Function," so you might want to read that section, too. In addition to my own small contributions, I recommend the following:

- Bruce Barnett's "Awk" (www.grymoire.com/Unix/Awk.html)
- Peteris Krumins' "Article series 'Awk One-Liners Explained'" (www.catonmat.net/series/awk-one-liners-explained)
- Peteris Krumins' *Awk One-Liners Explained* (www.catonmat.net/blog/awk-book/)

- Eric Pement's "Handy One-Line Scripts for awk" (www.pement.org/awk/awk1line.txt)

- Dale Dougherty & Arnold Robbins' *sed & awk*

- Alfred Aho, Peter J. Weinberger, and Brian W. Kernighan's *The AWK Programming Language* (notice the initials of the last names!)

Named for its three inventors, Aho, Weinberger, and Kernighan, awk allows you to look in files and input for patterns and then filter items and write reports. That might sound like sed, and there are several areas where the two overlap, but awk is an actual programming language, with variables, functions, arrays, system calls, and lots more, and sed is not. Does that mean you should always use awk instead of sed? Nope. It means you should use whichever one is right for the job.

On one of my servers, the mail spool file sometimes gets a little big, so I like to periodically check its size and triage when necessary. I started with a simple use of wc (from earlier in this chapter) to find out how many bytes the mail file is.

```
$ wc -c /var/mail/mail
2780599 /var/mail/mail
```

That's nice, but I only need the bytes, not the name of the file. I'll use awk to output just the actual size by specifying $1, which tells it to print the first column only.

```
$ wc -c /var/mail/mail | awk '{print $1}'
2780599
```

That's better. Those numbers, though… I can certainly do the math in my head, but it would be even quicker if I had the computer do the math for me.

```
$ wc -c /var/mail/mail |
➥awk '{print "mail is " $1/1024 " MB"}'
mail is 2715.43 MB
```

I told awk to print out the string "mail is " (note the space at the end), then to take the first column and divide that number by 1024, and finally to append the string " MB" (again, notice the space, this time at the beginning). The result is what you see as the output in the listing: mail is 2715.43 MB.

TIP: It would be smart to turn that command into a function, as it is kind of long and not very much fun to type. For that, see Chapter 12's "Create a New Temporary Function."

Let's do something similar, but complicate it a bit. Once again, I want to take columns of data and pull out a few to display as a mini report. The df -h command (see Chapter 13) shows the disk usage of file systems on the computer (I removed several lines to save space and to focus on the important ones):

```
$ df -h
Filesystem Size Used Avail Use% Mounted on
/dev/sda   4.9G 742M 4.1G  16% /
/dev/sdb   79G  36G  43G   46% /var
```

I don't want all that, so I'll use awk to rewrite what gets posted to the screen:

```
$ df -h |
➥awk '{ print $6 " has " $4 " of " $2 " left" }'
Mounted has Avail of Size left
/ has 4.1G of 4.9G left
/var has 43G of 79G left
```

Uh oh. The results look good, except for that first
line! Actually, awk did exactly what I asked it to (by
the way, re-ordering columns is perfectly fine): it
grabbed the sixth, fourth, and second columns and
wrote them out with the specified strings (note the
spaces, which make the results readable). The first line
is part of that, so there it is, but I don't want it. Here's
the fix:

```
$ df -h | awk
➥'NR>1 { print $6 " has " $4 " of " $2 " left" }'
/ has 4.1G of 4.9G left
/var has 43G of 79G left
```

I told awk to skip the first line using NR>1. NR is a
special variable in awk that stands for the *number of
records* (lines) awk has seen in the file so far. That
variable increments by 1 every time awk processes a
line. So NR>1 means that after the first line (>1), awk
should start printing what I ordered it to print. Good
boy, awk!

NOTE: Some of you may have looked at the previous
example and thought of this:

```
$ df -h | grep '^/' |
➥awk '{ print $6 " has " $4 " of " $2 " left" }'
```

You are absolutely correct! Instead of using NR>1
in awk, I could've told grep to leave out any line
that didn't start with /, which would have effectively

removed the first line of the output I got from `df`. Which one to use is up to you, but it once again shows that Linux commands often provide you with more than one way to do the job.

Conclusion

There's a wonderful saying called "Taylor's Law of Programming" that goes something like this:

Never write it in C if you can do it in `awk`.

Never do it in `awk` if `sed` can handle it.

Never use `sed` when `tr` can do the job.

Never invoke `tr` when `cat` is sufficient.

Avoid using `cat` whenever possible.

After reading this chapter and the chapters that cover those other commands, you should start seeing the logic behind Taylor's Law. It's funny, but its point is correct: Use the right command at the right time.

We've covered a lot of ground in this chapter, and when it comes to `sed` and `awk`, we've barely started travelling into those two enormous lands. There's a lot left to discover about all the filters in this chapter—and in this book—but it should be obvious to you now that they are an absolutely essential part of the Linux command line. UNIX is built on the idea of small programs that focus on one task, and filters embody that idea perfectly.

## 8

Ownerships and Permissions

From the beginning, Linux was designed to be a multiuser system (unlike Windows, which was originally designed as a single user OS, which is the source of much of its security problems even to this day). This meant that different users would be active simultaneously on the system, creating files, deleting directories, and reading various items. To keep everyone from stepping on each other's toes and damaging the underlying operating system itself, a scheme of permissions was created early on. Mastering the art of Linux permissions will aid you as you use your Linux box, whether it's a workstation used by one person or a server accessed by hundreds. The tools are simple, but the power they give you is complex. Time to jump in!

NOTE: When I updated this book for its second edition, I removed the section about `chgrp -v` and `chgrp -c` (which both tell you what `chgrp` is doing while it's doing it). You can find the original text on my website, www.granneman.com/linux-redactions.

Become Another User

```
su username
```

The su command (which stands for *switch user*, not, as is popularly imagined, *super user*) can allow one user to temporarily act as another, but it is most often used when you want to quickly become root in your shell, run a command or two, and then go back to being your normal, non-root user. Think of it as Clark Kent changing into his Superman duds, righting a few wrongs, and then going back to his non-super self.

Invoking su isn't difficult. Just enter su, followed by the user whose identity you want to assume, and then enter that user's password—not your own.

```
$ ls
/home/scott/libby
$ whoami
scott
$ su gromit
Password:
$ whoami
gromit
$ ls
/home/scott/libby
```

There's a new command in that example, one that's not exactly the most widely used: whoami. It just tells you who you are, as far as the shell is concerned. Here, you're using it to verify that su is working as you'd expected.

Become Another User, with His Environment Variables

```
su -l
```

The su command only works if you know the password of the target user. No password, no transformation. If it does work, you switch to the shell that the user has specified in the /etc/passwd file: sh, zsh, or bash, for instance. Most Linux users just use the default bash shell, so you probably won't see any differences there. Notice also in the previous example that you didn't change directories when you changed users. In essence, you've become gromit, but you're still using scott's environment variables. It's as if you found Superman's suit and put it on. You might look like Superman (yeah, right!), but you wouldn't have any of his powers.

The way to fix that is to use the -l option (or --login).

```
$ ls
/home/scott/libby
$ whoami
scott
$ su -l gromit
Password:
$ whoami
gromit
$ ls
/home/gromit
```

Things look mostly the same as the "Become Another User" example, but things are very different behind the scenes. The fact that you're now in gromit's home directory should demonstrate that something has changed. The -l option tells su to use a login shell, as though gromit actually logged in to the machine. You're now not just gromit in name, but you're using gromit's environment variables, and you're in gromit's home directory (where gromit would find himself when he first logged in to this machine). It's as though putting on Superman's skivvies also gave you the ability to actually leap tall buildings in a single bound!

Become root

```
su
```

At the beginning of this chapter, the point was made that most times su is used to become root. You could use su root, or better still, su -l root, but there is a quicker way.

```
$ whoami
scott
$ su
Password:
$ whoami
root
```

If su doesn't work, try sudo su instead. Different distros do it different ways—no surprise!

Become root, with Its Environment Variables

```
su -
```

Entering su all by its lonesome is equivalent to typing in su root—you're root in name and power, but that's

all. Behind the scenes, your non-root environment
variables are still in place, as shown here:

```
$ ls
/home/scott/libby
$ whoami
scott
$ su
Password:
$ whoami
root
$ ls
/home/scott/libby
```

When you use su -, you not only become root, you
also use root's environment variables.

```
$ ls
/home/scott/libby
$ whoami
scott
$ su -
Password:
$ whoami
root
$ ls
/root
```

Now that's better! Appending - after su is the same
as su -l root but requires less typing. You're root in
name, power, and environment, which means you're
fully root. To the computer, anything that root can
do, you can do. Have fun with your superpowers, but
remember that with great power comes great resp...
aw, you know how it ends!

Change the Group Owning Files and Directories

`chgrp`

By default, on virtually every Linux system, when you create a new file (or directory), you are that file's owner and group. For instance, let's say you're going to write a new script that can be run on your system.

```
$ touch script.sh
$ ls -l
-rw-r--r-- 1 scott scott script.sh
```

NOTE: The user name and group name happen to both be scott on this machine, but that's not necessarily the case on every machine. When a file is created, the user's UID (her User ID number) becomes the owner of the file, while the user's GID (her Group ID number) becomes the group for the file.

But what if you are part of an admins group on your machine and you want your script to be available to other members of your group so they can run it? In that case, you need to change your group from scott to admins using the chgrp command.

```
$ chgrp admins script.sh
$ ls -l
-rw-r--r-- 1 scott admins script.sh
```

NOTE: Yes, the script still won't run because it's not executable. That process is covered later in this chapter with chmod.

You should know a couple of things about chgrp.
When you run chgrp, you can use a group's name
or the group's numeric ID. How do you find the
number associated with a group? The easiest way is
just to use cat on /etc/group, the file that keeps track
of groups on your machine, and then take a look at
the results.

```
$ cat /etc/group
bind:x:118:
scott:x:1001:
admins:x:1002:scott,alice,bob
[list truncated for length]
```

The other point to make about chgrp involves
security: You can only change permissions for a group
if you are a member of that group. In other words,
Scott, Alice, or Bob can use chgrp to make admins a
group for a file or directory, but Carol cannot because
she's not a member of admins.

Recursively Change the Group Owning a Directory

chgrp -R

Of course, you might not want to change the group
of just one file or directory. If you want to change
the groups of several files in a directory, you can use
a wildcard. If you want to change the contents of
a directory and everything below it, use the -R (or
--recursive) option.

```
$ pwd
/home/scott/pictures/libby
$ ls -F
by_pool/  libby_arrowrock.jpg  libby.jpg  on_floor/
$ ls -lF *
-rw-r--r-- 1 scott scott libby_arrowrock.jpg
-rw-r--r-- 1 scott scott libby.jpg

by_pool/:
-rw-r--r-- 1 scott scott libby_by_pool_02.jpg
drwxr-xr-x 2 scott scott lieberman_pool

on_floor/:
-rw-r--r-- 1 scott scott libby_on_floor_01.jpg
-rw-r--r-- 1 scott scott libby_on_floor_02.jpg
$ chgrp -R family */*
$ ls -l *
-rw-r--r-- 1 scott family libby_arrowrock.jpg
-rw-r--r-- 1 scott family libby.jpg

by_pool:
-rw-r--r-- 1 scott family libby_by_pool_02.jpg
drwxr-xr-x 2 scott family lieberman_pool

on_floor:
-rw-r--r-- 1 scott family libby_on_floor_01.jpg
-rw-r--r-- 1 scott family libby_on_floor_02.jpg
```

CAUTION: If you used chgrp -R family *, you wouldn't change any of the dot files in the /home/scott/pictures/libby directory. However, chgrp -R family .* should not be used. It changes all the dot files in the current directory, but .* also matches .., so all the files in the parent directory are also changed, which is probably not what you want!

Change the Owner of Files and Directories

`chown`

Changing a file's group is important, but it's far more likely that you'll change owners. To change groups, use `chgrp`; to change owners, use `chown`. However, there is a big caveat about `chown`: only root (or those with `sudo`, as on Ubuntu) can change the owner of files! Yes, if you're not root, you cannot change who owns your own files.

TIP: Another way to allow others to have access to your files is to have root use the `useradd` or `usermod` commands to add the desired users to the group that controls the files. But notice that even there, root (or a user with `sudo`) has to do the work.

```
# ls -l
-rw-r--r-- 1 scott scott  libby_arrowrock.jpg
-rw-r--r-- 1 scott family libby.jpg
-rw-r--r-- 1 scott scott  libby_on_couch.jpg
# chown denise libby.jpg
# ls -l
-rw-r--r-- 1 scott  scott  libby_arrowrock.jpg
-rw-r--r-- 1 denise family libby.jpg
-rw-r--r-- 1 scott  scott  libby_on_couch.jpg
```

Some of the points previously made about `chgrp` in "Change the Group Owning Files and Directories" apply to `chown` as well. The `chgrp` command uses either a user's name or her numeric ID. The numeric ID for users can be seen by running `cat /etc/passwd` (or by running the `id` command), which gives you something like this:

```
bind:x:110:118::/var/cache/bind:/bin/false
scott:x:1001:1001:Scott,,,:/home/scott:/bin/bash
ntop:x:120:120::/var/lib/ntop:/bin/false
```

The first number you see is the numeric ID for that user (the second number is the numeric ID for the main group associated with the user).

CAUTION: Like `chgrp -R`, you can use `chown -R` to recursively change the owner of files and directories. Still, be aware of a little issue. If you use `chown -R scott *`, you do not change any of the dot files in the directory, which is fine. However, `chown -R scott .*` should not be used. It changes all the dot files in the current directory, but `.*` also matches `..`, so all the files in the parent directory are also changed, which is probably not what you want.

Change the Owner and Group of Files and Directories

```
chown owner:group
```

You've seen that you can use `chgrp` to change groups and `chown` to change owners, but it's possible to use `chown` to kill two birds with one stone. After `chown`, specify the user and then the group, separated by a colon, and finally the file or directory (this is one of many reasons why you should avoid using colons in user or group names).

```
$ ls -l
-rw-r--r-- 1 scott scott libby.jpg
$ chown denise:family libby.jpg
$ ls -l
-rw-r--r-- 1 denise family libby.jpg
```

You can even use chown to change only a group by
leaving off the user in front of the colon.

```
$ ls -l
-rw-r--r-- 1 scott scott libby.jpg
$ chown :family libby.jpg
$ ls -l
-rw-r--r-- 1 scott family libby.jpg
```

TIP: What if a user or group *does* have a colon in its
name? Just type the backslash in front of that colon,
which "escapes" the character and tells the system
that it's just a colon, and not a separator between a
user and group name:

```
$ chown denise:family\:parents libby.jpg
```

This works, but it's better to disallow colons in user
and group names in the first place!

Because chown does everything chgrp does, there's very
little reason to use chgrp, unless you feel like doing it
old-school.

NOTE: When you separate the user and group, you can
actually use either a . or : character. New recommen-
dations are to stick with the :, however, because the .
is deprecated.

Understand the Basics of Permissions

Before moving on to the chmod command, which allows you to change the permissions associated with a file or directory, let's review how Linux understands those permissions.

NOTE: Linux systems can use a more granular and powerful permission system known as Access Control Lists (ACLs). At this time, however, ACLs are still not widely used, so they're not covered here. For more info about ACLs, check out "Access Control Lists" at *Linux Magazine* (www.linux-mag.com/id/1802/) and "FilePermisionsACLs" at the Ubuntu Community Documentation site (https://help.ubuntu.com/community/FilePermissionsACLs). There's also a GNOME GUI editor for ACLs called Eiciel (http://rofi.roger-ferrer.org/eiciel/). If you want more of the technical details, Andreas Grünbacher's "POSIX Access Control Lists on Linux" (www.suse.de/~agruen/acl/linux-acls/online/) was written in 2003, but it still contains a wealth of relevant information.

Linux understands that three sets of users can work with a file or directory: the actual owner (also known as the file's user), a group, and everyone else on the system. Each of these sets is represented by a different letter, as shown in Table 8.1.

Table 8.1   **Users and Their Abbreviations**

User Group	Abbreviation
User (owner)	u
Group	g
Others	o

In the "List Permissions, Ownership, and More" section in Chapter 2, "Navigating Your File System," you learned about long permissions, which indicate what users can do with files and directories. In that section, you looked at three attributes: read, write, and execute, represented by r, w, and x, respectively. Additional possibilities are suid, sgid, and the sticky bit, represented respectively by s (or s on some systems), s (or s), and t (or T). Keep in mind, however, that all of these can have different meanings depending on whether the item with the attribute is a file or a directory. Table 8.2 summarizes each attribute, its abbreviation, and what it means.

Table 8.2 **Permission Letters and Their Meanings**

File Attribute	Abbreviation	Meaning for File	Meaning for Directory
Readable	r	Can view	Can list with ls
Writable	w	Can edit	Can delete, rename, or add files
Executable	x	Can run as program	Can access to read files and subdirectories or to run files
suid	s	Any user can execute the file with owner's permissions	Not applicable
sgid	s	Any user can execute the file with group's permissions	All newly created files in a directory belong to the group owning the directory

File Attribute	Abbreviation	Meaning for File	Meaning for Directory
suid or sgid, but no x	S	Any user could execute the file with owner's permissions (if suid is set) or group's permissions (if sgid is set), but file is not executable	Not applicable
Sticky bit	t	Not applicable to Linux	User cannot delete or rename files, unless he is the file's or containing directory's owner
Sticky, but no x	T	Not applicable to Linux	User can only delete or rename her files, but cannot access to read files and subdirectories

NOTE: The root user can always do anything to any file or directory, so the previous table doesn't apply to root. (Of course, root cannot magically execute things that are not executable, so it can't do *anything*, but you get my drift.)

Each of these file attributes is covered in more detail in the following sections. Now that you understand the basics, let's look at using the chmod command to change the permissions of files and directories.

Change Permissions on Files and Directories Using Alphabetic Notation

```
chmod [ugo] [+-=] [rwx]
```

You can use two notations with chmod: alphabetic or numeric. Both have their advantages, but it's sometimes easier for users to learn the alphabetic system first. Basically, the alphabetic method uses a simple formula: the user group you want to affect (u, g, o); followed by a plus sign (+) to grant permission, a minus sign (−) to remove permission, or an equal sign (=) to set exact permission; followed by the letters (r, w, x, s, t) representing the permission you want to alter. For instance, let's say you want to allow members of the family group to be able to change a picture.

```
$ ls -l
-rw-r--r-- 1 scott family libby.jpg
$ chmod g+w libby.jpg
$ ls -l
-rw-rw-r-- 1 scott family libby.jpg
```

Easy enough. But what if you had wanted to give both the family group and all other users write permission on the file?

```
$ ls -l
-rw-r--r-- 1 scott family libby.jpg
$ chmod go+w libby.jpg
$ ls -l
-rw-rw-rw- 1 scott family libby.jpg
```

Of course, because you're really giving all users—the owner, the group, and the world—read and write access, you could have just done it like this:

```
$ ls -l
-rw-r--r-- 1 scott family libby.jpg
$ chmod a=rw libby.jpg
$ ls -l
-rw-rw-rw- 1 scott family libby.jpg
```

You realize you made a mistake, and need to remove the capability of the family group and the world to alter that picture, and also ensure that the world can't even see the picture.

```
$ ls -l
-rw-rw-rw- 1 scott family libby.jpg
$ chmod go-w libby.jpg
$ ls -l
-rw-r--r-- 1 scott family libby.jpg
$ chmod o-r libby.jpg
$ ls -l
-rw-r----- 1 scott family libby.jpg
```

Instead of the -, you could have used the =:

```
$ ls -l
-rw-rw-rw- 1 scott family libby.jpg
$ chmod g=r libby.jpg
$ ls -l
-rw-r--rw- 1 scott family libby.jpg
$ chmod o= libby.jpg
$ ls -l
-rw-r----- 1 scott family libby.jpg
```

Notice on the last chmod that o equaled nothing, effectively removing all permissions for all other users on the system. Now that's fast and efficient!

The disadvantage to the alphabetic system is shown in the last example: If you want to make changes to two or more user groups and those changes are different for each user group, you end up running chmod at least two times. The next section shows how numeric permissions get around that problem.

Change Permissions on Files and Directories Using Numeric Permissions

```
chmod [0-7][0-7][0-7]
```

Numeric permissions (also known as octal permissions) are built around the binary numeric system. We're going to skip the complicated reasons why the permissions have certain numbers and focus on the end meaning: read (r) has a value of 4, write (w) is 2, and execute (x) is 1. Remember that Linux permissions recognize three user groups—the owner, the group, and the world—and each user group can read, write, and execute (see Table 8.3).

Table 8.3 **Permissions and Numeric Representations**

	Owner	Group	World
Permissions	r; w; x	r; w; x	r; w; x
Numeric representation	4; 2; 1	4; 2; 1	4; 2; 1

Permissions under this schema become a matter of simple addition. Here are a few examples:

- A user has read and write permissions for a file or directory. Read is 4, write is 2, and execute is 0 (because it's not granted). 4 + 2 + 0 = 6.

- A user has read and execute permissions for a file. Read is 4, write is 0 (because that permission hasn't been granted), and execute is 1. 4 + 0 + 1 = 5.

- A user has read, write, and execute permissions for a directory. Read is 4, write is 2, and execute is 1. 4 + 2 + 1 = 7.

Under this method, the most a user group can have is 7 (read, write, and execute), and the least is 0 (cannot read, write, or execute). Because there are three user groups, you have three numbers, each between 0 and 7, and each representing what permissions that user group has associated with it. Table 8.4 shows the possible numbers and what they mean.

Table 8.4   **Numeric Permissions Represented with `ls -l`**

Number	`ls -l` Representation
0	`- - -`
1	`- -x`
2	`-w-`
3	`-wx`
4	`r- -`
5	`r-x`
6	`rw-`
7	`rwx`

Although a wide variety of permissions can be set, a few tend to reappear constantly. Table 8.5 shows common permissions and what they mean.

Table 8.5   **Common Permissions Represented with** `ls -l`

chmod Command	ls -l Representation	Meaning
chmod 400	-r--------	Owner can read; no one else can do anything
chmod 644	-rw-r--r--	Everyone can read; only owner can edit
chmod 660	-rw-rw----	Owner and group can read and edit; world can do nothing
chmod 664	-rw-rw-r--	Everyone can read; owner and group can edit
chmod 700	-rwx------	Owner can read, write, and execute; no one else can do anything
chmod 744	-rwxr--r--	Everyone can read; only owner can edit and execute
chmod 755	-rwxr-xr-x	Everyone can read and execute; only owner can edit
chmod 777	-rwxrwxrwx	Everyone can read, edit, and execute (not usually a good idea)

CAUTION: Yes, you can set `chmod 000` on a file or directory, but that obviously means that no one can read or change the file's contents except root. However, both root and the owner of the file can still use `chmod` to change permissions again back to normal. Your `chmod 000` changed who can alter what is *in* the file, but didn't change who can set permissions *on* the file.

Octal permissions should now make a bit of sense. They require a bit more cogitation to understand than alphabetic permissions, but they also allow you to set changes in one fell swoop. Let's revisit the examples from "Change Permissions on Files and Directories Using Alphabetic Notation" but with numbers instead.

Let's say you want to allow members of the `family` group to be able to change a picture.

```
$ ls -l
-rw-r--r-- 1 scott family libby.jpg
$ chmod 664 libby.jpg
$ ls -l
-rw-rw-r-- 1 scott family libby.jpg
```

What if you had wanted to give both the `family` group and all other users write permission on the file?

```
$ ls -l
-rw-r--r-- 1 scott family libby.jpg
$ chmod 666 libby.jpg
$ ls -l
-rw-rw-rw- 1 scott family libby.jpg
```

You realize you made a mistake, and you need to remove the capability of the `family` group and the world to alter that picture and also ensure that the world can't even see the picture.

```
$ ls -l
-rw-rw-rw- 1 scott family libby.jpg
$ chmod 640 libby.jpg
$ ls -l
-rw-r----- 1 scott family libby.jpg
```

This example shows the difference between using numbers and using letters. The numeric method uses chmod 640, while the letter method would use chmod a=rw,go-w,o-r or chmod u=rw,g=r,o=. Personally, I find numeric notation far easier to remember, use, and type. Learn both methods, but pick the one that feels more natural to you.

TIP: If you still want some help with octal permissions, there's a great tool that makes things a lot easier at permissions-calculator.org.

Change Permissions Recursively

`chmod -R`

You've probably noticed by now that many Linux commands allow you to apply them recursively to files and directories, and chmod is no different. With the -R (or --recursive) option, you can change the permissions of hundreds of file system objects in seconds—just be sure that's what you want to do.

```
$ pwd
/home/scott/pictures/libby

$ ls -lF
drwxrw----  2 scott scott     120 by_pool/
-rw-r--r--  1 scott scott   73786 libby_arrowrock.jpg
-rw-r--r--  1 scott scott   18034 libby.jpg
drwxrw----  2 scott scott     208 on_floor/
$ ls -l *
-rw-r--r--  1 scott scott   73786 libby_arrowrock.jpg
-rw-r--r--  1 scott scott   18034 libby.jpg

by_pool:
-rw-r--r--  1 scott scott  413929 libby_by_pool_02.jpg
-rwxr-xr-x  2 scott scott   64983 lieberman_pool.jpg

on_floor:
-rw-r--r--  1 scott scott  218849 libby_on_floor_01.jpg
-rw-r--r--  1 scott scott  200024 libby_on_floor_02.jpg
$ chgrp -R family *
$ chmod -R 660 *
chmod: 'by_pool': Permission denied
chmod: 'on_floor': Permission denied
```

"Permission denied?" What happened? Take a look
at Table 8.2. If a file is executable, it can be run as a
program, but a directory must be executable to allow
users access inside it to read its files and subdirectories.
Running chmod -R 660 * removed the x permission
from everything—files and directories. When chmod
went to report what it had done, it couldn't because it
couldn't read inside those directories, since they were
no longer executable.

So what should you do? There really isn't a simple
answer. You could run chmod using a wildcard that
only affects files of a certain type, like this:

```
$ chmod -R 660 *.jpg
```

That would only affect images and not directories, so you wouldn't have any issues. If you have files of more than one type, however, it can quickly grow tedious, as you'll have to run chmod once for every file type.

If you have many subdirectories within subdirectories, or too many file types to deal with, you can be really clever and use the find command to look for all files that are not directories and then change their permissions. You'll learn more about that in Chapter 11.

The big takeaway here: When changing permissions recursively, be careful. You might not get what you expected and end up preventing access to files and subdirectories accidentally.

Set and Then Clear suid

```
chmod u[+-]s
chmod 4[0-7][0-7][0-7]
```

In the "Understand the Basics of Permissions" section, you looked at several possible permissions. You've focused on r, w, and x because those are the most common, but others can come in handy at times. Let's take a look at suid, which only applies to executable files, never directories.

After suid is set, suid means that a user can execute a file with the owner's permissions, as though it was the owner of the program running it. You can see a common example of suid in action by looking at the permissions for the passwd command, which allows users to set and change their passwords.

```
$ ls -l /usr/bin/passwd
-rwsr-xr-x 1 root root /usr/bin/passwd
```

You can see that passwd is set as suid because it has an s where the user's x should be. The root user owns passwd, but it's necessary that ordinary users be allowed to run the command, or they wouldn't be able to change their passwords on their own. To make the passwd command executable for everyone, x is set for the user, the group, and all users on the system. That's not enough, however. The answer is to set passwd as suid root, so anyone can run it with root's permissions for that command.

NOTE: You might see both an s and an S to indicate that suid is set. You see an s if the owner already had execute permissions (x) before you set suid, and an S if the owner didn't have execute set before suid was put in place. The end result is the same, but the capitalization tells you what was in place originally.

Now let's be honest—as an ordinary user, it's not very likely that you'll need to change programs to suid. In fact, it can be a big security hole, so please think carefully before you do it! It's still good to know about it for that once-in-a-while case in which you need to use it.

TIP: Want to find out how many programs on your Linux box are set suid? Run this command (on my server, there were only 22, which ain't too bad):

```
$ find / -xdev -perm -4000 -type f
➡ -print0 | xargs -0 ls -l | wc -l
```

When you find that it's time to put suid into action, and you've carefully thought through the security implications, you can set and unset suid in two ways: using letters or using numbers. Let's say that you, acting as root, have installed a program named *foobar* that absolutely *requires* that the suid bit is set. The alphabet method would look like this:

```
$ ls -l
-rwxr-xr-- 1 root admins foobar
$ chmod u+s foobar
$ ls -l
-rwsr-xr-- 1 root admins foobar
```

Now anyone in the admins group can run foobar as though they were root. But note that anyone not in the admins group is shut out because it only has read permission for the program. If it was necessary for everyone on the system to be able to run foobar as root, the permissions would be -rwsr-xr-x.

Removing suid is a matter of using u- instead of u+.

```
$ ls -l
-rwsr-xr-- 1 root admins foobar
$ chmod u-s foobar
$ ls -l
-rwxr-xr-- 1 root admins foobar
```

Setting suid via octal permissions is a bit more complicated, only because it introduces a new facet to the numeric permissions you've been using. You'll recall that numeric permissions use three digits, with the first representing what is allowed for the owner, the second for the group, and the third for all other users. It turns out that there's actually a fourth digit that appears to the left of the owner's number. That digit is a 0 the vast majority of the time, however, so it's not necessary to display or use it. In other words, chmod 644 libby.jpg and chmod 0644 libby.jpg are exactly the same thing. You only need that fourth digit when you want to change suid (or sgid or the sticky bit, as you'll see in the following sections).

The number for setting suid is 4, so you'd change foobar using numbers like this:

```
$ ls -l
-rwxr-xr-- 1 root admins foobar
$ chmod 4754 foobar
$ ls -l
-rwsr-xr-- 1 root admins foobar
```

Removing suid is a matter of purposely invoking the 0 because that sets things back to the default state, without suid in place.

```
$ ls -l
-rwsr-xr-- 1 root admins foobar
$ chmod 0754 foobar
$ ls -l
-rwxr-xr-- 1 root admins foobar
```

TIP: One important thing you should know about suid: It will not work on any *interpreted* program, which means any script that starts with #!. If you think about it, this is a very smart move, security-wise! For more, read www.faqs.org/faqs/unix-faq/faq/part4/ section-7.html.

Set and Then Clear sgid

```
chmod g[+-]s
chmod 2[0-7][0-7][0-7]
```

Closely related to suid is sgid. sgid can apply to both
files and directories. For files, sgid is just like suid,
except that a user can now execute a file with the
group's permissions instead of an owner's permissions.
For example, on your system the crontab command is
probably set as sgid, so that users can ask cron to run
programs for them, but as the much more restricted
crontab group rather than the all-powerful root user.

```
$ ls -l /usr/bin/crontab
-rwxr-sr-x 1 root crontab /usr/bin/crontab
```

When applied to directories, sgid does something
interesting: Any subsequent files created in that
directory belong to the group assigned to the
directory. An example helps make this clearer.

Let's say you have three users—Alice, Bob, and
Carol—who are all members of the admins group.
Alice's username is alice, and her primary group is
also alice, an extremely common occurrence on most
Linux systems. Bob and Carol follow the same pattern,
with their usernames and primary groups being,
respectively, bob and carol. If Alice creates a file in a
directory shared by the admins group, the owner and
group for that file is alice, which means that the other
members of the admins group are unable to write to
that file. Sure, Alice could run chgrp admins document
(or chown :admins document) after she creates a new
file, but that quickly grows incredibly tedious.

If the shared directory is set to sgid, however, any
new file created in that directory is still owned by the
user who created the file, but it's also automatically
assigned to the directory's group, in this case, admins.
The result: Alice, Bob, and Carol can all read and
edit any files created in that shared directory, with a
minimum of tedium.

Unsurprisingly, you can set sgid with either letters or
numbers. Using letters, sgid is just like suid, except
that a g instead of a u is used. Let's look at sgid applied
to a directory, but keep in mind that the same process
is used on a file.

```
$ ls -1F
drwxr-xr-x 11 scott admins bin/
$ chmod g+s bin
$ ls -1F
drwxr-Sr-x 11 scott admins bin/
```

NOTE: You might see both an s and an s to indicate
that sgid is set. You see an s if the group already had
execute permissions (x) before you set sgid, and an s
if the group didn't have execute set before sgid was
put in place. The end result is the same, but the capitalization tells you what was in place originally.

Removing sgid is pretty much the opposite of adding it.

```
$ ls -1F
drwxr-Sr-x 11 scott admins bin/
$ chmod g-s bin
$ ls -1F
drwxr-xr-x 11 scott admins bin/
```

If you haven't already read the previous section,
"Set and Then Clear suid," go back and do so, as
it explains the otherwise mysterious fourth digit
that appears just before the number representing the
owner's permissions. In the case of suid, that number
is 4; for sgid, it's 2.

```
$ ls -1F
drwxr-xr-x 11 scott  admins bin/
$ chmod 2755 bin
$ ls -1F
drwxr-Sr-x 11 scott  admins bin/
```

You remove sgid the same way you remove suid:
with a 0 at the beginning, which takes sgid out of
the picture.

```
$ ls -1F
drwxr-Sr-x 11 scott  admins bin/
$ chmod 0755 bin
$ ls -1F
drwxr-xr-x 11 scott  admins bin/
```

NOTE: You know what creating a new file in a sgid
directory will do, but be aware that other file system
processes can also be affected by sgid. If you copy
a file with cp into the sgid directory, it acquires the
group of that directory. If you move a file with mv into
the sgid directory, however, it keeps its current group
ownership and does not acquire that of the directory's
group. Finally, if you create a new directory inside the
sgid directory using mkdir, it not only inherits the
group that owns the sgid directory, but also attains
sgid status itself.

Set and Then Clear the Sticky Bit

```
chmod [+-]t
chmod 1[0-7][0-7][0-7]
```

Besides being a fun phrase that rolls off the tongue, what's the sticky bit? In the old days of UNIX, if the sticky bit was set for an executable file, the OS knew that the file was going to be run constantly, so it was kept in swap space so it could be quickly and efficiently accessed. Linux is a more modern system, so it ignores the sticky bit when it's set on files.

That means that the sticky bit is used on directories. After it is set on a folder, users cannot delete or rename files in that folder unless they are that file's owner or the owner of the directory that has the sticky bit set on it. If the sticky bit isn't set and the folder is writable for users, that also means that those users can delete and rename any files in that directory. The sticky bit prevents that from happening. The most common place you'll see it is in your /tmp directory, which is world-writable by design, but the individual files and folders within /tmp are protected from other users by the sticky bit.

```
$ ls -l /
drwxrwxrwt 12 root root 496 tmp
[Results truncated for length]
```

NOTE: You may see both a t and a T to indicate that
the sticky bit is set. You see a t if the world already
had execute permissions (x) before you set the sticky
bit, and a T if the world didn't have execute set before
the sticky bit was put in place. The end result is the
same, but the capitalization tells you what was in
place originally.

Like so many other examples using chmod in this
chapter, it's possible to set the sticky bit with either
letters or numbers.

```
$ ls -1F
drwxrwxr-x 2 scott family libby_pix/
$ chmod +t libby_pix
$ ls -1F
drwxrwxr-t 2 scott family libby_pix/
```

Two things might be a bit confusing here. First,
although previous uses of the alphabetic method for
setting permissions required you to specify who was
affected by typing in a u, g, or o, for instance, that's
not necessary with the sticky bit. A simple +t is all that
is required.

Second, note that the t appears in the world's execute
position, but even though the directory isn't world-
writable, it still allows members of the family group
to write to the directory, while preventing those
members from deleting files unless they own them.

Removing the sticky bit is about as straightforward as
you could hope.

```
$ ls -1F
drwxrwxr-t 2 scott family libby_pix/
$ chmod -t libby_pix
$ ls -1F
drwxrwxr-x 2 scott family libby_pix/
```

Setting the sticky bit using octal permissions involves the fourth digit already covered in "Set and Then Clear suid" and "Set and Then Clear sgid." Where suid uses 4 and sgid uses 2, the sticky bit uses 1 (see a pattern?).

```
$ ls -1F
drwxrwxr-x 2 scott family libby_pix/
$ chmod 1775 libby_pix
$ ls -1F
drwxrwxr-t 2 scott family libby_pix/
```

Once again, a 0 cancels out the sticky bit.

```
$ ls -1F
drwxrwxr-t 2 scott family libby_pix/
$ chmod 0775 libby_pix
$ ls -1F
drwxrwxr-x 2 scott family libby_pix/
```

The sticky bit isn't something you'll be using on many directories on your workstation, but on a server it can be incredibly handy. Keep it in mind, and you'll find that it solves some otherwise thorny permission problems.

TIP: In the interest of speeding up your time on the command line, it's possible to set combinations of suid, sgid, and the sticky bit at the same time. In the same way that you add 4 (read), 2 (write), and 1 (execute) together to get the numeric permissions for users, you can do the same for `suid`, `sgid`, and the sticky bit.

Number	Meaning
0	Removes sticky bit, `sgid`, and `suid`
1	Sets sticky bit
2	Sets `sgid`
3	Sets sticky bit and `sgid`
4	Sets `suid`
5	Sets sticky bit and `suid`
6	Sets `sgid` and `suid`
7	Sets sticky bit, `sgid`, and `suid`

Be sure to note that using a `0` removes `suid`, `sgid`, and the sticky bit all at the same time. If you use `0` to remove `suid` but you still want the sticky bit set, you need to go back and reset the sticky bit.

Conclusion

Permissions are vitally important for the security and even sanity of a Linux system, and they can seem overwhelming at first. With a bit of thought and learning, however, it's possible to get a good handle on Linux permissions and use them to your advantage. The combination of `chgrp` to change group ownership, `chown` to change user ownership (and group ownership as well), and the powerful `chmod` gives Linux users a wealth of tools that enables them to set permissions in a way that works best for them.

## 9

Archiving and Compression

Although the distinction is sometimes made opaque in casual conversation, there is in fact a world of difference between *archiving* files and *compressing* them. Archiving means that you take 10 files and combine them into one file, with no difference in size. If you start with 10 100KB files and archive them, the resulting single file is 1000KB. On the other hand, if you compress those 10 files, you might find that the resulting files range from only a few kilobytes to close to the original size of 100KB, depending upon the original file type and how you performed the compression.

NOTE: In fact, you might end up with a bigger file *after* compression! If the file is already compressed, compressing it again adds extra overhead, resulting in a slightly bigger file.

All of the archive and compression formats in this chapter—zip, gzip, bzip2, and tar—are popular, but zip is probably the world's most widely used format. That's because of its almost universal use on Windows and Mac OS X, so things compressed using zip also work on Linux. If you're sending archives out to users and you don't know which operating systems they're using, zip is a safe choice to make.

gzip was designed as an open-source replacement for an older UNIX program, compress. It's found on virtually every UNIX-based system in the world, including Linux and Mac OS X, but it's not present on Windows (without third-party software, that is). If you're sending files back and forth to users of UNIX-based machines, gzip is a safe choice.

The bzip2 command is the new kid on the block. Designed to supersede gzip, bzip2 creates smaller files, but at the cost of speed. That said, computers are so fast nowadays that most users won't notice much difference between the time it takes gzip or bzip2 to compress a group of files.

NOTE: Wikipedia has a good article comparing a huge number of compression formats ("List of archive formats"), which you can find at http://en.wikipedia.org/wiki/List_of_archive_formats.

---

zip, gzip, and bzip2 are focused on compression (although zip also archives). The tar command does one thing—archive—and it has been doing it for a long time. It's found almost solely on UNIX-based machines. You'll definitely run into tar files (also called tarballs) if you download source code, but almost every Linux user can expect to encounter a tarball some time in his career.

NOTE: When I updated this book for its second edition,
I removed the section about `gzip -[0-9]` (which lets
you adjust compression levels with `gzip`) and `bzip2`
`-[0-9]` (which does the same thing, but for `bzip`).
You can find the original text on my website,
www.granneman.com/linux-redactions.

Archive and Compress Files Using `zip`

```
zip
```

Around since 1989, and now ubiquitous on most
commonly-used operating systems, `zip` both archives
and compresses files, thus making it great for sending
multiple files as email attachments, backing up items,
or saving disk space. Using it is simple. Let's say you
want to send a TIFF to someone via email. A TIFF
image is uncompressed, so it tends to be pretty large.
Zipping it up should help make the email attachment
a bit smaller.

```
$ ls -lh
-rw-r--r-- scott scott 1006K young_edgar_scott.tif
$ zip grandpa.zip young_edgar_scott.tif
  adding: young_edgar_scott.tif (deflated 19%)
$ ls -lh
-rw-r--r-- scott scott 1006K young_edgar_scott.tif
-rw-r--r-- scott scott  819K grandpa.zip
```

In this case, you shaved off about 200KB on the
resulting zip file, or 19%, as `zip` helpfully informs
you. Not bad. You can do the same thing for several
images.

```
$ ls -l
-rw-r--r-- scott scott  251980 edgar_at_intl_
➥shoe.tif
-rw-r--r-- scott scott 1130922 edgar_baby.tif
-rw-r--r-- scott scott 1029224 young_edgar_scott.tif
$ zip grandpa.zip edgar_at_intl_shoe.tif edgar_
➥baby.tif young_edgar_scott.tif
  adding: edgar_at_intl_shoe.tif (deflated 4%)
  adding: edgar_baby.tif (deflated 12%)
  adding: young_edgar_scott.tif (deflated 19%)
$ ls -l
-rw-r--r-- scott scott  251980 edgar_at_intl_
➥shoe.tif
-rw-r--r-- scott scott 1130922 edgar_baby.tif
-rw-r--r-- scott scott 2074296 grandpa.zip
-rw-r--r-- scott scott 1029224 young_edgar_scott.tif
```

It's not too polite, however, to zip up individual files
this way. For three files, it's not so bad. The recipient
will unzip grandpa.zip and end up with three individual
files. If the payload was 50 files, however, the user
would end up with files strewn everywhere. Better to
zip up a directory *containing* those 50 files so when the
user unzips it, he's left with a tidy directory instead.

```
$ ls -1F
drwxr-xr-x scott scott edgar_scott/
$ zip grandpa.zip edgar_scott
  adding: edgar_scott/ (stored 0%)
  adding: edgar_scott/edgar_baby.tif (deflated 12%)
  adding: edgar_scott/young_edgar_scott.tif
➥ (deflated 19%)
  adding: edgar_scott/edgar_at_intl_shoe.tif
➥ (deflated 4%)
$ ls -1F
drwxr-xr-x scott scott     160 edgar_scott/
-rw-r--r-- scott scott 2074502 grandpa.zip
```

Whether you're zipping up a file, several files, or a directory, the pattern is the same: the `zip` command, followed by the name of the zip file you're creating, and finished with the item(s) you're adding to the zip file.

Get the Best Compression Possible with `zip`

```
zip -[0-9]
```

It's possible to adjust the level of compression that `zip` uses when it does its job. The command uses a scale from 0 to 9, in which 0 means "no compression at all" (which is like `tar`, as you'll see later), 1 means "do the job quickly, but don't bother compressing very much," and 9 means "compress the heck out of the files, and I'll wait as long as it takes." The default is 6, but modern computers are fast enough that it's probably just fine to use 9 all the time.

Say you're interested in researching Herman Melville's *Moby-Dick*, so you want to collect key texts to help you understand the book: *Moby-Dick* itself, Milton's *Paradise Lost*, and the Bible's book of Job. Let's compare the results of different compression rates.

```
$ ls -l
-rw-r--r-- scott scott  102519 job.txt
-rw-r--r-- scott scott 1236574 moby-dick.txt
-rw-r--r-- scott scott  508925 paradise_lost.txt
$ zip -0 moby.zip *.txt
  adding: job.txt (stored 0%)
  adding: moby-dick.txt (stored 0%)
  adding: paradise_lost.txt (stored 0%)
```

```
$ ls -l
-rw-r--r-- scott scott  102519 job.txt
-rw-r--r-- scott scott 1236574 moby-dick.txt
-rw-r--r-- scott scott 1848444 moby.zip
-rw-r--r-- scott scott  508925 paradise_lost.txt
$ zip -1 moby.zip *txt
updating: job.txt (deflated 58%)
updating: moby-dick.txt (deflated 54%)
updating: paradise_lost.txt (deflated 50%)
$ ls -l
-rw-r--r-- scott scott  102519 job.txt
-rw-r--r-- scott scott 1236574 moby-dick.txt
-rw-r--r-- scott scott  869946 moby.zip
-rw-r--r-- scott scott  508925 paradise_lost.txt
$ zip -9 moby.zip *txt
updating: job.txt (deflated 65%)
updating: moby-dick.txt (deflated 61%)
updating: paradise_lost.txt (deflated 56%)
$ ls -l
-rw-r--r-- scott scott  102519 job.txt
-rw-r--r-- scott scott 1236574 moby-dick.txt
-rw-r--r-- scott scott  747730 moby.zip
-rw-r--r-- scott scott  508925 paradise_lost.txt
```

In tabular format, the results look like this:

Book	zip -0	zip -1	zip -9
Moby-Dick	0%	54%	61%
Paradise Lost	0%	50%	56%
Job	0%	58%	65%
Total (in bytes)	1848444	869946	747730

The results you see would vary depending on the file types (text files typically compress well) and the sizes of the original files, but this gives you a good idea of what you can expect. Unless you have a really slow machine or you're just naturally impatient, you should just use `-9` all the time to get the maximum compression.

NOTE: If you want to be clever, define an alias in your `.bash_aliases` file that looks like this:

```
alias zip='zip -9'
```

That way you'll always use `-9` and won't have to think about it.

Archive and Compress Files of a Specified Type in Directories and Subdirectories

```
zip -i
zip -r
```

You can see that it's easy to use the `zip` command to compress files and directories. But what if you only want certain kinds of files in your zip file? And what if those files are located in subdirectories? You can use `zip` to meet both needs. Let's take them one at a time.

In either case, let's assume the directory structure shown in the following code:

```
$ ls reading/*
Authors_and_Texts.txt

reading/lovecraft:
Beyond the Wall of Sleep.jpg
Beyond the Wall of Sleep.txt
The Call of Cthulhu.jpg
The Call of Cthulhu.txt
```

```
reading/machen:
The Great God Pan.jpg
The Great God Pan.txt
```

Notice there are two kinds of files in the lovecraft folder: txt and jpg. If you only want the txt files in your zip file, you would use this:

```
$ cd reading/lovecraft
$ zip lovecraft.zip . -i \*.txt
  adding: Beyond the Wall of Sleep.txt (deflated 57%)
  adding: The Call of Cthulhu.txt (deflated 58%)
$ ls
Beyond the Wall of Sleep.jpg
Beyond the Wall of Sleep.txt
The Call of Cthulhu.jpg
The Call of Cthulhu.txt
lovecraft.zip
```

There are three things you need to pay attention to:

- To indicate where you want zip to start, use the ., which means the current directory (as I mentioned back in Chapter 2's "View Hidden Files and Folders").

- To tell zip that you want only files of a certain type, use the -i (or --include) option.

- Finally, to specify the actual files, you enter *.txt, which might not seem correct at first. Shouldn't it be just *.txt? It turns out that you need the backslash there in order to allow zip to do the matching, not the bash shell.

This works, but what if you want to get all the `txt`
files in all subdirectories? To do that, start above the
folder containing the files you want, and then run the
following:

```
$ ls -F
reading/
$ zip -r weird_fiction.zip reading/ -i \*.txt
  adding: reading/Authors_and_Texts.txt (deflated
➥58%)
  adding: reading/Lovecraft/Beyond the Wall of
➥Sleep.txt (deflated 57%)
  adding: reading/Lovecraft/The Call of Cthulhu.txt
➥(deflated 58%)
  adding: reading/Machen/The Great God Pan.txt
➥(deflated 60%)
$ ls -F
reading/
weird_fiction.zip
```

This time, the big change is that we add the `-r` (or
`--recurse-paths`) option, which tells `zip` to start at
the current directory and proceed down the directory
structure it finds.

Notice also that instead of using the `.`, I specified
`reading/` as the starting point. Why? Because I wanted
the resulting zip file to be at the same level as the
`reading` directory. If I had instead wanted `weird_
fiction.zip` to be *inside* `reading`, I would've started in
that directory and then used `zip -r weird_fiction.zip
. -i *.txt`.

Password-Protect Compressed Zip Archives

```
zip -P
zip -e
```

The zip program allows you to encrypt and password-protect your zip archives using the -P option. You shouldn't use this option. It's completely insecure, as you can see in the following example (the actual password is 12345678):

```
$ zip -P 12345678 moby.zip *.txt
```

Because you had to specify the password on the command line, anyone viewing your shell's history (and you might be surprised how easy it is for other users to do so) can see your password in all its glory. Don't use the -P option!

Instead, just use the -e option, which encrypts and password-protects your zip file just like -P does. The difference, however, is that you're prompted to type the password in invisibly, so it won't be saved in the history of your shell events.

```
$ zip -e moby.zip *.txt
Enter password:
Verify password:
  adding: job.txt (deflated 65%)
  adding: moby-dick.txt (deflated 61%)
  adding: paradise_lost.txt (deflated 56%)
```

The only part of this that's saved in the shell is zip -e moby.zip *.txt. The actual password you type disappears into the ether, unavailable to anyone viewing your shell history.

Oh, and how do people unzip your password-protected archive? You could type zip -P *password* moby.zip, but that would be a bad idea, as the password would be visible in your history. Instead, just unzip the file like normal. If a password is needed, you'll be prompted to enter a password that isn't then saved to history. Much easier and safer!

CAUTION: The security offered by the zip program's password protection isn't that great. In fact, it's pretty easy to find a multitude of tools floating around the Internet that can quickly crack a password-protected zip archive. Think of password-protecting a zip file as the difference between writing a message on a postcard and sealing it in an envelope: It's good enough for ordinary folks, but it won't stop anyone who's determined.

Also, the version of zip included with some Linux distros may not support encryption, in which case you'll see a zip error: "Encryption not supported." The only solution: recompile zip from source. Ugh.

Unzip Files

`unzip`

Expanding a zip archive isn't hard at all. To create a zipped archive, use the zip command; to expand that archive, use the unzip command.

```
$ unzip moby.zip
Archive:  moby.zip
  inflating: job.txt
  inflating: moby-dick.txt
  inflating: paradise_lost.txt
```

The unzip command helpfully tells you what it's doing as it works. To get even more information, add the -v option (which stands, of course, for *verbose*).

```
$ unzip -v moby.zip
Archive:  moby.zip
 Length   Method   Size   Ratio  CRC-32   Name
 -------  ------   ------  -----  ------   ----
  102519  Defl:X    35747   65%  fabf86c9 job.txt
 1236574  Defl:X   487553   61%  34a8cc3a moby-dick.txt
  508925  Defl:X   224004   56%  6abe1d0f paradise_
↪lost.txt
 -------          ------    ---          -------
 1848018          747304    60%          3 files
```

There's quite a bit of useful data here, including the method used to compress the files, the ratio of original to compressed file size, and the cyclic redundancy check (CRC) used for error correction.

Test Files That Will Be Unzipped

`unzip -t`

Sometimes zipped archives become corrupted. The worst time to discover this is after you've unzipped the archive and deleted it, only to discover that some or even all of the unzipped contents are damaged and won't open. Better to test the archive first before you actually unzip it by using the -t (for *test*) option.

```
$ unzip -t moby.zip
Archive:  moby.zip
    testing: bible/                    OK
    testing: bible/genesis.txt         OK
    testing: bible/job.txt             OK
    testing: moby-dick.txt             OK
    testing: paradise_lost.txt         OK
No errors detected in compressed data of moby.zip.
```

If you're worried about the integrity of a zip file, then use -t to check it out. It would be a smart thing to do, and although it might take some extra time, it could be worth it in the end.

TIP: A related option is -l (which stands for "list"). Looking at a zip file and can't remember what's in it? Wanting to make sure that a file you need is contained within a zip file? Worried about unzipping a file that spews out 100 files into your current directory instead of unzipping a directory that merely *contains* 100 files? Then first give zip -l a try!

Archive and Compress Files Using gzip

```
gzip
```

Using gzip is a bit easier than zip in some ways. With zip, you need to specify the name of the newly created zip file or zip won't work; with gzip, though, you can just type the command and the name of the file you want to compress.

```
$ ls -l
-rw-r--r-- scott scott  508925 paradise_lost.txt
$ gzip paradise_lost.txt
$ ls -l
-rw-r--r-- scott scott  224425 paradise_lost.txt.gz
```

NOTE: As I discussed earlier in this chapter, the zip command allows you to specify how much compression you want on a scale from 0 to 9. The gzip command works exactly the same way.

You should be aware of a very big difference between `zip` and `gzip`: When you zip a file, `zip` leaves the original behind so you have both the original and the newly zipped file, but when you gzip a file, you're left with only the new gzipped file. The original is gone.

If you want `gzip` to leave behind the original file, you need to use the `-c` (or `--stdout` or `--to-stdout`) option, which outputs the results of `gzip` to the shell, but you need to redirect that output to another file. If you use `-c` and forget to redirect your output, you get nonsense like this:

```
$ gzip -c paradise_lost.txt
w`
  I
�1�,(33�찔�i'+��M�S3�t1*f%eY�'[q��
D��}d]C%g�       R�@,r�e▒trB3+3/��|*��0D@▒s
BAqn��,Y8*#"]]RU
```

Not good. Instead, output to a file.

```
$ ls -l
-rw-r--r-- scott scott  508925 paradise_lost.txt
$ gzip -c paradise_lost.txt > paradise_lost.txt.gz
$ ls -l
-rw-r--r-- scott scott 497K paradise_lost.txt
-rw-r--r-- scott scott 220K paradise_lost.txt.gz
```

Much better! Now you have both your original file *and* the zipped version.

TIP: If you accidentally use the `-c` option without specifying an output file, just start pressing Ctrl+C several times until `gzip` stops.

Archive and Compress Files Recursively Using gzip

```
gzip -r
```

If you want to use gzip on several files in a directory, just use a wildcard. You might not end up gzipping everything you think you will, however, as this example shows.

```
$ ls -F
bible/  moby-dick.txt  paradise_lost.txt
$ ls -l *
-rw-r--r-- scott scott 1236574 moby-dick.txt
-rw-r--r-- scott scott  508925 paradise_lost.txt

bible:
-rw-r--r-- scott scott 207254 genesis.txt
-rw-r--r-- scott scott 102519 job.txt
$ gzip *
gzip: bible is a directory -- ignored
$ ls -l *
-rw-r--r-- scott scott 489609 moby-dick.txt.gz
-rw-r--r-- scott scott 224425 paradise_lost.txt.gz

bible:
-rw-r--r-- scott scott 207254 genesis.txt
-rw-r--r-- scott scott 102519 job.txt
```

Notice that the wildcard didn't do anything for the files inside the bible directory because gzip by default doesn't walk down into subdirectories. To get that behavior, you need to use the -r (or --recursive) option along with your wildcard.

```
$ ls -F
bible/  moby-dick.txt  paradise_lost.txt
$ ls -l *
-rw-r--r-- scott scott 1236574 moby-dick.txt
-rw-r--r-- scott scott  508925 paradise_lost.txt

bible:
-rw-r--r-- scott scott 207254 genesis.txt
-rw-r--r-- scott scott 102519 job.txt
$ gzip -r *
$ ls -l *
-rw-r--r-- scott scott 489609 moby-dick.txt.gz
-rw-r--r-- scott scott 224425 paradise_lost.txt.gz

bible:
-rw-r--r-- scott scott 62114 genesis.txt.gz
-rw-r--r-- scott scott 35984 job.txt.gz
```

This time, every file—even those in subdirectories—
was gzipped. However, note that each file is
individually gzipped. The gzip command cannot
combine all the files into one big file, like you can
with zip. To do that, you need to incorporate tar, as
you'll see later in the section "Archive and Compress
Files with tar and gzip."

Uncompress Files Compressed
with gzip

gunzip

Getting files out of a gzipped archive is easy with the
gunzip command.

```
$ ls -l
-rw-r--r-- scott scott  224425 paradise_lost.txt.gz
$ gunzip paradise_lost.txt.gz
$ ls -l
-rw-r--r-- scott scott  508925 paradise_lost.txt
```

In the same way that gzip removes the original file,
leaving you solely with the gzipped result, gunzip
removes the .gz file, leaving you with the final
gunzipped result. If you want to ensure that you have
both, you need to use the -c option (or --stdout or
--to-stdout) and pipe the results to the file you want
to create.

```
$ ls -l
-rw-r--r-- scott scott  224425 paradise_lost.txt.gz
$ gunzip -c paradise_lost.txt.gz > paradise_lost.txt
$ ls -l
-rw-r--r-- scott scott  508925 paradise_lost.txt
-rw-r--r-- scott scott  224425 paradise_lost.txt.gz
```

It's probably a good idea to use -c, especially if you
plan to keep behind the .gz file or pass it along to
someone else. Sure, you could use gzip and create
your own archive, but why do the extra work?

NOTE: If you don't like the gunzip command, you can
also use gzip -d (or --decompress or --uncompress).

Test Files That Will Be
Unzipped with gunzip

```
gunzip -t
```

Before gunzipping a file (or files) with gunzip, you
might want to verify that they're going to gunzip

correctly without any file corruption. To do this, use the -t (or --test) option.

```
$ gunzip -t paradise_lost.txt.gz
$
```

That's right: If nothing is wrong with the archive, gunzip reports nothing back to you. If there's a problem, you'll know, but if there's not a problem, gunzip is silent. That can be a bit disconcerting, but that's how UNIX-based systems work. They're generally only noisy if there's an issue you should know about, not if everything is working as it should.

NOTE: You can also use the -t option with gzip as well, to test the archive when you're creating it.

Archive and Compress Files Using bzip2

bzip2

Working with bzip2 is pretty easy if you're comfortable with gzip, as the creators of bzip2 deliberately made the options and behavior of the new command as similar to its progenitor as possible.

```
$ ls -l
-rw-r--r-- scott scott 1236574 moby-dick.txt
$ bzip2 moby-dick.txt
$ ls -l
-rw-r--r-- scott scott 367248 moby-dick.txt.bz2
```

NOTE: As I discussed earlier in this chapter, the zip and gzip commands allows you to specify how much compression you want on a scale from 0 to 9. The bzip2 command works exactly the same way. Ah, consistency!

Just like gzip, bzip2 leaves you with just the .bz2 file. The original moby-dick.txt is gone. To keep the original file, you use the -k (or --keep) option.

```
$ ls -l
-rw-r--r-- scott scott 1236574 moby-dick.txt
$ bzip2 -k moby-dick.txt
$ ls -l
-rw-r--r-- scott scott 1236574 moby-dick.txt
-rw-r--r-- scott scott  367248 moby-dick.txt.bz2
```

Even compressed, *Moby-Dick* is still a pretty big file. Good thing it's such a great read!

Uncompress Files Compressed with bzip2

```
bunzip2
```

In the same way that bzip2 was purposely designed to emulate gzip as closely as possible, the way bunzip2 works is very close to that of gunzip.

```
$ ls -l
-rw-r--r-- scott scott 367248 moby-dick.txt.bz2
$ bunzip2 moby-dick.txt.bz2
$ ls -l
-rw-r--r-- scott scott 1236574 moby-dick.txt
```

You'll notice that bunzip2 is similar to gunzip
in another way: Both commands remove the
original compressed file, leaving you with the final
uncompressed result. If you want to ensure that you
have both the compressed and uncompressed files, you
need to use the -k option (or --keep), just like you do
with bzip2 when you're creating the archive.

```
$ ls -l
-rw-r--r-- scott scott 367248 moby-dick.txt.bz2
$ bunzip2 -k moby-dick.txt.bz2
$ ls -l
-rw-r--r-- scott scott 1236574 moby-dick.txt
-rw-r--r-- scott scott  367248 moby-dick.txt.bz2
```

It's a good thing when commands use options that are
easy to remember. I want to keep the file, so I use -k
or --keep. Got it!

NOTE: If you're not feeling favorable toward bunzip2,
you can also use bzip2 -d (or --decompress or
--uncompress).

Test Files That Will Be Unzipped with bunzip2

```
bunzip2 -t
```

Before bunzipping a file (or files) with bunzip, you
might want to verify that they're going to bunzip
correctly without any file corruption. To do this, use
the -t (or --test) option.

```
$ bunzip2 -t paradise_lost.txt.gz
$
```

Just as with `gunzip`, if there's nothing wrong with the archive, `bunzip2` doesn't report anything back to you. If there's a problem, you'll know, but if there's not a problem, `bunzip2` is silent.

Archive Files with `tar`

```
tar -cf
```

Remember, `tar` doesn't compress; it merely archives (the resulting archives are known as *tarballs*, by the way). Instead, `tar` uses other programs, such as `gzip` or `bzip2`, to compress the archives that `tar` creates. Even if you're not going to compress the tarball, you still create it the same way with the same basic options: `-c` (or `--create`), which tells `tar` that you're making a tarball, and `-f` (or `--file`), which is the specified filename for the tarball.

```
$ ls -l
-rw-r--r-- scott scott  102519 job.txt
-rw-r--r-- scott scott 1236574 moby-dick.txt
-rw-r--r-- scott scott  508925 paradise_lost.txt
$ tar -cf moby.tar *.txt
$ ls -l
-rw-r--r-- scott scott  102519 job.txt
-rw-r--r-- scott scott 1236574 moby-dick.txt
-rw-r--r-- scott scott 1853440 moby.tar
-rw-r--r-- scott scott  508925 paradise_lost.txt
```

Pay attention to two things here. First, add up the file sizes of `job.txt`, `moby-dick.txt` and `paradise_lost.txt`, and you get 1848018 bytes. Compare that to the size of `moby.tar`, and you see that the tarball is only 5422 bytes bigger. Remember that `tar` is an archive tool, not a compression tool, so the result is at least the same size as the individual files put together, plus a little bit for overhead to keep track of what's in the tarball. Second, notice that tar, unlike gzip and bzip2, leaves the original files behind. This isn't a surprise, considering the background of the tar command as a backup tool (The name stands for *tape archive*, and it harks back to a time when backups were done using massive banks of tapes.)

What's really cool about tar is that it's designed to work across entire directory structures, so you can archive a large number of files and subdirectories in one fell swoop.

```
$ ls -lF
drwxr-xr-x scott scott     168 moby-dick/
$ ls -l moby-dick/*
-rw-r--r-- scott scott  102519 moby-dick/job.txt
-rw-r--r-- scott scott 1236574 moby-dick/
➥moby-dick.txt
-rw-r--r-- scott scott  508925 moby-dick/paradise_
➥lost.txt

moby-dick/bible:
-rw-r--r-- scott scott 207254 genesis.txt
-rw-r--r-- scott scott 102519 job.txt
$ tar -cf moby.tar moby-dick/
$ ls -lF
drwxr-xr-x scott scott     168 moby-dick/
-rw-r--r-- scott scott 2170880 moby.tar
```

The tar command has been around forever, and it's obvious why: It's so darn useful! But it gets even more useful when you start factoring in compression tools, as you'll see in the next section.

NOTE: The `tar` command has a (somewhat deserved) reputation for being a bit, oh, *arcane*. The awesome nerd comic strip xkcd makes a great joke at `tar`'s expense at http://xkcd.com/1168/.

Archive and Compress Files with `tar` and `gzip`

```
tar -pzcvf
```

If you look back at "Archive and Compress Files Using `gzip`" and "Archive and Compress Files Using `bzip2`" and think about what was discussed there, you'll probably start to figure out a problem. What if you want to compress a directory that contains 100 files, contained in various subdirectories? If you use `gzip` or `bzip2` with the `-r` (for *recursive*) option, you'll end up with 100 individually compressed files, each stored neatly in its original subdirectory. This is undoubtedly not what you want. Attach 100 `.gz` or `.bz2` files to an email? Yikes!

That's where `tar` comes in. First you'd use `tar` to archive the directory and its contents (those 100 files inside various subdirectories) into a tarball, and then you'd use `gzip` or `bzip2` to compress the tarball. Because `gzip` is the most common compression program used in concert with `tar`, we'll focus on that.

You could do it this way:

```
$ ls -l moby-dick/*
-rw-r--r-- scott scott  102519 moby-dick/job.txt
-rw-r--r-- scott scott 1236574 moby-dick/
➥moby-dick.txt
```

```
-rw-r--r-- scott scott  508925 moby-dick/paradise_
➥lost.txt

moby-dick/bible:
-rw-r--r-- scott scott 207254 genesis.txt
-rw-r--r-- scott scott 102519 job.txt
$ tar -cf moby.tar moby-dick/ | gzip -c >
➥moby.tar.gz
$ ls -l
drwxr-xr-x scott scott 168 moby-dick
-rw-r--r-- scott scott  20 moby.tar.gz
```

This method works, but it's just too much typing!
There's a much easier way that should be your
default. It involves three new options for tar: -p (or
--preserve-permissions or --same-permissions), which
makes sure that permissions are preserved; -z (or
--gzip), which invokes gzip from within tar so you
don't have to do so manually; and -v (or --verbose),
which isn't required here but is always useful, as it
keeps you notified as to what tar is doing as it runs.

```
$ ls -l moby-dick/*
-rw-r--r-- scott scott  102519 moby-dick/job.txt
-rw-r--r-- scott scott 1236574 moby-dick/
➥moby-dick.txt
-rw-r--r-- scott scott  508925 moby-dick/paradise_
➥lost.txt

moby-dick/bible:
-rw-r--r-- scott scott 207254 genesis.txt
-rw-r--r-- scott scott 102519 job.txt
$ tar -pzcvf moby.tar.gz moby-dick/
moby-dick/
moby-dick/job.txt
moby-dick/bible/
```

```
moby-dick/bible/genesis.txt
moby-dick/bible/job.txt
moby-dick/moby-dick.txt
moby-dick/paradise_lost.txt
$ ls -l
drwxr-xr-x scott scott    168 moby-dick
-rw-r--r-- scott scott 846049 moby.tar.gz
```

The usual extension for a file that has had the `tar`
and then the `gzip` commands used on it is `.tar.gz`;
however, you could use `.tgz` or `.tar.gzip` if you like.

NOTE: It's entirely possible to use `bzip2` with `tar`
instead of `gzip`. Your command would look like this
(note the `-j` option, which is where `bzip2` comes in):

```
$ tar -pjcvf moby.tar.bz2 moby-dick/
```

In that case, the extension should be `.tar.bz2`,
although you may also use `.tar.bzip2`, `.tbz2`, or `.tbz`.
(I would actually avoid using `.tbz`, as the extension
alone doesn't make clear if the file was compressed
using `gzip` or `bzip2`, which could be a bit confusing.)

Test Files That Will Be Untarred and Uncompressed

```
tar -zvtf
```

Before you take apart a tarball (whether or not it was
also compressed using `gzip`), it's a really good idea to
test it. First, you'll know if the tarball is corrupted,
saving yourself hair pulling when files don't seem
to work. Second, you'll know if the person who
created the tarball thoughtfully tarred up a directory
containing 100 files, or instead thoughtlessly tarred up

100 individual files, which you're just about to spew all over your desktop.

To test your tarball (once again assuming it was also zipped using `gzip`), use the `-t` (or `--list`) option.

```
$ tar -zvtf moby.tar.gz
drwxr-xr-x scott/scott        0 moby-dick/
-rw-r--r-- scott/scott  102519 moby-dick/job.txt
drwxr-xr-x scott/scott        0 moby-dick/bible/
-rw-r--r-- scott/scott  207254 moby-dick/bible/
➥genesis.txt
-rw-r--r-- scott/scott  102519 moby-dick/bible/
➥job.txt
-rw-r--r-- scott/scott 1236574 moby-dick/
➥moby-dick.txt
-rw-r--r-- scott/scott  508925 moby-dick/paradise_
➥lost.txt
```

This tells you the permissions, ownership, file size, and time for each file. In addition, because every line begins with `moby-dick/`, you can see that you're going to end up with a directory that contains within it all the files and subdirectories that accompany the tarball, which is a relief.

Be sure that the `-f` is the last option because after that you're going to specify the name of the `.tar.gz` file. If you don't, `tar` complains:

```
$ tar -zvft moby.tar.gz
tar: You must specify one of the `-Acdtrux' options
Try `tar --help' or `tar --usage' for more
information.
```

Now that you've ensured that your `.tar.gz` file isn't corrupted, it's time to actually open it up, as you'll see in the following section.

NOTE: If you're testing a tarball that was compressed using `bzip2`, just use this command instead:

```
$ tar -jvtf moby.tar.bz2
```

Untar and Uncompress Files

```
tar -pzvxf
```

To create a `.tar.gz` file, you used a set of options: `-pzcvf`. To untar and uncompress the resulting file, you only make one substitution: `-x` (or `--extract`) instead of `-c` (or `--create`).

```
$ ls -l
-rw-r--r-- rsgranne rsgranne 846049 moby.tar.gz
$ tar -pzvxf moby.tar.gz
moby-dick/
moby-dick/job.txt
moby-dick/bible/
moby-dick/bible/genesis.txt
moby-dick/bible/job.txt
moby-dick/moby-dick.txt
moby-dick/paradise_lost.txt
$ ls -l
drwxr-xr-x rsgranne rsgranne    168 moby-dick
-rw-r--r-- rsgranne rsgranne 846049 moby.tar.gz
```

Make sure you always test the file before you open it, as covered in the previous section, "Test Files That Will Be Untarred and Uncompressed." That means the order of commands you should run will look like this:

```
$ tar -zvtf moby.tar.gz
$ tar -pzvxf moby.tar.gz
```

NOTE: If you're opening a tarball that was compressed using `bzip2`, just use this command instead (of course, use the `-t` option to test first!):

```
$ tar -pjvxf moby.tar.bz2
```

Conclusion

Back in the days of slow modems and tiny hard drives, archiving and compression was a necessity. These days, it's more of a convenience, but it's still something you'll find yourself using all the time. For instance, if you ever download source code to compile it, more than likely you'll find yourself face-to-face with a file such as `sourcecode.tar.gz`. In the future, you'll probably see more and more of those files ending with `.tar.bz2`. And if you exchange files with Windows users, you're going to run into files that end with `.zip`. Learn how to use your archival and compression tools—you're going to be using them far more than you think.

10

Finding Files, Directories, Words, and Phrases

Every year, hard drives get bigger and cheaper, a nice combination. With all the technical toys we have in our lives now—digital cameras, video cameras, MP3 players, as well as movies and music we find on the Net—we certainly have plenty of stuff to fill those hard drives. Every digital pack rat has to pay the price, however, and that too often tends to be an inability to find the files he wants. It can be hard to find that one photo of your brother in the midst of 10,000 other pictures, or that paper you wrote that's somewhere in a folder with 600 other documents. Fortunately, Linux has powerful tools at your disposal that can help you quickly and efficiently retrieve a necessary file.

TIP: Looking for the `find` command? That's the subject of the next chapter!

NOTE: When I updated this book for its second edition, I removed info about `locate -n` (which lets you control how many results get returned from `locate`). You can find the original text on my website, www.granneman.com/linux-redactions.

Search a Database of Filenames

`locate`

Know the name of a file, or even part of the name, but don't know where it resides on your system? That's what `locate` is for. The `locate` command looks for files, programs, and directories matching your search term. Any matching results are printed to your terminal, one after the other.

NOTE: To save space, I've replaced the first part of the path—`/home/scott`—with an ellipsis.

```
$ locate haggard
…/txt/rider haggard
…/txt/rider haggard/Queen of the Dawn.txt
…/txt/rider haggard/Allan and the Ice-Gods.txt
…/txt/rider haggard/Heu-Heu or The Monster.txt
```

Your search results show up quickly because `locate` isn't searching your system in real time. Instead, `locate` searches a database of filenames that is automatically updated daily (more about that in "Update the Database Used by `locate`" later in this chapter). Because `locate` searches a pre-existing database, its results appear almost instantaneously.

On your computer, though, you're probably using `slocate` instead of `locate`—you're just not aware of it, as many distros create a soft link for /usr/bin/ `locate` that points to /usr/bin/`slocate`. The `slocate` command (which stands for *secure locate*) is a more recent version that won't search directories that the user doesn't have permission to view (for instance, if you're not root, results from /root shouldn't show up when you search with `locate`). Before `slocate`, `locate` would spit back many errors complaining about permission problems; with `slocate`, those errors are a thing of the past.

NOTE: Increasingly, Linux distros are moving from `slocate` to `mlocate` (which stands for *merging locate*), so you may see that on your computer instead. Instead of re-indexing your entire hard drive, `mlocate` re-uses existing databases in an effort to speed things up and not give your hard drive a workout every night. Fortunately, `mlocate` was designed to be backward compatible with `slocate`, so everything I say here should apply just as well.

To verify how `slocate` works, try the following. Note that the first search, done when you're a normal user and not root, fails to return any results. Use `su` to become root (or run the command with `sudo`), run `locate` again, and bingo! Search results appear (`slocate.db` is the database file used by `slocate`, by the way).

```
$ locate slocate.db
$ su -
# locate slocate.db
/var/lib/slocate/slocate.db.tmp
/var/lib/slocate/slocate.db
```

Because it's transparent to the user that she's running slocate, and because locate uses fewer letters and is therefore quicker to type, we're going to refer to locate in this book, even though slocate (or perhaps mlocate) is the actual command that's being run.

Search a Database of Filenames Without Worrying About Case

`locate -i`

In the previous section, you tested locate by searching for any files or directories with the word *haggard* in the name, so you could find your collection of public domain H. Rider Haggard novels. The results looked like this:

```
$ locate haggard
…/txt/rider haggard
…/txt/rider haggard/Queen of the Dawn.txt
…/txt/rider haggard/Allan and the Ice-Gods.txt
…/txt/rider haggard/Heu-Heu or The Monster.txt
```

This worked because the directory containing the novels had the word *haggard* in it. But if that directory had instead been named H Rider Haggard, the search would have failed due to Linux's case sensitivity (discussed in Chapter 1, "Things to Know About Your Command Line"). Sure enough, when you use the `-i` option, a *case-insensitive* search is performed, finding files with both *haggard* and *Haggard* (and, in fact, *HAGGARD*, *HaGgArD*, and so on) in the path.

```
$ locate -i haggard
.../txt/rider haggard
.../txt/rider haggard/Queen of the Dawn.txt
.../txt/rider haggard/Allan and the Ice-Gods.txt
.../txt/rider haggard/Heu-Heu or The Monster.txt
.../txt/H. Rider Haggard
.../txt/H. Rider Haggard/King Solomons Mines.txt
.../txt/H. Rider Haggard/Allan Quatermain.txt
```

It turns out that there were more Haggard novels available than it first seemed (it also turns out that I was sloppy and need to combine those two folders into one!). Remember to use `-i` when you want to maximize your `locate` results, as you can otherwise miss important files and folders that you wanted to find.

NOTE: For more on H. Rider Haggard, see http://en.wikipedia.org/wiki/Rider_Haggard. He's a fun, if very dated, read.

Update the Database Used by `locate`

`updatedb`

The first section of this chapter that introduced `locate`, "Search a Database of Filenames," mentioned that the reason the command is so fast is because it is actually searching a database containing your machine's file and directory names. When `locate` is installed, it automatically sets itself up to scan your hard drive and update that database, usually in the middle of the night. That's great for convenience, but not so great if you need to find a file you just placed on your computer.

For instance, what if you install Rootkit Hunter, a program that looks for rootkits (used by miscreants to take control of your Linux box), and then you want to look at the files the program has installed? The `locate` command won't be able to help you because it doesn't know about those files and won't know about them until its database is updated at a later time. You can, however, manually update the database used by `locate` at any time by running `updatedb`. Because that command indexes virtually every file and folder on your computer, you need to be root to run it (or use `sudo` on distributions like Ubuntu that discourage root use).

```
# apt-get install rkhunter
# exit
$ locate rkhunter
$ su -
# updatedb
# exit
$ locate rkhunter
/usr/local/rkhunter
/usr/local/rkhunter/bin
/usr/local/rkhunter/etc
```

In the preceding commands, you first install `rkhunter`, the package name for Rootkit Hunter, and then exit root. You search for `rkhunter`, but it's nowhere to be seen. You become root again, run `updatedb` to scan your hard drive, and let the `locate` database know about any changes, and then exit root. Finally, you search for `rkhunter` with `locate` again, and this time you're successful.

One thing you should be aware of, however: The speed with which `updatedb` works depends upon the amount of stuff on your hard drive and the speed of your computer. Got a fast processor, a fast hard drive, and few files? Then `updatedb` will work quickly. Do you have a slow CPU, a 5,400 rpm drive, and a kajillion files? Expect `updatedb` to take quite a while. If you're interested in knowing just how long it takes to run, preface `updatedb` with the `time` command, like this:

```
# time updatedb
```

When `updatedb` finishes, `time` tells you how long it took to get the `locate` database squared away. That is useful information to have in your head for next time in case you ever need to use `updatedb` and you're in a hurry.

NOTE: If you're using the newer `mlocate`, then `updatedb` will actually run pretty quickly compared to the `updatedb` used with `slocate`, since `mlocate`'s `updatedb` re-uses existing databases. If your distro is still using `slocate`, it turns out that the `updatedb` command is exactly the same as running `slocate -u`, and `updatedb` is actually just a link to `slocate`. The same is not true for the `updatedb` that ships with `mlocate`—that version of `updatedb` is its own separate program entirely.

Searching Inside Text Files for Patterns

`grep`

The `locate` command searches the names of files and directories, but it can't search inside those files. To do that, you use `grep`. Essentially, you give `grep` a pattern for which you want to search, point it at a file or a group of files (or even a whole hard drive) that you want to search, and then `grep` outputs a list of lines that match your pattern.

```
$ grep pain three_no_more_forever.txt
all alone and in pain
```

In this case, you used `grep` to see if the word *pain* was in a file containing a poem by Peter Von Zer Muehlen titled "Three No More Forever." Sure enough, the word *pain* is in the file, so `grep` prints the line containing your search term on the terminal. But what if you want to look in several of Peter's poems at once? Wildcards to the rescue!

```
$ grep pain *
fiery inferno in space.txt:watch the paint peel,
three_no_more_forever.txt:all alone and in pain
the speed of morning.txt:of a Chinese painting.
8 hour a day.txt:nice paint job too
ghost pain.txt:Subject: ghost pain
```

Notice that `grep` finds all uses of the string `pain`, including `paint` and `painting`. Also pay attention to how `grep` shows you the filename for each file that contains the search term, as well as the line containing that term. So far, it's been pretty easy to search inside files with grep. So it's a perfect time to complicate matters, as you'll discover in the following sections.

The Basics of Searching Inside Text Files for Patterns

In the previous section, you learned that grep works by looking for the existence of a pattern in a group of files. Your first use of grep was extremely basic, but now you need to get a bit more complex, and to do that, you need to understand the patterns for which grep searches. Those patterns are built using one of the most powerful tools in the Linux toolbox: *regular expressions*, also known as *regex* or *regexp*. To take full advantage of grep, you really need to grok regular expressions; however, regex is a book all in itself, so we're only going to cover the basics here.

TIP: Want to learn more about regular expressions? You can search the Internet, and you'll find a lot of good stuff, but I'd head to www.regular-expressions. info first. As for print, *Sams Teach Yourself Regular Expressions in 10 Minutes* (by Ben Forta; ISBN: 0672325667) is a great book that'll really help you as you explore and learn regex.

One thing that confuses new users when they start playing with grep is that the command has several versions, as shown in Table 10.1.

Table 10.1   **Different Versions of** `grep`

Interpret Pattern As	`grep` Command Option	Separate Command
Basic regular expression	`grep -G` (or `--basic-regexp`)	`grep`
Extended regular expression	`grep -E` (or `--extended-regexp`)	`egrep`
List of fixed strings, any of which can be matched	`grep -F` (or `--fixed-strings`)	`fgrep`
Perl regular expression	`grep -P` (or `--perl-regexp`)	Not applicable

To summarize this table, `grep` all by itself works with basic regular expressions. If you use the `-E` (or `--extended-regexp`) option or the `egrep` command, you can use extended regex. Two other, more complicated, choices are `grep` with the `-F` (or `--fixed-strings`) option or the `fgrep` command, which allows you to use multiple search terms that could be matched, and `grep` with the `-P` (or `--perl-regexp`) option, which allows Perl programming mavens to use that language's sometimes unique approach to regex.

NOTE: In this book, unless otherwise stated, we're using just plain `grep` for basic regex.

A few possible points of confusion need to be clarified before you continue. If you're unclear about any of these, use the listed resources as a jumping-off point to learn more.

Wildcards are not equivalent to regular expressions. Yes, both wildcards and regular expressions use the * character, for instance, but they have subtly but importantly different meanings. Where certain characters (? and *, for example) are used as wildcards to indicate substitution, the same characters in regex are used to indicate the number of times a preceding item is to be matched. For instance, with wildcards, the ? in c?t replaces one and only one letter, matching cat, cot, and cut, for instance, but not ct. With regular expressions, the ? in c[a-z]?t indicates that the letters *A* through *Z* are to be matched either zero or one time(s), thereby corresponding to cat, cot, cut, and also ct. The asterisk, as used in c[a-z]*t, would instead mean "any number of letters," so it would match cat, cot, cut, and also strings like chart, cooooooot, or c is less than t—or ct.

TIP: To learn more about differences between wildcards and regular expressions, see "Regular Expressions Explained" (www.castaglia.org/proftpd/doc/contrib/regexp.html) and "Wildcards Gone Wild" (http://www.linux-mag.com/id/1528/).

Another potentially perplexing thing about grep is that you need to be aware of special characters in your grep regex. For instance, in regular expressions, the string [a-e] indicates a regex range, and means any one character matching a, b, c, d, or e. When using [or] with grep, you need to make it clear to your shell whether the [and] are there to delimit a regex range or are part of the words for which you're searching. Here's the list of common special characters that you need to watch for:

. ? [ ] ^ $ | \

Finally, there is a big difference between how the shell interprets single quotes and double quotes, which can bite you when you're trying to use regular expressions. Single quotes (' and ') tell the shell that you are searching for a string of characters, while double quotes (" and ") let your shell know that you want to use shell variables. For instance, using grep and regex in the following way to look for all usages of the phrase "hey you!" in a friend's poetry wouldn't work:

```
$ grep hey you! *
grep: you!: No such file or directory
8 hours a day.txt:hey you! let's run!
friends & family.txt:in patience they wait
speed of morning.txt:they say the force
```

Because you simply wrote out *hey you!* with nothing around it, grep was confused. It first looked for the search term *hey* in a file called you! but it was unsuccessful, as that isn't the actual name of a file. Then it searched for *hey* in every file contained in the current working directory, as indicated by the * wildcard, with three good results. It's true that the first of those three contained the phrase you were searching for, so in that sense your search worked, but not really. This search was crude and didn't deliver the desired results. Let's try again.

This time you'll use double quotes around your search term. That should fix the problem you had when you didn't use anything at all.

```
$ grep "hey you!" *
bash: !" *: event not found
```

Even worse! Actually, the quotation marks also cause a
big problem and give even worse results than you saw
before. What happened? The ! is a shell command
that references your command history. Normally,
you'd use the ! by following it with a process ID
(PID) number that represents an earlier command you
ran, like !264. Here, though, bash sees the !, looks for
a PID after it, and then complains that it can't find
an earlier command named " * (a double quote, a
space, and an asterisk), which would be a very weird
command indeed.

Like I said, quotation marks indicate that you are
using shell variables in your search term, which is in
fact not what you wanted at all. So double quotes
don't work. Let's try single quotes.

```
$ grep 'hey you!' *
txt/pvzm/8 hours a day.txt:hey you! let's run!
```

Much better results! The single quotes told grep that
your search term didn't contain any shell variables,
and was just a string of characters that you wanted to
match. Lo and behold, there was a single result, the
exact one you wanted.

The lesson? Know when to use single quotes, when
to use double quotes, and when to use nothing. If
you're searching for an exact match, use single quotes,
but if you want to incorporate shell variables into
your search term (which will be rare indeed), use
double quotes. If you're searching for a single word
that contains just numbers and letters, it's safe to
leave off all quotes entirely. If you want to be safe, I
recommend defaulting to single quotes, even around
a single word, as you greatly lower your chances for
nasty surprises.

Search Recursively for Text in Files

```
grep -R
```

The * wildcard allows you to search several files in the same directory, but to search in several subdirectories at once, you need the -R (or --recursive) option. Let's look for the word *hideous*, a favorite of horror writers of the nineteenth and early twentieth centuries, amongst a collection of old-fashioned but still wonderful tales (these results are greatly truncated, as any Lovecraft fan would know!).

```
$ grep -R hideous *
Machen/The Great God Pan.txt:know, not in
➥your most fantastic, hideous dreams can you have
Machen/ The Great God Pan.txt:hideously
➥contorted in the entire course of my practice
Lovecraft/Beyond the Wall of Sleep.txt:some hideous
➥but unnamed wrong, which
Lovecraft/Beyond the Wall of Sleep.txt:blanket over
➥the hideous face, and awakened the nurse.
Lovecraft/The Call of Cthulhu.txt:hideous a chain. I
➥think that the professor, too, intended to
Lovecraft/The Call of Cthulhu.txt:voodoo meeting;
➥and so singular and hideous were the rites
```

TIP: Of course, if you get too many results, you should pipe the results to less:

```
$ grep -R hideous * | less
```

Another tactic would be to send the output of the command into a text file, and then open that file in whatever text editor you prefer:

```
$ grep -R hideous * > hideous_in_horror.txt
```

That's a great way to search and store your results in case you need them later.

Oh, and if you're a programmer who needs a more powerful search tool than `grep`, check out `ack` at betterthangrep.com. And yes, it's named for Bill the Cat!

Search for Words and Highlight the Results

`grep --color=auto`

Visual cues are a good thing. In particular, color can really make something pop so that it's obvious. If you're looking for words using `grep`, adding the `--color=auto` option can help you find them quickly and easily (since this book isn't printed in color, I made the colored words in the results bold instead):

```
$ grep -R hideous *
Machen/The Great God Pan.txt:know, not in
➥your most fantastic, hideous dreams can you have
Machen/The Great God Pan.txt:hideously
➥contorted in the entire course of my practice
Lovecraft/Beyond the Wall of Sleep.txt:some hideous
➥but unnamed wrong, which
Lovecraft/Beyond the Wall of Sleep.txt:blanket over
➥the hideous face, and awakened the nurse.
Lovecraft/The Call of Cthulhu.txt:hideous a chain. I
➥think that the professor, too, intended to
Lovecraft/The Call of Cthulhu.txt:voodoo meeting;
➥and so singular and hideous were the rites
```

See? It's easy to find the word, because grep called it out for you!

TIP: You may find that grep is showing colors even though you haven't specified `--color=auto`. In my Ubuntu install, for instance, I was seeing these results (since this book isn't printed in color, I made the colored words in the results bold instead):

```
$ grep Finny family.txt
My son's name is Finny.
$ grep --color=auto Finny family.txt
My son's name is Finny.
```

What was going on? I suspected that Ubuntu had set up grep to use `--color=auto` by default. To check, I ran the following command, which showed me that I was correct:

```
$ type grep
grep is aliased to 'grep --color=auto'
```

As I discussed in Chapter 4's "Discover How a Command Will Be Interpreted," the type command tells you how bash will interpret a command. In this case, grep was an alias. If you suspect that a command has some options aliased to it, try type.

Search for Text in Files, Ignoring Case

`grep -i`

By default, searches performed with grep are case-sensitive. In the previous section, you searched amongst H. P. Lovecraft stories for the word *hideous* (a favorite of that author). But what about *Hideous*?

```
$ grep Hideous Lovecraft/*
Lovecraft/The Whisperer in Darkness.txt: them.
➥Hideous though the idea was, I knew…
```

The earlier search for *hideous* found 463 results (wow!) and *Hideous* returned one. Is there any way to combine them? Yes, with the `-i` (or `--ignore-case`) option, which searches for both, and also searches for *HiDeOuS*, *HIDEOUS*, and all other possible combinations.

```
$ grep -i hideous h_p_lovecraft/*
Lovecraft/The Call of Cthulhu.txt:voodoo meeting;
➥and so singular and hideous were the rites
Lovecraft/The Call of Cthulhu.txt:stated, a very
➥crude bas-relief of stone, comprising a hideous
Lovecraft/The Whisperer in Darkness.txt: them.
➥Hideous though the idea was, I knew…
```

Keep in mind that you're probably increasing the number of results you're going to get, perhaps by quite a bit. If that's a problem, check the Tip at the end of "Search Recursively for Text in Files" for some advice about dealing with it.

Search for Whole Words in Files

`grep -w`

Think back to the earlier section "The Basics of Searching Inside Text Files for Patterns," in which you first learned about grep. You searched for the word *pain*, and grep obediently returned a list showing you where *pain* had been used.

```
$ grep pain *
fiery inferno in space.txt:watch the paint peel,
three_no_more_forever.txt:all alone and in pain
the speed of morning.txt:of a Chinese painting.
8 hour a day.txt:nice paint job too
ghost pain.txt:Subject: ghost pain
```

By default, grep searches for all occurrences of the string
pain, showing you lines that contain *pain*, but also *paint*
and *painting*. If *painless*, *Spain*, or *painstaking* had been in
one of the files that were searched, those lines would
have shown up as well. But what if you only wanted
lines in which the exact word *pain* appeared? For that,
use the -w (or --word-regexp) option.

```
$ grep -w pain *
three_no_more_forever.txt:all alone and in pain
ghost pain.txt:Subject: ghost pain
```

This option can really help narrow your search results
when you receive too many to easily sort through.

Show Line Numbers Where
Words Appear in Files

grep -n

The grep command shows you the line containing the
term for which you're searching, but it doesn't really
tell you where in the file you can find that line. To
find out the line number, utilize the -n (or --line-
number) option.

```
$ grep -n pain *
fiery inferno in space.txt:56:watch the paint peel,
three_no_more_forever.txt:19:all alone and in pain
the speed of morning.txt:66:of a Chinese painting.
8 hour a day.txt:78:nice paint job too
ghost pain.txt:32:Subject: ghost pain
```

Now that you know the line numbers for each
instance of the string pain, it is a simple matter to go
directly to those lines in virtually any text editor. Nice!

Search the Output of Other Commands for Specific Words

`[command] | grep`

The grep command is powerful when used by itself,
but it really comes alive when you use it as a filter
for the output of other programs. For instance, let's
say you have all your John Coltrane MP3s organized
in separate subfolders for each album (66 in all...yes,
Coltrane is that good), with the year at the beginning.
A partial listing might look like this (the -1 option is
used with ls so there is one result on each line):

```
$ ls -1
1956 Coltrane For Lovers
1957 Blue Train
1957 Coltrane [Prestige]
1957 Lush Life
1957 Thelonious Monk With John Coltrane
[Results truncated]
```

Now, what if you just wanted to see a list of the
albums you own that Coltrane released in 1960? Pipe

the results of ls -l to grep, and you'll get your answer
in seconds.

```
$ ls -l | grep 1960
1960 Coltrane Plays The Blues
1960 Coltrane's Sound
1960 Giant Steps
1960 My Favorite Things
```

After you start thinking about it, you'll find literally
hundreds of uses for grep in this way. Here's another
powerful one. The ps command lists running
processes, while the -f option tells ps to give the full
listing, with lots of information about each process,
and the -u option, followed by a username, restricts
the output to processes owned by that user. Normally,
ps -fU scott would result in a long list, too long
if you're looking for information about a specific
process. With grep, however, you can easily restrict
the output.

NOTE: To save space, some of the information you'd
normally see with ps has been removed.

```
$ ps -fU scott | grep firefox
scott 17623 /bin/sh /opt/firefox/firefox
scott 17634 /opt/firefox/firefox-bin
scott  1601 grep firefox
```

The ps command lists all processes owned by the
scott user (64, in fact), but pipes that output to grep,
which lists only those lines that contain the word
firefox in them. Unfortunately, the last line of output
is erroneous: You only care about the actual Firefox
program, not the search for firefox using grep. To

hide the search for `firefox` in the `grep` results, try
this instead:

```
$ ps -fU scott | grep [f]irefox
scott 17623 /bin/sh /opt/firefox/firefox
scott 17634 /opt/firefox/firefox-bin
```

The `grep` search term used square brackets to specify a
regex range—[f]—which in this case runs all the way
from f to f. The search found `firefox` on those lines
output by `ps` in which Firefox was running; however,
it didn't match the line for `grep` because that line was
actually [f]irefox, which wouldn't match. The `grep`
command here can't match the original string `ps -ef
| grep [f]irefox` because it contained [and], and the
`grep` search for [f]irefox resolves to searching for the
exact word *firefox*. This is a bit confusing, but if you
try it yourself and think about it a bit, it'll make some
sense. At any rate, it works. Give it a try!

TIP: If you're really feeling lazy, you should check out
the `pgrep` command, which combines the last several
paragraphs into one simple package.

See Context for Words Appearing in Files

`grep [-ABC]`

When dealing with data, context is everything. As
you've learned, `grep` outputs the actual line containing
the search term, but you can also tell `grep` to include
lines before and after the match. In the previous section,

"Search the Output of Other Commands for Specific Words," you used grep to work with a list of John Coltrane albums. One of his best was *A Love Supreme*. What three albums came out before that one? To get the answer, use the -B (or --before-context=#) option.

```
$ ls -1 | grep -B 3 "A Love Supreme"
1963 Impressions
1963 John Coltrane & Johnny Hartman
1963 Live At Birdland
1964 A Love Supreme
```

If you want to find out what came after *A Love Supreme*, use the -A (or --after-context=#) option instead.

```
$ ls -1 | grep -A 3 "A Love Supreme"
1964 A Love Supreme
1964 Coltrane's Sound
1964 Crescent
1965 Ascension
```

To get the full historical context for *A Love Supreme*, try the -C (or --context=#) option, which combines before and after.

```
$ ls -1 | grep -C 3 "A Love Supreme"
1963 Impressions
1963 John Coltrane & Johnny Hartman
1963 Live At Birdland
1964 A_Love Supreme
1964 Coltrane's Sound
1964 Crescent1965 Ascension
```

This can be a bit confusing when you have more than one match in a file or group of files. For instance,

Coltrane released several live albums, and if you want to see the albums just before and after those, you're going to get more complex results.

```
$ ls -1 | grep -C 1 Live
1963 John Coltrane & Johnny Hartman
1963 Live At Birdland
1964 A Love Supreme
--
1965 Last Trane
1965 Live in Seattle
1965 Major Works of John Coltrane
--
1965 Transition
1966 Live at the Village Vanguard Again!
1966 Live in Japan
1967 Expression
1967 Olatunji Concert Last Live Recording
1967 Stellar Regions
```

The -- characters separate each matched group. The first two groups of results are obvious—an album with *Live* in the title, preceded and followed by another album—but the last section is a bit more complicated. Several albums containing the word *Live* in the title are right next to each other, so the results are bunched together. It might look a bit weird, but if you look at each instance of *Live*, you'll notice that the album before and after it is in fact listed.

The results are even more informative if you incorporate the -n option, which lists line numbers (because you're using ls -1, it's the line number of that ls listing).

```
$ ls -1 | grep -n -C 1 Live
37-1963 John Coltrane & Johnny Hartman
38:1963 Live At Birdland
39-1964 A Love Supreme
--
48-1965 Last Trane
49:1965 Live in Seattle
50-1965 Major Works of John Coltrane
--
52-1965 Transition
53:1966 Live at the Village Vanguard Again!
54:1966 Live in Japan
55-1967 Expression
56:1967 Olatunji Concert Last Live Recording
57-1967 Stellar Regions
```

Now -c gives you even more information about
each line, as indicated by the character after the line
number. A : indicates that the line matches, while -
means that it's a line before or after a match. Line 54,
1966 Live in Japan, does double duty. It comes after
1966 Live at the Village Vanguard Again!, which
should mean it has a -, but it is itself a match, which
necessitates :. Because a match is more important, that
wins and : is ultimately used.

Show Lines Where Words Do Not Appear in Files

`grep -v`

In the jazz world, John Coltrane still rules nearly
40 years after his death; likewise, Led Zeppelin is
recognized as one of the all-time great rock 'n' roll
bands. While they were together, Led Zeppelin
released nine albums; however, many of them had the

band's name in the album title (yes, the fourth release
didn't really have a title, but most critics still recognize
it as *Led Zeppelin IV*, so humor me). What if you want
to see a list of MP3 folders containing Led Zeppelin's
albums, but exclude those that actually have the words
Led Zeppelin in the title? With the -v (or --invert-
match) option, you can show only results that *do not*
match the given pattern.

```
$ ls -1
1969 Led Zeppelin
1969 Led Zeppelin II
1970 Led Zeppelin III
1971 Led Zeppelin IV
1973 Houses Of The Holy
1975 Physical Graffiti
1976 Presence
1979 In Through The Out Door
1982 Coda
$ ls -1 | grep -v "Led Zeppelin"
1973 Houses Of The Holy
1975 Physical Graffiti
1976 Presence
1979 In Through The Out Door
1982 Coda
```

With -v, you can really start to narrow your results to
show only the exact items you need.

List Files Containing Searched-for Words

```
grep -l
```

The grep command lists the lines containing the term
for which you searched, but there might be times

when you don't want to know the lines; instead, you want to know the names of the files that contain those matched lines. Previously in "Search for Text in Files, Ignoring Case," you looked for lines in H. P. Lovecraft stories that contained the word *hideous*. With the -l (or --files-with-matches) option, you can instead produce a list of those files (the -i is for case-insensitive searches, remember).

```
$ grep -il hideous Lovecraft/*
Lovecraft/The Call of Cthulhu.txt
Lovecraft/From Beyond.txt
Lovecraft/The Case of Charles Dexter Ward.txt
[Results truncated]
```

This type of result is particularly useful when combined with other commands. For example, if you wanted to print a list of Lovecraft's stories containing the word *hideous*, you could combine grep with the lpr command (for more on lpr, search for it on my website, www.granneman.com) as follows:

```
$ grep -il hideous Lovecraft/* | lpr
```

Keep in mind that this command would print out the list of stories, not the stories themselves. (There is a way to do that, though, and here's a hint: It involves cat.)

List the Number of Occurrences of Words in Files

```
grep -c
```

The eighteenth-century British poet and mystic William Blake famously said of Milton's *Paradise Lost*

that he was "of the Devil's party without knowing it."
In other words, the character of Satan in *Paradise Lost*
was a lot more interesting than that of God. To fully
participate in the debate around Blake's comment,
you'd need to do a lot of reading, starting with
Paradise Lost (which I did, back when I was working
on a Ph.D. in Seventeenth Century British Literature).

Even though we don't have time for everyone to do
their reading, we can still contribute to the discussion,
albeit in a limited way. Let's use the `-c` (or `--count`)
option for `grep` to find out how many times Milton
uses the words "Satan" and "God" in *Paradise Lost*:

```
$ grep -c Satan "Paradise Lost.txt"
12
$ grep -c God "Paradise Lost.txt"
327
```

Whoa! Only 12 mentions of Satan in *Paradise Lost*? No
way. That's not the epic I remember reading. Wait a
second… it was written in the seventeenth century.
Capitalization was a lot more free-form then. Let's try
the command with a case-insensitive option:

```
$ grep -ci Satan "Paradise Lost.txt"
72
$ grep -ci God "Paradise Lost.txt"
329
```

Now that's more like it! Still, it appears that when it
comes to a word count, Milton may not have been "of
the Devil's party" after all (take that, William Blake!).

NOTE: The -c option actually reports the number of *lines* in which a word appears, not the actual number of *times* the word appears. In other words, if you search for the word "hideous," a line like "The old hideous man was hideously hideous" will give you a count of 1, not 3.

Search for Words Inside Search Results

grep | grep

What if you want a list of albums released by John Coltrane in the last three years of his career? Simple enough.

```
$ ls -1 | grep 196[6-7]
1966 Live at the Village Vanguard Again!
1966 Live in Japan
1967 Expression
1967 Olatunji Concert Last Live Recording
1967 Stellar Regions
```

The range [6-7] limits what would otherwise be a much longer list to the years 1966–1967. So far, so good, but what if you don't want to include any of his live albums (which would normally be a horrible mistake, but let's pretend here)? Here's how to do it:

```
$ ls -1 | grep 196[6-7] | grep -v Live
1967 Expression
1967 Stellar Regions
```

The -v option (which you learned about previously in "Show Lines Where Words Do Not Appear in Files") worked to strip out lines containing Live, but the really interesting thing here is how you took the output of ls -1, piped that to grep 196[6-7], and then piped the output from that filter to a second instance of grep, this one with -v Live. The final results are exactly what you wanted: a list of all John Coltrane's albums, released between 1966–1967, that do not contain Live in the title. And that, my friends, shows you the power of the Linux command line in a nutshell!

Conclusion

This chapter focused on two commands that you'll be using often: locate and grep. Though they're related—both assist the Linux user in finding files and information on his computer—they go about it in different ways. The locate command searches the names of files using a database of filenames to speed up its work, while the grep command looks in real time within the contents of files to pull out the search terms.

As cool as both locate and grep are, they're just the beginning when it comes to searching your file system. The next chapter is about one of the most powerful and versatile commands on a Linux system, a command that perfectly complements, and in fact can work in tandem with, locate and grep. That command? The mighty find. Turn that page and let's get going!

## 11

The `find` Command

In the last chapter, we covered commands that let you search for files (`locate`) and data within files (`grep`). The third command in the powerful triumvirate is `find`. While `locate` searches a database for files, which makes it fast but dependent upon a constantly updated database, `find` searches for files on the fly using criteria that you specify. Since `find` has to parse through your file structure, it's much slower than `locate`, but you can do lots of things with `find` that aren't possible with `locate`.

Throughout this chapter, we're going to work on an external hard drive that contains music and related files and is mounted at /media/music. Also notice that there are spaces in the filenames, which explains the quotation marks you will see in various commands. You'll see that `find` allows us to slice and dice the files in a variety of ways.

NOTE: When I updated this book for its second edition, I removed info about find -fprint (which prints the results of the find command to a file). You can find the original text on my website at www.granneman. com/linux-redactions.

Find Files by Name

```
find -name
```

The find command is basically used to look for files by name, or part of a name (hence, the -name option). By default, find is automatically recursive and searches down through a directory structure. Let's look for all MP3 files sung by the unique group The Shaggs on the music drive:

```
$ cd /media/music
$ find . -name Shaggs
./Outsider/Shaggs
```

What? This can't be correct! The find command found the folder, but not the songs. Why? Because we didn't use any wildcards, find looked for files specifically named "Shaggs." There is only one item with that precise name: the folder that contains the songs. (Since a folder is a special kind of file, it's counted!)

We need to use wildcards, but in order to prevent the shell from interpreting the wildcards in ways we don't intend, we need to surround what we're searching for with quotation marks. Let's try the search again with our new improvements:

```
$ find . -name "*Shaggs*"
./Outsider/Shaggs
./Outsider/Shaggs/Gimme Dat Ting (Live).mp3
./Outsider/Shaggs/My Pal Foot Foot.mp3
./Outsider/Shaggs/I Love.mp3
./Outsider/Shaggs/You're Somethin' Special To
➥ Me.mp3
./Outsider/Shaggs/Things I Wonder.mp3
```

We surrounded the wildcards with quotation marks; lo and behold, we found the folder and the files.

NOTE: Another option to `find` that you've been using without realizing it is `-print`. The `-print` option tells `find` to list the results of its search on the terminal. The `-print` option is on by default, so you don't need to include it when you run `find`.

Another important aspect of `find` is that the format of your results is dependent upon the path searched. Previously, we used a relative path, so our results were given to us as relative paths. What would happen if we used an absolute path—one that begins with a /—instead?

```
$ find / -name "*Shaggs*"
/media/music/Outsider/Shaggs
/media/music/Outsider/Shaggs/Gimme Dat Ting
➥ (Live).mp3
/media/music/Outsider/Shaggs/My Pal Foot Foot.mp3
/media/music/Outsider/Shaggs/I Love.mp3
/media/music/Outsider/Shaggs/You're Somethin'
➥ Special To Me.mp3
/media/music/Outsider/Shaggs/Things I Wonder.mp3
```

If you search using a relative path, your results use
a relative path; if you search using an absolute path,
your results use an absolute path. We'll see other uses
of this principle later in the chapter. For now, just
keep this important idea in mind.

NOTE: To find out more about the Shaggs, see http://
www.allmusic.com/artist/the-shaggs-mn0000418794
and http://en.wikipedia.org/wiki/The_Shaggs. You
haven't lived until you've played "My Pal Foot Foot" at
your next party!

Find Files by Ownership

```
find -user
find -group
```

In addition to searching for files by name, you can
also search for files by owner. Do you want to find
the files on the music drive owned by scott? Use find
with the -user option, followed by the user name (or
the user number, which you can find in /etc/passwd):

```
$ find . -user scott
```

Whoa! There are way too many results! It might be
easier to look for files that are *not* owned by scott.
To do so, put a ! in front of the option you wish to
reverse:

```
$ find . ! -user scott
./Punk/Stooges/Fun House/01 Down on the Street.mp3
$ ls -l "Punk/Stooges/Fun House/01 Down on the
➥Street.mp3"
gus music ./Punk/Stooges/Fun House/01 Down on the
➥Street.mp3
```

Ah… one song by The Stooges is owned by `gus` instead of `scott`. Keep in mind that you can always use the ! as a NOT operator (which is saying, for example, "Find files where the user is *not* `scott`").

If you instead want to look for files owned by a particular group, just use -group, followed by the group's name or number. On the music drive, `scott` should be the owner and `music` should be the group. Let's see if there are any files that are *not* in the `music` group:

```
$ find . ! -group music
./Disco/Brides of Funkenstein/Disco to Go.mp3
./Disco/Sister Sledge/He's The Greatest
➡ Dancer.mp3
./Disco/Wild Cherry/Play That Funky Music.mp3
./Electronica/New Order/Substance/11 - Bizarre
➡ Love Triangle.mp3
```

There are only four results out of a large number of files that aren't in the `music` group. Notice that, once again, we used ! to say, "Find the files that are *not* owned by the `music` group."

Find Files by File Size

`file -size`

Sometimes you'll want to find files based on their size. The `find` command can assist here as well. To specify a size, use the -size option, followed by a letter representing the size scheme you wish to use. If you don't provide a letter, the default is used; however, you should understand that you probably won't find what you want, and why. If you don't append a letter after the number, the default is in bytes (which is then divided by 512 and rounded up to the next integer). This is too much math. It's easier to use a suffix after the number that represents the size in more common terms, as shown in Table 11.1.

Table 11.1   **Find Files by Size**

Suffix	Meaning
b	512-byte blocks (the default)
c	Bytes
k	Kilobytes (KB)
M	Megabytes (MB)
G	Gigabytes (GB)

NOTE: Strictly speaking, even though the man page for `find` calls these Kilobytes, Megabytes, and Gigabytes, those are the wrong terms, as I explained in Chapter 6's "View the First Several Bytes, Kilobytes, or Megabytes of a File." A lot of programs still use the old terms, which are now incorrect. For more on this, see http://en.wikipedia.org/wiki/Mebibyte.

Let's say we want to find every Clash song from their immortal album, *London Calling*, that is 10MB. (Yes, these were encoded at a super-high rate.) This job is easy enough with `find`:

```
$ cd Punk/Clash/1979_London_Calling
$ find . -size 10M
./07 - The Right Profile.mp3
./08 - Lost In The Supermarket.mp3
./09 - Clampdown.mp3
./12 - Death Or Glory.mp3
```

That's weird. Only four songs? Here's where you need to understand a "gotcha" associated with using find: If you say 10M, then find looks for files that are exactly 10MB in size (rounded to 10MB, of course). If you want files larger than 10MB, you need to place a plus sign (+) in front of the given size; if you want files smaller than 10MB, use a minus sign (-) in front of the size:

```
$ find . -size +10M
./03 - Jimmy Jazz.mp3
./15 - Lover's Rock.mp3
./18 - Revolution Rock.mp3
```

Now we have a problem. Specifying 10M gives us files that are exactly 10MB, excluding those that are bigger, while specifying +10M gives us files that are larger than 10MB, excluding those that are exactly 10MB. How do we get both? If you want to learn how to obtain files that are 10MB and larger, see the "Show Results If Either Expression Is True (OR)" section later in this chapter.

TIP: If you want to find large text files, use c after your number. As Table 11.1 shows, c changes the search size to bytes. Every character in a text file is a byte, so an easy way to remember c is to associate it with the "characters" in a text file.

For instance, to find enormous text files, you can use this code:

```
$ find /home/scott/documents -size +500000c
```

Find Files by File Type

```
find -type
```

One of the most useful options for find is -type, which allows you to specify the type of object you wish to look for. Remember that everything on a UNIX system is a file (covered back in Chapter 1, "Things to Know About Your Command Line," in the "Everything Is a File" section), so what you're actually indicating is the type of file you want find to ferret out for you. Table 11.2 lists the file types you can use with find.

Table 11.2   **Finding Files by Type**

File Type Letter	Meaning
f	Regular file
d	Directory
l	Symbolic (soft) link
b	Block special file
c	Character special file
p	FIFO (First In First Out)
s	Socket

Let's say we want a quick list of all the versions of Frank Sinatra's great song "Come Fly With Me" we have on the music drive. You might start with this series of commands (results have been truncated; there were actually 14 listed):

```
$ cd "Jazz - Vocal/Frank Sinatra"
$ find . -name "*Come Fly With Me*"
./1962 Live In Paris/26 - Come Fly With Me.mp3
./1957 Come Fly With Me
./1957 Come Fly With Me/01 - Come Fly With Me.mp3
./1966 Sinatra At The Sands/01 - Come Fly With
➡ Me.mp3
```

Notice the second result? That's a directory for
Sinatra's great 1957 album, also named "Come Fly
With Me." I only want files, not directories, so I need
to use -type f to limit my results to just files:

```
$ find . -name "*Come Fly With Me*" -type f
./1962 Live In Paris/26 - Come Fly With Me.mp3
./1957 Come Fly With Me/01 - Come Fly With Me.mp3
./1966 Sinatra At The Sands/01 - Come Fly With
➡ Me.mp3
```

This list is helpful, but since the name of every album
directory begins with the year the album was released,
we can pipe the results to the sort command (covered
in Chapter 7's "Sort the Contents of a File") and trace
the changes Sinatra made with the song over time:

```
$ find . -name "*Come Fly With Me*" -type f
➡ | sort
./1957 Come Fly With Me/01 - Come Fly With Me.mp3
./1962 Live In Paris/26 - Come Fly With Me.mp3
./1966 Sinatra At The Sands/01 - Come Fly With
➡ Me.mp3
```

It can be incredibly beneficial to use a pipe to filter
the list you generate with find; as you get better with
find, you'll discover that you do this more and more.

Find Files by Time

```
find -amin|-cmin|-mmin
find -atime|-ctime|-mtime
find -anewer|-cnewer|-newer|-newerXY
```

So far we've talked about using find to list files based
on name, ownership, file size, and file type. But what
about time? The find command has that one covered,
in spades.

For instance, I once had to detect all the files in a
directory and its subdirectories that were older than
four hours. With find, it was easy:

```
$ find . -mmin +240
```

This means "List all files that were modified more
than 240 minutes ago." When you use find in this
way, you have to specify a number (most of the time,
as you'll see). That number can be expressed in one of
three ways, shown in Table 11.3.

Table 11.3   Numeric Arguments for Finding Files
by Time

Numeric Argument	Meaning
+n	Greater than n
-n	Less than n
n	Exactly n

One thing to remember is that n can be the number
of minutes or the number of hours, depending upon
the specific test you're using. And that brings me to
the next thing you need to know: Some of the tests

`find` uses check when the files were *accessed*, some when the files were *changed*, and some when the files were *modified*. At first, those sound like synonyms for each other. But to your Linux box, they are actually very different.

- **Accessed** means the contents were read, but nothing was altered, as with `less`.

- **Changed** means the metadata (or file status) was altered but not the contents, as with `chmod`, `chown`, `link`, and `rename`.

- **Modified** means the data was altered by editing it.

TIP: You can see these yourself with any file on your Linux machine by running the `stat` command against a file, like this (I'm showing just the relevant output here, but you really should check `stat` out, as it provides some very useful info):

```
$ stat foobar.txt
Access: 2013-04-14 16:57:24.768011000 -0500
Modify: 2012-12-01 22:27:24.424000023 -0600
Change: 2012-12-01 22:27:24.424000023 -0600
```

Now that we know the differences between *access*, *modify*, and *change*, let's finally proceed to the tests you can use with `find`. I've grouped them together logically in Table 11.4 so that they hopefully make more sense. Remember that `n` in Table 11.4 can mean any of the numeric arguments in Table 11.3.

Table 11.4   **Tests for Finding Files by Time**

Test	Meaning
Minutes	
`-amin` *n*	Accessed *n* minutes ago
`-cmin` *n*	Status changed *n* minutes ago
`-mmin` *n*	Data modified *n* minutes ago
Hours (fractional parts of days are ignored)	
`-atime` *n*	Accessed *n*$\star$24 hours ago
`-ctime` *n*	Status changed *n*$\star$24 hours ago
`-mtime` *n*	Data modified *n*$\star$24 hours ago

NOTE: You might be wondering about creation time and why it's not an option. The reason it doesn't appear is because the Linux kernel doesn't track creation times for files.

Want to discover files that were accessed more than 45 minutes ago? Use `-amin +45`.

What if you need files that changed status in the last 24 hours? Use `-ctime 0`. (Remember, `find` throws out the fractional parts of days, and since you want less than 1 day, you use `0`—it's confusing, I know.)

How about files whose data was modified between two and four days ago? Use `-mtime +2 -a -mtime +4`. (We're ANDing our expressions, as we discuss next in "Show Results If the Expressions Are True (AND).") Yes, you will get some files from the day before (probably), but those can be removed with `grep -v` (see Chapter 10's "Show Lines Where Words Do Not Appear in Files"). Remember, `-atime`, `-ctime`, and `-mtime` are using *n*`*24` hours from *your current time*, so you have to expect some broad results.

> **NOTE:** There are other time-based expressions you can use with `find` that I just don't have space to cover here. One of them might be just what you need, so be sure to check out `-anewer`, `-cnewer`, `-newer`, and `-newerXY`.

Show Results If the Expressions Are True (AND)

```
find -a
```

A key feature of `find` is the ability to join several options to more tightly focus your searches. You can link together as many options as you'd like with `-a` (or `-and`). For example, if you want to find the song "Let It Bleed" performed by the world's greatest rock 'n' roll band, The Rolling Stones, you might use just `-name "*Let It Bleed*"` at first, but that wouldn't necessarily work. The Stones recorded an album also titled *Let It Bleed*, so we need to distinguish between files and directories. We, therefore, also need to use `-type f`. Combine them as follows:

```
$ cd Rolling_Stones
$ find . -name "*Let It Bleed*" -a -type f
./1972 More Hot Rocks/17 - Let It Bleed.mp3
./1995 Stripped/08 - Let It Bleed.mp3
./1969 Let It Bleed/5 - Let It Bleed.mp3
```

That's cool, but how many Stones tunes do we have? Pipe the results of `find` to `wc` (short for "word count," covered in Chapter 7's "Count the Number of Words, Lines, and Characters in a File"), but use the

-l option, which gives you the number of lines instead of the word count:

```
$ cd Rolling_Stones
$ find . -name "*mp3*" -a -type f | wc -l
1323
```

One thousand, three hundred and twenty three Rolling Stones songs. Sweet! In this case, you *can* always get what you want.

NOTE: If you have no idea what that last sentence means, get yourself a copy of the album *Let It Bleed* now. Don't forget to play it loud.

Show Results If Either Expression Is True (OR)

```
find -o
```

Earlier, in the section "Find Files by File Size," we saw that we could use `find` to list every Clash song on *London Calling* that was exactly 10MB, and we could use `find` to list songs on *London Calling* that were more than 10MB, but we couldn't do both at the same time with -size. In the previous section, we saw that -a combines options using AND; however, we can also utilize -o (or -or) to combine options using OR.

We can find all the songs by The Clash, on any album, that are 10MB or larger by using the following command:

```
$ cd Clash
$ find . -size +10M -o -size 10M
./1977 The Clash/01 - Clash City Rockers.mp3
./1977 The Clash/13 - Police And Thieves.mp3
./1979 London Calling/15 - Lover's Rock.mp3
./1979 London Calling/18 - Revolution Rock.mp3
./2007 The Sandinista Project/04 - Jason
➡Ringenberg - Ivan Meets G.I. Joe.m4a
./1980 Sandinista!/01 - The Magnificent Seven.mp3
./1980 Sandinista!/02 - Hitsville U.K.mp3
[Results greatly truncated for length]
```

Oops... we also got results from *The Sandinista Project*, an album of covers of Clash songs, which we didn't want. We need to exclude results from *The Sandinista Project*, so we'll use a ! in front of the expression, as discussed earlier in this chapter in "Find Files by Ownership."

But which expression? To exclude *The Sandinista Project*, you might think that we would add ! -name "*Project*" at the end of our command, giving us find . -size +10M -o -size 10M ! -name "*Project". But that won't work, for several reasons.

The -name is wrong because -name only looks at the actual filename, and ignores everything before the / in front of the filename. The word we want to exclude—*Project*—is a directory, so -name will never see it. Instead, we want to use -wholename, which searches the entire path, including the filename.

The other problem is the way I structured the command. At this point, we have two expressions joined by OR along with another expression for wholename on top of that. To make sure that OR does what we want, we need to surround it with parentheses, which combines the statements (kind

of like algebra!). However, you need to escape the
parentheses with backslashes so the shell doesn't
misinterpret them, and you also need to put spaces
before and after your statement, or it won't work. The
combination gives us this command:

```
$ find . \( -size +10M -o -size 10M \) -a
➥ ! -wholename "*Project*"
./1977 The Clash/01 - Clash City Rockers.mp3
./1977 The Clash/13 - Police And Thieves.mp3
./1979 London Calling/15 - Lover's Rock.mp3
./1979 London Calling/18 - Revolution Rock.mp3
./1980 Sandinista!/01 - The Magnificent Seven.mp3
./1980 Sandinista!/02 - Hitsville U.K.mp3
```

The Sandinista Project is a great album, but I just want
to know about Clash songs performed by The Clash.
Thanks to the `find` command, I can.

NOTE: Read about *London Calling* at Allmusic.com
(www.allmusic.com/album/london-calling-
mw0000189413) or Wikipedia (http://en.wikipedia.org/
wiki/London_calling).

We can also use `-o` to find out how many songs we
have on the music drive. We might start with this
command, which we run from the root of /media/
music, and which uses `-a` (be patient; we'll get to `-o`):

```
$ find . -name "*mp3" -a -type f | wc -l
105773
```

One hundred and five thousand? That's not right. Ah,
now it's obvious. We were only searching for mp3 files,
but a few songs were encoded in the M4A format.
Let's look for mp3 or m4a files and count the results
with `wc -l`:

```
$ find . \( -name "*mp3" -o -name "*.m4a" \) -a
➡-type f | wc -l
106666
```

893 m4a files sounds about right. I forgot the FLAC files! Let's add another -o to the mix:

```
$ find . \( -name "*mp3" -o -name "*.m4a*" -o -name
➡"*.flac" \) -a -type f | wc -l
109709
```

Now that's more like it: almost 110,000 songs and still growing!

NOTE: In the previous version of this book, I had the following files and formats:

23,407 mp3

0 m4a

18,224 ogg (I have 0 now)

556 flac

That was 42,187 music files in total. Clearly, I've been busy since then!

Show Results If the Expression Is Not True (NOT)

```
find -n
```

We have already used ! to negate expressions in earlier sections in this chapter (see "Find Files By Ownership" and "Show Results If Either Expression Is True (OR)"), but let's take another, longer look at this operator. In the previous section, we used find to determine how many mp3, m4a, ogg, and flac files we have on the music drive. But how many total files do we have on the drive? A very simple `find` command will give us the answer.

```
$ find . | wc -l
122255
```

Hmm...122,255 total files, but only 109,709 are `mp3`, `m4a`, or `flac` (as we discovered in the previous section). What are the other 12,546? Let's construct a `find` command that excludes files that end in `.mp3`, `.m4a`, or `.flac` while also excluding directories. Wrap these four conditions in parentheses, and then place `!` before the command to indicate our wish to negate these items and instead look for things that do not match these specifications:

```
$ find . ! \( -name "*mp3" -o -name "*m4a" -o
➥-name "*flac" -o -type d \)
./Rock - Folk/Band/1970 Stage Fright/Art/
➥Cover.png
./Rock - Folk/Bob Dylan/2007 Dylan Hears a Who/
➥Art/Cover.jpg
./Rock - British Blues/Rolling Stones/1973 0908
➥ Wembley, London/Info.txt
./Classical - Opera/Puccini/Turandot/1972
➥ Sutherland, Pavarotti, Caballe/Libretto.pdf
./Rock - Pop/ABBA/1993 Abba Gold Greatest Hits/
➥01 - Dancing Queen.MP3
./Rock/Neil Young/1970 0301 Tea Party, Boston/
➥Info.htm
./Rock - Punk/Clash/2007 The Sandinista Project/
➥Booklet.pdf
./Jazz - Vocal/Frank Sinatra/1963 The Concert
➥ Sinatra/07 - This Nearly Was Mine.Mp3
[Results truncated for length]
```

Now we have the answer, or at least we're starting to get an answer. We have PDFs, text, and HTML files, and files that end in MP3 instead of mp3 (we also have JPEGs, PNGs, and even music videos). The find command, like all of Linux, is case-sensitive (as discussed in Chapter 1), so a search for "*mp3*" will not turn up songs that have the .MP3 suffix. Is there any quick and easy way to change these files so that they have the correct lowercase extension? Sure. And we'll use find to do it.

TIP: The -name expression is case sensitive, but the -iname expression is not (the "i" stands for "insensitive"). So if we wanted to find all mp3 files regardless of the case of the extension, we'd use find . -iname "*mp3*", which would find files ending in mp3, MP3, Mp3, and mP3.

Execute a Command on Found Files

`find -exec`

Now we enter the area in which find really shows off its power: the ability to execute commands on the files that it, uh, finds. After listing the options that help narrow down your search—such as -name, -type, or -user—append -exec (short for "execute") along with the commands you want to run on each individual file. You use the symbols {} to represent each file, and end your command with \ to escape the semicolon so your shell doesn't interpret it as an indication of command stacking (which we discussed in Chapter 5, "Building Blocks").

In the previous section, for example, I discovered that some of the files on the music drive ended with MP3.

Since I prefer lowercase extensions, I need to convert all instances of MP3 to mp3 to make the files consistent. We can do this with the -exec option for find. First, let's verify that there are files that end with MP3 (of course, I'm only showing a few of the many results):

```
$ find . -name "*MP3"
./Blues - Delta/Robert Johnson/1990 Complete
➥ Recordings/29 - Malted Milk.MP3
./Blues - Delta/Robert Johnson/1990 Complete
➥ Recordings/16 - Dead Shrimp Blues.MP3
./Blues - Delta/Robert Johnson/1990 Complete
➥ Recordings/11 - Terraplane Blues.MP3
```

Let's use find with -exec to change the file extension. The program we can use with -exec is rename, which changes parts of filenames:

```
$ find . -name "*MP3"
➥ -exec rename 's/MP3/mp3/g' {} \;
```

TIP: There are at least two different versions of the rename command, each with a different syntax and options. In this instance, I'm using the one written by Larry Wall (inventor of the Perl programming language) that uses—no surprise!—Perl-like syntax for the substitution. The best post I've seen on this issue is "A Tale of Two Renames" by Tim Heaney, available at http://chnsa.ws/68.

To check which one you have, look at man rename and scroll down to the AUTHOR section. If you don't have rename on your Linux box (and you very well may not), you'll need to install it using the instructions in Chapter 14, "Installing Software."

The rename command is followed with instructions
for the name change in this format: s/old/new/. (The
s stands for *substitute*) Now let's see if our command
worked:

```
$ find . -name "*MP3"
./Blues - Delta/Robert Johnson/1990 Complete
➡ Recordings/29 - Malted Milk.mp3
./Blues - Delta/Robert Johnson/1990 Complete
➡ Recordings/16 - Dead Shrimp Blues.mp3
./Blues - Delta/Robert Johnson/1990 Complete
➡ Recordings/11 - Terraplane Blues.mp3
```

TIP: We used s/old/new in this instance, but you'll
often want to use s/old/new/g instead (the g stands
for "global"). If each filename has only one instance
of old to change into new—as in "Terraplane Blues.
mp3"—then s/MP3/mp3 works just fine. But what if
Robert Johnson, in a stunning bit of futuristic guess-
work, had written a song called "Corrupted mp3
Blues"? Now the filename would be "Corrupted MP3
Blues.MP3." In order to change both instances of MP3
to mp3, we use s/MP3/mp3/g. This tells rename we want
to change MP3 to mp3, not just the first one, which is
what s/MP3/mp3/ does.

Yep—all instances of MP3 were changed to mp3. Let's try
a similar process with another situation. In the previous
section, we noticed that many of the results discovered
were m3u, or playlist, files. Unfortunately, many of
these files had underscores in the filenames, which I
want to change into spaces. Let's first generate a list
of m3u files that have underscores. We can search for
*_*m3u, which uses wildcards around an underscore to
discover files that include that character in their names:

```
$ find . -name "*_*m3u"
./Holiday_-_Christmas/Christmas_With_The_Rat_
➥Pack.m3u
./Holiday_-_Christmas/Boots_For_Your_Stockings.m3u
./Classical_-_Baroque/Handel/Chamber_Music.m3u
./Classical_-_Opera/Famous_Arias.m3u
./R&B_-_Doo_Wop/Doo_Wop_Box.m3u
./Electronica/Aphex_Twin/I_Care_Because_You_Do.m3u
```

Now let's find m3u files with underscores in their
names; when one is found, we can run rename against
it. We're substituting "_" with "\ " (we escape the
space so that find understands what we're looking for
and the shell doesn't get confused) to fix the problem:

```
$ find . -name "*_*m3u"
➥ -exec rename 's/_/\ /g' {} \;
$ find . -name "*_*m3u"
$
```

The command worked as planned. Begone,
underscores!

NOTE: Before running commands on the files found by
find, we must first figure out which files are going to be
forevermore fixed (try saying that out loud!). That's just
prudence. You don't want to change the wrong files!

Execute a Command on Found Files More Efficiently

```
find +
find | xargs
```

Recently I was working on a client's server that
had filled up with 1.5 million temp files thanks to a

misconfiguration. Yes, one and a half million. Now, you might think that using find piped to a simple rm would work, but if you tried that, you'd see the following:

```
$ ls | less
sess_000000001.txt
sess_000000002.txt
sess_000000003.txt
[Results truncated by 1.5 million]
$ find . -name "sess_*" -exec rm {} \;
/bin/rm Argument list too long
```

Due to a limit in the Linux kernel, you can't feed a super-huge number of arguments to a command without seeing that error. Uh oh. We have to get rid of all those files, but how?

The newfangled solution is to use find like this (and then wait patiently for 1.5 million files to disappear):

```
$ find . -name "sess_*" -exec rm {} +
```

This is different from the previous section's use of -exec in two ways: the lack of the \; and the use of the + (in fact, the + at the end allows us to drop the \;). Normally, find executes rm once for every file it finds, which is woefully inefficient and also leads to the "argument list too long" problem, but the + tells find to instead chunk the files it identifies together and run rm on each chunk, not on each file.

So why not use the + method for find all the time? Because it's relatively new in the UNIX timeline, only appearing since 2006, and not all versions of find on all systems support it. You can test if yours does, with something harmless like find . -exec ls {} +. If you see results instead of an error message, your version of find supports the + (and be prepared to press Ctrl+C if the huge listing shows no signs of stopping!).

The classic, I-was-here-first-and-should-work-everywhere solution is to use xargs. That command reads from STDIN and then uses what it reads in as arguments against commands you specify. The reason xargs works is because it processes input in chunks instead of one at a time (see where find got the idea for the +?), meaning that it is run fewer times by your system and can get around the "argument list too long" error. Want to see how big those chunks would be? Run xargs --show-limits (press Ctrl+D to stop xargs) for the numbers.

NOTE: Pipes and xargs are similar in that both take output from a command and use it—and, on top of that, xargs almost always uses pipes!—but they have significant differences. A pipe takes the output of the first command and uses it as the *input* to the second command. The xargs command, however, takes the output of the first command (thanks to the pipe) and uses it as the *arguments* to the second command.

For example, ls -1 | wc -1 takes the output of ls -1 and uses that as input for wc -1, because wc uses STDIN, but ls -1 | echo outputs nothing, because echo expects arguments, not STDIN. Since echo takes arguments, ls -1 | xargs echo works because xargs turns out the output of ls -1 into arguments for echo. (Yes, it's silly to echo the results of ls, but I'm trying to make a point!)

Going back to my initial example of 1.5 million files, instead of using the -exec action with find, let's pipe the results of find to xargs and use that command to delete those files:

```
$ find . -name "sess_*" | xargs rm
$ ls
[Nothing! 1.5 million files gone!]
```

Now, it took a looooong time for that command to run—deleting 1.5 million files takes a good chunk of time—but it worked, which made everyone happy.

TIP: Although you often see find piped to xargs, you can of course use xargs with different commands. It's just that 90% of the examples you'll find on the Web seem to start with find!

Execute a Command on Found Files Containing Spaces

```
find -print0 | xargs -0
```

In the previous section, I had to delete 1.5 million files, all named something like sess_000000001.txt, so I used find with xargs, like this:

```
$ find . -name "sess_*" | xargs rm
```

That worked only because sess_000000001.txt and its horde of siblings didn't have spaces in their names. If the files had instead been named sess 000000001.txt, I would have seen these results:

```
$ find . -name "sess_*" | xargs rm
rm: cannot remove './sess': No such file or
➥directory
rm: cannot remove '000000001.txt': No such file or
➥directory
rm: cannot remove './sess': No such file or
➥directory
rm: cannot remove '000000002.txt': No such file or
➥directory
^C
```

That ^c at the end was me pressing Ctrl+C to stop 3 million lines from streaming by (two lines for each file, since the filename has one space in it). Clearly, those spaces are causing a problem. But why?

The xargs command uses spaces to split output, so when find sends over sess 000000001.txt, xargs sees that as rm sess and rm 000000001.txt. Since those don't exist, rm in turn complains. And by the way, this could actually be dangerous—if you had a file named 000000001.txt, it would now be gone.

It's not just spaces that could cause xargs to mangle the command. Characters like quotation marks, apostrophes, newlines, and backslashes can also lead to unexpected results and failures. To get around these issues, you should instead use this command:

```
$ find . -name "sess_*" -print0 | xargs -0 rm
```

Normally find sends over each full filename followed by an invisible newline character (that's why you see each of find's results on its own line). The -print0 action tells find to instead follow each full filename by the null character. Meanwhile, the -0 option tells xargs that it should use the null character instead of a space for separating output. Since both find and xargs are working together, you don't get any errors. And as a bonus, the -0 tells xargs to ignore quotation marks and any of the other characters that can cause it to fail.

Conclusion

It should now be obvious that find is one powerful tool! Yet there are still an enormous number of things that find can do, so you really should look at man find or read several of the excellent tutorials available on the Web that cover the more arcane—yet useful—aspects of the command. Sure, you can use `find` to search for and list files and folders using an amazing variety of options. It really becomes invaluable, however, when you use the `-exec` option to run commands on the discovered files, or when you pipe the output to other commands. This is one of the greatest commands available to you on your Linux box, so start using it!

Your Shell

So far in this book you've been running commands in your bash shell, but you haven't focused on the shell itself. In this chapter, you look at commands that affect your use of the shell: history, which lists everything you've entered on the command line, alias, which allows you to create shortcuts for commands, and function, which is like alias times twenty. All are useful, and all can save you lots of time when you're using the command line. Laziness is a good thing when it comes to computer users, and these are definitely commands that will help you be as lazy as possible when using your Linux box.

View Your Command-Line History

```
history
```

Every time you type a command in your shell, that command is saved in a file named .bash_history in your home directory (the dot in front of the filename means that it's hidden unless you use ls -a). By default, that file holds the last 500 lines entered on the command line. (It's possible to increase that number; to find out how, start with http://chnsa.ws/ul.) If you want to view that list of commands, just enter the history command.

```
$ history
  496  ls
  497  cd rsync_ssh
  498  ls
  499  cat linux
  500  exit
```

CAUTION: Now you understand why you need to be careful typing passwords and other sensitive information on the command line: Anyone who can view your .bash_history file is able to see those passwords. Be careful and think about what you enter directly on the command line!

Need to find a particular command in your history? You have a few ways to do so. The first is manual. Because you're looking at 500 results, they're going to stream by so fast that you can't see any until you get to the end. To step through the results one screen at a time, turn to your old friend less:

```
$ history | less
```

If you don't want to use `less`, you can instead type `history` followed by a number, where that number determines how many lines of prior commands your terminal displays. So `history 50`, for instance, would show my last fifty commands. Now you can jump through your results much more easily.

Being able to step back through commands is nice, but it's also tedious. To automate things, pipe the `history` command to `grep` (discussed in Chapter 10, "Finding Files, Directories, Words, and Phrases") and narrow things down quickly, like so:

```
$ history | grep pandoc
105 pandoc -o temp.html temp.md
```

There it is! If only there was an easy way to run that command again... oh wait! There is. Just keep reading!

TIP: If you find that you use the `history | grep` construction a lot (I know I do), making an alias for that in your `.bash_aliases` file makes things a bit easier:

```
alias histg="history | grep"
```

What's an alias, you ask? The answer awaits you just a few sections ahead!

Run the Last Command Again

`!!`

If you want to run the last command you used again, enter two exclamation points. That looks in the history file and runs the last command in the list.

```
$ pwd
/home/scott
$ !!
pwd
/home/scott
```

Notice that you first see the actual command that's going to run, and then the results of that command. By default, the command appears just as a courtesy to let you know what's happening, because it's already running by the time you see it. If it's a command that takes only a split second to run, by the time you see the command, you'll also see the output.

Obviously, this can lead to surprises. What if the command you *think* is going to run is not in fact the command that runs (because pages of output separate the last command and the current prompt, or because you've told bash not to keep certain commands in history, and you forgot)?

There is a way to fix that problem before it ever occurs, however. Add the following to .bashrc and then reload the file:

```
# Verify substituted history expansion before running
shopt -s histverify
```

The first line is a comment, while the second line tells bash to display any command you pull out of history and display it without actually running it. Yes, this means you'll have to manually press Enter, but I consider that a small price to pay for getting to review what's about to happen before it happens.

If typing !! is too much trouble for you, you can always just press the Up arrow, and you will cycle through the previous history of commands. When you get to the one you want, press Enter.

TIP: This is a good one. If you run a multi-line command, `bash` by default saves each line as a separate entry. This means that you can't easily run that multi-line command again using the Up arrow or `!!`. However, if you edit your `.bashrc` file to add the following two lines (the first is a comment, so it's not strictly necessary, but it helps to explain what you're doing to future you), you'll solve that particular problem.

```
# Save each line of a multi-line command in
➥the same history entry
shopt -s cmdhist
```

Reload your `.bashrc` file (discussed back in Chapter 1, "Things to Know About Your Command Line") and you will be in multi-line command heaven.

This is a truly useful way to have your computer do tedious work for you.

Run a Previous Command Using Numbers

```
! [##]
```

When you run `history`, it automatically places a number in front of every previous command. If you'd like to run a previous command and you know the number that `history` has assigned to it, just enter an exclamation point immediately followed by that command's history number, and it will run again.

```
$ pwd
/home/scott
$ whoami
scott
$ !499
pwd
/home/scott
```

If you're unsure about the number, run `history` again
to find out. Be aware that the `pwd` command in this
example was number 499 the first time, but after I
ran it again using !499, it became 498 because it was
pushed down on the list by my new command.

Run a Previous Command Using a String

`! [string]`

The capability to run a command again by referencing
its number is nice, but it requires that you know the
command's number in `history`, which can be no
fun to discover (piping the output of `history` to `grep`
would help, but it's still not optimal). Often a better
way to reference a previously entered command is
by the actual command's name. If you follow the
exclamation point by the first few letters of that
command, your shell runs the first command it finds
when looking backward in `.bash_history`.

```
$ cat /home/scott/todo.txt
Buy milk
Buy dog food
Renew Ars Technica subscription
$ cd /home/scott/pictures
```

```
$ !cat
cat /home/scott/todo.txt
Buy milk
Buy dog food
Renew Ars Technica subscription
```

If the cat command is found three times in your
history—at 35 (cat /home/scott/todo), 412 (cat
/etc/apt/sources.list), and 496 (cat /home/scott/
todo)—and you enter !cat, the one found at 496 is
the one that runs. If you want to run the cat found
at 412, you need to run either !412 or follow the
exclamation with enough information so it can tell
you're referencing the command listed as 412.

```
$ !cat /etc
cat /etc/apt/sources.list
deb http://us.archive.ubuntu.com/ubuntu precise main
deb-src http://us.archive.ubuntu.com/ubuntu precise
➥main
```

Because humans have a far easier time remembering
words instead of numbers, you may find that this is a
good method for invoking past commands. If you're
ever unsure of which command you're actually going
to invoke, run history and take a look.

Search for a Previous
Command and Run It

```
^-r (Ctrl-r)
^-s (Ctrl-s)
^-g (Ctrl-g)
```

I've covered several ways to run previous commands,
and they're all very handy, but I've saved the best for

last. Let's say that your history contains the following
lines in it:

```
1471 ssh hlp@azathoth.miskatonic-expedition.com
1472 cd /var/www
1473 chmod 755 ~/bin/backup.sh
1474 ssh hlp@nyarlathotep.miskatonic-expedition.com
1475 find /var/www -name "bootstrap.js"
1476 cd ~/bin
1477 ssh hlp@cthulhu.miskatonic-expedition.com
```

You're now 500 lines past all that, and you want
to SSH (covered in Chapter 16, "Working on the
Network") back into nyarlathotep.miskatonic-
expedition.com, but you just don't feel like typing all
that out. You certainly don't feel like hitting the Up
arrow hundreds of times (good!), and you're also feeling
too lazy for a history | grep ssh to find out the line
number of the right command. The answer? Search!

Press ctrl-r (represented as ^-r, and sometimes c-r, in
the usual documentation) and you'll see the following
appear at the bottom of your terminal window:

```
(reverse-i-search)'':
```

Start typing ss and as you do, bash will search your
history backwards from newest to oldest, hence, the
words "reverse" and "search" in the prompt. As you
type the letters, the match will appear, regardless of
where the ss might be. So, for instance, you might see
this right away:

```
(reverse-i-search)'ss': less /etc/inputrc
```

As you type the h, however, turning your search
term into ssh, the first result looking backward in

your history will appear (hence, the letter *i* in the prompt, which stands for "incremental." Assuming you had not used SSH to connect to any other servers for the last 500 lines or so of history, you would now see this:

```
(reverse-i-search)'ssh': ssh hlp@cthulhu.
➥miskatonic-expedition.com
```

That's not the one you want, but now you've got the right term. To search backwards in your history while keeping the same search term—ssh in this case—press Ctrl-r again. The "r" stands for "reverse" so now you would see the one you do want:

```
(reverse-i-search)'ssh': ssh hlp@nyarlathotep.
➥miskatonic-expedition.com
```

However, suppose you're too fast on the draw and you press Ctrl-r *again*, which means you shoot past the one you want and now see a match from further back in history:

```
(reverse-i-search)'ssh': ssh hlp@azathoth.
➥miskatonic-expedition.com
```

No biggie. You went too far back, and now you want to go the other direction, so you press Ctrl-s, which searches forward in your history (and which you can press as many times as you'd like, of course). Since you did that, you're back to where you want to be:

```
(reverse-i-search)'ssh': ssh hlp@nyarlathotep.
➥miskatonic-expedition.com
```

At this point, you can press Enter, which will either display the command (if you followed my advice earlier in "Run the Last Command Again") so you can press Enter again once you've reviewed it, or just run the command (if you didn't follow my advice).

TIP: If Ctrl-s does nothing, you're experiencing a conflict with that particular key binding. On many Linux computers, Ctrl-s sends an XOFF flow control (for more on that, see https://en.wikipedia.org/wiki/Software_flow_control), which by now is pretty ancient and hardly needed by anyone except a tiny few edge cases. To temporarily disable XOFF, enter this in your terminal and press Enter:

```
$ stty -ixon
```

Ctrl-s should work now, but as soon as you log out and log back in again, XOFF will once again be off. To turn the darn thing off permanently, edit .bashrc and put these lines in it:

```
# Disable XOFF flow control so that Ctrl-s
➥does forward history searching
stty -ixon
```

Save the file, reload it (source ~/.bashrc), and you should be good to go.

But what if, once you're actually viewing the command you found, you say to yourself, "Self, that's not really what I want to do. Not only is that not the command I want to run, I don't want to be searching for commands at all!" At that point, to get out of searching through your history, just press Ctrl-g, which aborts the process.

Now that is awesome, but what if we could make it even awesomer? Well guess what—we can!

Remember how Ctrl-r and Ctrl-s do an *incremental* search through your history? Needless to say, this can produce a lot of false positives. Let's say I'm on my server azathoth and I want to SSH to nyarlathotep. I press Ctrl-r and type ssh and I get the following, in order (actually, reverse order, but you get what I'm saying), as I keep pressing Ctrl-r:

```
cat ~/.ssh/config
ssh hlp@nyarlathotep.miskatonic-expedition.com
cd ~/.ssh
man ssh
less intern-ssh-instructions.txt
```

Notice how the incremental search is finding the string ssh no matter where it is on the history line. That's nice if I'm truly searching, but I really just want to SSH into nyarlathotep and not have to wade through all those other matches. Here's how to make sure that happens.

Edit your ~/.inputrc (see "Special Files That Affect Your Command Line" in Chapter 1) and add the following:

```
# When pressing up or down arrows, show only
# history that matches what was already typed
"\e[A":history-search-backward
"\e[B":history-search-forward
```

Save the file and reload it: type bind -f ~/.inputrc and press Enter. (Next time you log in via a different shell, bash will automatically source the file, so you only need to enter that command if you're trying out something new.) Now on your command line, do not press Ctrl-r to start searching your history; instead, just type ssh and press the Up arrow (the \e[A in the example; \e[B corresponds to the Down arrow). And look what pops up first!

```
$ ssh hlp@nyarlathotep.miskatonic-expedition.com
```

Press Enter and I would now be connecting to nyarlathotep. Why? Because now when I press the Up arrow, it searches for what I typed, just like Ctrl-r did, but it only shows results from my history file that match the string I typed *at the beginning of the line*. I no longer see every line that has ssh in it, only those that have ssh first in the line. Try it out, and trust me, you will not believe how you ever lived without it before!

NOTE: To check whether reloading .inputrc worked, enter the following command, press Enter, and you should see the following:

```
$ bind -P | grep history-search
history-search-backward can be found on "\e[A".
history-search-forward can be found on "\e[B".
```

That tells us that searching backward is bound to the Up arrow, and searching forward is bound to the Down arrow, exactly what we want. If instead you see the following, you have a problem:

```
$ bind -P | grep history-search
history-search-backward is not bound to any keys
history-search-forward is not bound to any keys
```

The easiest solution is to simply open a new shell and run the test above to see if it works. If it does, close your old shell and start using the new one. If it still doesn't work, carefully check your ~/.inputrc— something is wrong in that file.

Display All Command Aliases

```
alias
```

If you use a command all the time, or if a command is
just particularly long and onerous to type, it behooves
you to make that command an *alias*. After you create
an alias, you simply type its name, and the command
(or commands) referenced by the alias runs. Of course,
if a command is particularly complicated or involves
several lines, you should instead turn it into a script or
function (for more on functions, see the end of this
chapter). But for small things, aliases are perfect.

As you will see very soon, aliases are either temporary
and stored in memory until you end your shell session,
or "permanent" and stored in a file in your home
directory. (I put "permanent" in quotation marks
because you can always delete them.) You might
find them in .bashrc, but you really should use bash_
aliases instead. (For more on both .bashrc and .bash_
aliases, see the end of Chapter 1.)

Most Linux distributions come with several aliases
already defined for you; to see that list, just enter alias
on the command line.

```
$ alias
alias la="ls -a"
alias ll="ls -l"
[list truncated for length]
```

Most distributions purposely keep the default aliases to
a minimum. It's up to you to add new ones, as you'll
shortly see.

View a Specific Command Alias

```
alias [alias name]
```

After you've defined several aliases, it can be hard to find a specific one if you type in the alias command. If you want to review what a specific alias does, just follow alias with the name of the specific alias about which you want to learn more.

```
$ alias wgetpage
alias wgetpage="wget --html-extension --recursive
➥--convert-links --page-requisites --no-parent"
```

Now you know exactly what the wgetpage alias does, quickly and easily.

NOTE: You'll learn more about wget in Chapter 16.

Create a New Temporary Alias

```
alias [alias name]="[command]"
```

If you find yourself typing a command over and over again, maybe it's time to make it an alias. For instance, to see just the subdirectories in your current working directory, you'd use ls -d */. To create a temporary alias for that command, use the following:

```
$ ls -d */
by_pool/  libby_pix/  on_floor/
$ alias lsd="ls -d */"
$ lsd
by_pool/  libby_pix/  on_floor/
```

You should realize a couple of things about using `alias` in this way. Your alias name can't have an `=` in it, which makes sense, because it's immediately followed by an `=` when you're defining it. You can, however, have an `=` in the actual alias itself. Also, an alias created in this fashion only lasts as long as this shell session is active. Log out, and your alias is gone.

Want to create an alias that lasts past when you log out? Then read the next section, "Create a New Permanent Alias."

Create a New Permanent Alias

```
alias [alias name]='[command]'
```

If you want your aliases to stick around between shell sessions, you need to add them to the file your shell uses to store aliases. Most of the time that file is either `.bashrc` or `.bash_aliases`; in this case, you're going to use `.bash_aliases`. No matter which file it is, be careful editing it, as you can cause yourself problems later when logging in. If you want to be really careful, create a backup of the file before editing it. Better safe than sorry.

NOTE: How can you find out which file you should use? Simple: Type `ls -a ~`. If you see `.bash_aliases`, use that; otherwise, look in `.bashrc` and see if other aliases are defined in there (and then tell it to use `.bash_aliases`!). If you don't see any aliases in there, take a look at `.profile`, which is occasionally used. For more on these files, see the end of Chapter 1.

To add an alias to .bash_aliases, open it with your favorite text editor and add a line like the following:

```
alias lsd="ls -d */"
```

The same rule discussed in "Create a New Temporary Alias" applies here as well: Your alias name can't have an = in it. After adding your alias to .bash_aliases, save the file and close it. But the alias doesn't work yet. The .bash_aliases file (or .bashrc if that's what you used) needs to be reloaded for the new alias to work:

```
$ source ~/.bash_aliases
```

Now your new alias will work.

NOTE: Some people discourage aliases that take a normal command and change its behavior, like alias rm="rm -i", because they say that you will get too dependent upon your alias and will forget that it's missing when you use another computer, potentially doing some damage. I think that's a pretty silly argument. If an alias makes things easier for you, use it. I'm sure that you have enough brains to remember that a different machine won't have your aliases on it.

Remove an Alias

```
unalias
```

All good things must come to an end, and sometimes an alias outlives its usefulness. To remove an alias, use the unalias command.

```
$ ls -d */
by_pool/  libby_pix/  on_floor/
$ alias lsd="ls -d */"
```

```
$ lsd
by_pool/  libby_pix/  on_floor/
$ unalias lsd
$ lsd
$
```

Note, though, that this command only works
permanently for temporary shell aliases, discussed
previously in "Create a New Temporary Alias." The
lsd alias in the previous example is now gone for
good. If you use the unalias command on an alias
found in .bash_aliases, it too will be gone, but only
as long as you're logged in. When you log out and log
back in, or reload .bash_aliases, the alias is back.

To remove aliases from .bash_aliases, you need to edit
the file and manually remove the line containing the
alias. If you think there's a chance you might want to
reuse the alias again sometime, just put a pound sign
(which comments it out) in front of the alias, like this:

```
# alias lsd="ls -d */"
```

Save .bash_aliases, reload it with the source ~/.bash_
aliases command, and the alias won't work any
longer. But if you ever need it again, open .bash_
aliases, remove the pound sign, save and reload the
file, and it's good to go again.

Create a New Temporary Function

```
function [function name] { }
[function name] () { }
```

If you need something more complex than an alias
but less complex than a script, you want a function.

The official *GNU Bash Reference Manual* describes a shell function as "a way to group commands for later execution using a single name for the group," which is absolutely correct. In many ways, you invoke a function like you invoke an alias: You simply type the name of the function, followed by any arguments you want to pass along. The big difference, as you'll see later in this chapter in "When to Use an Alias and When to Use a Function," is that a function allows you to do things that you just can't do with an alias.

There are two ways to declare a function. You could use the function command, followed by your function name, with the commands you want to run in the function inside the curly braces { and }. Or you can use a method that's more comfortable to programmers in which you start with the function name and then follow it with an empty pair of parentheses and then the curly braces. Which you choose is up to you, but I'm more used to the latter, so that's what I'll use in my examples.

Short, temporary functions can be created on a single line, as in this example, which first creates a new directory with mkdir -p and then cds into it:

```
$ mkcd () { mkdir -p "$1"; cd "$1"; }
$ mkcd lovecraft
$ pwd
/home/scott/lovecraft
```

If you use the single-line method, then you *must* use semicolons after each command, even the last one.

NOTE: You probably figured this out already, but the $1 in the function is a *positional parameter* that is replaced with the first argument you type after the function name. The last section of this chapter, "When to Use an Alias and When to Use a Function," goes into much greater detail about those terms and what they mean.

Functions can also stretch over multiple lines. If you create it on the command line (which is how you make a temporary function, after all), you're going to see something you might not have seen before. When you type the first line of your new function and press Enter, a *secondary prompt* will appear that looks like a >. This is bash telling you that it needs more input in order to complete the command. In this case, since you're creating a function, it's waiting for that final } and a press of the Enter key. Until then, as you enter the lines of your function and press Enter, each subsequent line will start with the > to indicate that bash is still waiting.

It's difficult to show that process in a book, but the following example should give you the idea. I pressed Enter after each of the four lines shown below; after the first one, a secondary prompt appeared and kept appearing until I finished the function with its final } and Enter.

```
$ mkcd () {
>    mkdir -p "$1"
>    cd "$1"
> }
```

No matter how you create it, a function created via the command line lasts only as long as your shell session is active. Log out, and your function, like the passenger pigeon, is gone.

Want to create a function that sticks around even after you log out? Then read the next section, "Create a New Permanent Function."

TIP: You can find some very useful and instructive functions if you use your favorite search engine to look for "bash useful functions" or the like.

Create a New Permanent Function

```
function [function name] { }
[function name] () { }
```

If you want your functions to stick around between shell sessions, you need to add them to a file used by your shell. Most of the time that file is either `.bashrc` or `.bash_aliases`; in my case, I prefer to use `.bash_aliases` since it already exists and since I've already sourced it in `.bashrc`.

Some people suffer cognitive dissonance when they're told to use a file named `.bash_aliases` to store functions. If you're one of those people, you can always create a file named `.bash_functions` in your home directory and source it in your `.bashrc` as follows:

```
if [ -f ~/.bash_functions ]; then
  source ~/.bash_functions
fi
```

If you create a *lot* of functions or your functions file becomes too big, you can instead put them into

separate files in a hidden directory, and source them in
your `.bashrc`:

```
if [ -d ~/.bash_functions ]; then
  for file in ~/.bash_functions/*; do
    source "$file"
  done
fi
```

Notice the `-d` instead of the `-f` as in the previous
example; that, of course, stands for "directory" while
the other option stood for "file."

To add a function to `.bash_aliases`, open it with your
favorite text editor and add your function. If it's short
and will work on one line, you can do this:

```
mkcd () { mkdir -p "$1"; cd "$1"; }
```

If it needs to be (or you want it to be) several lines,
which is often better for readability, do something like
this instead:

```
knownhosts () {
  [ "${1}" ] || return
  local date=$(date +%Y-%m-%d-%H.%M.%S)
  sed -i_${date} -e "${1}d" ~/.ssh/known_hosts
}
```

Let me explain what's going on here. This is a
function that I've found useful with SSH (covered
in Chapter 16's "Securely Log In to Another
Computer"). Periodically, a server's public SSH key
may change, requiring you to edit the known_hosts
file in ~/.ssh to remove the line referring to that
server so another public key can be obtained from it.

Fortunately, SSH tells you which line to change in its error message, as you see in the excerpt below:

```
Offending key in /home/scott/.ssh/known_hosts:8
```

I have to manage a lot of servers, and I was tired of opening my known_hosts file constantly to delete lines, so I wrote the function. To use it, you simply type the name of the function followed by the line number the SSH error message provided:

```
$ knownhosts 8
```

The line is deleted, so you can now connect to the server in question and get another public key. Easy. So how's it work?

The first line—["${1}"] || return—verifies that an argument (in this case, a line number) was submitted after the command. If not, it simply returns from, or exits, the function (often a very good thing to add to your functions, by the way!).

The second line—local date=$(date +%Y-%m-%d-%H.%M.%S)—creates a local variable called date with the output of the date command. By default, all variables created within a function are global; that is, they still exist after the function returns. In contrast, a local variable is only available within the function. Once the function returns, the variable no longer exists. In this case, the date variable will hold the current date, for example, 2015-07-25-22.21.41.

The third line— sed -i_${date} -e "${1}d" ~/.ssh/known_hosts—uses sed (covered in Chapter 7's "Transform Text in a File") to do a few things. The -i option tells sed to edit the file in place, but to first make a backup copy and add the value of the date variable to that backup copy, so that it will look like this: known_hosts_2015-07-25-22.21.41. (Yes, this means that over time you'll end up with a bunch of backup files in ~/.ssh, but this isn't a big deal: Just clean them out periodically.) The -e option deletes the problematic server entry from the file. The number entered as an argument to the function—8 in this example—is passed to the function using the ${1} parameter.

NOTE: Notice I used {} around the variables. Those are optional, but really help to disambiguate variables from surrounding text. For example, compare ${1}d and $1d. They're both the same thing, but the former is far more readable.

No matter how you enter your function in .bash_aliases, after you're finished, save the file and close it. You now need to reload the .bash_aliases file for the new function to work, so run this command:

```
$ source ~/.bash_aliases
```

Now your new function will work. I hope it makes you more productive!

Display All Functions

If you want to see a list of all your aliases, you just use the alias command. Unfortunately, there's no equivalent for functions. Instead, you can use this handy little function that does a really useful thing: It lists all your functions!

```
listfunc () {
  for func in $(compgen -A function | grep -v _);
  do
    declare -f $func;
    echo -e "\r";
  done
}
```

This uses a `for` loop, command substitution (covered in Chapter 5, "Building Blocks"), the `grep` command that is covered in Chapter 10, and two commands that I'm not going to describe and will instead leave as research homework for you (`compgen` and `declare`). Put that function in your `.bash_aliases` file and then, when you want to use it, just enter `listfunc` on your command line. Voila!

NOTE: If you do some reading, you'll see that some people point out that you can use `declare -f` to see all your functions. That's true, but you'll also see every other function that's available to your shell, including all those that came with your particular distro. When I ran that function I gave you earlier in this section (`listfunc`), I found out that the functions I had added manually took 59 lines. When I ran `declare -f`, all the other functions on my system not created by me added up to 2213 lines!

Remove a Function

`unset -f [function name]`

Getting rid of an alias is easy: just use `unalias`. However, there's no `unfunction`. Instead, when you're finished with a function, use the `unset` command along

with the `-f` option (which stands for—surprise!—
"function").

```
$ mkcd () { mkdir -p "$1"; cd "$1"; }
$ mkcd lovecraft
$ pwd
/home/scott/lovecraft
$ unset -f mkcd
$ mkcd cthulhu
mkcd: command not found
```

Note, though, that this command works permanently
for temporary shell functions only, discussed
previously in "Create a New Temporary Function."
The mkcd function in the previous example is now
gone for good. If you use the unset command on a
function found in .bash_aliases (or .bash_functions),
it too will be gone, but only as long you're logged
in. When you log out and log back in, or reload
.bash_aliases, the function is back.

To remove functions from .bash_aliases, you need
to edit the file and manually remove the line(s)
containing the function. If you think there's a chance
you might want to reuse the function again sometime,
just put a pound sign (which comments it out) in front
of the function's line(s), like this:

```
# mkcd () { mkdir -p "$1"; cd "$1"; }
```

Save .bash_aliases, reload it with the source ~/.bash_
aliases command, and the function won't work any
longer. But if you ever need it again, open .bash_
aliases, remove the pound sign, save and reload the
file, and it's good to go.

When to Use an Alias and When to Use a Function

So I've covered aliases and functions, but when is it appropriate to use one instead of the other?

There are a few similarities between the two. Both aliases and functions are loaded into memory with your shell. (Modern computers are so robust, and functions take up so little memory, that you really don't need to worry about any adverse impact.) And both aliases and functions can only be used by your current shell and therefore can only affect your current shell environment (unlike scripts).

However, the differences are what's important. In fact, the official *GNU Bash Reference Manual* says this about aliases: "For almost every purpose, shell functions are preferred over aliases." Why is that?

For one thing, bash always executes aliases *after* functions, but for all practical matters, you shouldn't even notice.

What about purposes? Aliases are mostly—not entirely, but mostly—used to turn a long command into something much shorter and more memorable (for example, `alias wgetpage="wget --html-extension --recursive --convert-links --page-requisites --no-parent"`), or for adding desired arguments onto commands (for example, `alias lsd="ls -d */"`). Functions are for much longer or more complex sequences of commands, often with logic and loops. So, for instance, you could do the following with a function (for details, see the previous section "Display All Functions"), but there's no way you could do anything like it with an alias:

```
listfunc () {
  for func in $(compgen -A function | grep -v _);
  do
    declare -f $func;
    echo -e "\r";
  done
}
```

But the big difference—and this is going to take a
bit of explaining—is how aliases and functions treat
arguments. As you will see, aliases basically pass any
arguments along to the end of the aliased command
in the same order in which you entered them. Shell
functions, however, allow you to capture arguments
and then rearrange, test, remove, and manipulate them.

NOTE: An `argument` is input that is passed to a command. For instance, given the function `mkcd () {`
`mkdir -p "$1"; cd "$1"; }`, when you type `mkcd`
`cthulhu` and press Enter, `cthulhu` is an argument.
Parameters are defined by the function or program, so
using the previously defined function, the `$1` defines
the parameter. (To be specific, `$1` is a *positional
parameter* that refers to the first argument; you can
use other numbered positional parameters to refer to
other arguments if your function requires it.) Think of
it this way: When you define it, it's a parameter; when
it's actually getting used, it's an argument.

You might want to try using a positional parameter
with an alias, but that's a losing battle. The argument
to an aliased command always gets used at the end, as
you can see here:

```
$ alias lstest="ls -l $1 | grep tar"
$ lstest /bin
grep: /bin: Is a directory
$ unalias lstest
```

Why did this fail? Because bash automatically appends
your argument—/bin—at the end, right after the grep
tar. So instead of creating ls -l /bin | grep tar,
you're actually constructing ls -l | grep tar /bin.
That's why grep reports an error: You're telling it to
look for the word "tar" in a directory name, which
ain't gonna work, instead of in a file or list of files,
which will.

Now that we understand where bash places arguments
to an alias—always appended to the end of the
command(s)—let's contrast that with the failed alias
from earlier in this section, but using a function instead:

```
$ lstest () { ls -l $1 | grep tar; }
$ lstest /bin
-rwxr-xr-x root root tar*
-rwxr-xr-x root root unicode_start*
```

This example works because a function allows you
to place the argument where you want, which in this
case is right after the first command, ls -l $1.

You'll find that both aliases and functions have their
places in your toolbox, and the more familiar you get
with Linux, the more you'll start relying on them.

Conclusion

One of your goals as a Linux user should be reducing the amount of characters you have to type to accomplish your goals. The original developers of UNIX were strong believers in that concept—that's why you enter `ls` instead of `list` and `mkdir` instead of `makedirectory`. The commands you've learned in this chapter—`history`, `alias`, and `function`— aid in that process. Tired of typing a long and complicated command? Reference it with `history`, or create an alias or function for it. You'll save keystrokes, and your keyboard (and, more importantly, your hands and wrists) will thank you for it.

Monitoring System Resources

A good computer user has to be a bit of a systems administrator, always checking the health of her machine to make sure that everything is running smoothly. To help achieve that goal, Linux has several commands to monitor system resources. In this chapter, you're going to look at several of those commands. Many of them have multiple uses, but all—in the best UNIX tradition of small tools that solve a single task well—are especially good at one particular aspect of system monitoring. Their tasks range from keeping track of the programs running on your computer (ps and top) to ending errant processes (kill) to listing all open files (lsof) to reporting your system's usage of RAM (free) and hard disk space (df and du). Learn these tools well. You'll find yourself using them in all sorts of situations.

Discover How Long Your Computer Has Been Running

```
uptime
```

Want to know how long your computer has been up and running? That's the job of the uptime command. It's pretty dang easy to use:

```
$ uptime
22:07:10 up 22 days, 23:29,  1 user,  load average:
➥0.46, 0.63, 0.52
```

So why would you use the uptime command to find out how long your computer has been running? Well, bragging rights isn't a bad reason at all. 22 days isn't bad, but I've seen way bigger numbers. If you search around, you'll see folks comparing uptimes to see who has the longest, which is always fun.

A more useful reason is finding out if your reboot happened successfully. For instance, sometimes I'll SSH (see Chapter 16, "Working on the Network") into a remote server, restart it, wait a few moments, and then SSH in again. A quick way to find out if the reboot succeeded? You guessed it—uptime!

View All Currently Running Processes

```
ps aux
```

Every once in a while, a program you're running locks up and stops responding, requiring that you close it. Or you might want to know what programs a certain user is running. Or you might just want to know about the processes currently running on your machine. In any of those cases and many others, you want to use the ps command that lists open processes on your computer.

Just to make your life even more complicated, ps has many versions, and they have different types of options. They can even have different meanings, depending on whether those options are preceded by a hyphen, so that u and -u mean completely different things. Up to now, this book has been pretty strict about preceding all options with a hyphen, but for ps, it's not, as it makes things a bit easier and more uniform.

To see all the processes that any user is running on your system, follow ps with these options: a (which means *all users*), u (*user-oriented*, or show the user who owns each process), and x (*processes without controlling ttys or terminal screens*, another way of saying "show every process"). Be forewarned that a fairly long list is going to zoom by on your screen: 132 lines on this computer.

```
$ ps aux
USER     PID %CPU %MEM    VSZ   RSS TTY    STAT START
➡TIME COMMAND
scott 24224  4.1  4.2 1150440 44036 ?      R     11:02
➡12:03 /home/scott/.cxoffice/bin/wine-preloader
scott  5594  0.0  0.1   3432  1820 pts/6 S+    12:14
➡0:00 ssh scott@humbug.machine.com
scott 14957  0.3  7.5 171144 78628 ?      Sl    13:01
➡0:35 /usr/lib/openoffice2/program/soffice.bin
➡-writer
scott 12369  0.0  0.0      0     0 ?      Z     15:43
➡0:00 [wine-preloader] <defunct>
scott 14680  0.0  0.1   3860  1044 pts/5 R+    15:55
➡0:00 ps aux
```

TIP: If you run `ps aux`, you'll notice that by default the output gets cut off at the edge of your terminal window. This of course means that you will not be able to see some information that could be very useful or important. To see the lines of output in their entirety, add the `-w` option (for *wrap*) like this: `ps aux -w`.

The `ps` command gives you a lot of information, including the user who owns the process, the unique process ID number (PID) that identifies the process, the percentage of the CPU (`%CPU`) and memory (`%MEM`) that the process is using, the current status (`STAT`) of the process, and the name of the process itself.

The `STAT` column can have different letters in it, with the following being the most important:

`STAT` **Letter**	**Meaning**
R	Running
S	Sleeping
T	Stopped
Z	Zombie

A `Z` is bad news because it means that the process has basically hung and cannot be stopped (fortunately, it does *not* mean that it will try to eat your brain). If you're having a problem with a program and `ps` indicates that it has a status of `Z`, you're probably going to have to reboot the machine to completely kill it.

Because `ps aux` provides you with a lot of data, it can be difficult to find the program for which you're searching. Piping the output of `ps aux` to `grep` can be an easy way to limit the results to a particular command.

```
$ ps aux | grep [f]irefox
scott 25205  0.0  0.0  4336     8 ?           S
➥Feb08  0:00 /bin/sh /opt/firefox/firefox
scott 25213  1.1 10.9 189092 113272 ?        Rl
➥Feb08 29:42 /opt/firefox/firefox-bin
```

Now you know just the instances of Firefox running
on this machine, including who's running the
program, how much of a load on the machine that
program is, and how long that program has been
running. Useful!

TIP: Why did you search for [f]irefox instead of
firefox? To find the answer, take a look in Chapter
10, "Finding Files, Directories, Words, and Phrases,"
in the "Search the Output of Other Commands for
Specific Words" section.

View a Process Tree

```
ps axjf
```

In the Linux world, processes don't just appear
out of thin air. Often, starting one program starts
other programs. All processes on a Linux system,
for instance, ultimately come from init, the mother
of all processes, which always has a PID of 1. The
ps command can provide you with a text-based
representation of this process tree so you can visually
see what processes have spawned others. To see the
process tree, use the a and x options, used in the
previous section, along with two others: j (for *BSD
job control format*, which determines the columns you'll
see) and f (the evocatively named *ASCII art forest*).

NOTE: Normally, you'd see the following columns:

```
PPID PID PGID SID TTY TPGID STAT UID TIME
➥COMMAND
```

In the interests of making the command tree easier to understand, most of the columns you'd actually see with `ps axjf` have been removed in the following code listing. Oh, and it's truncated, too.

```
$ ps axjf
PPID    PID  COMMAND
   1   7558  /usr/sbin/gdm
7558   7561   \_ /usr/sbin/gdm
7561   7604       \_ /usr/X11R6/bin/X :0
7561   8225       \_ /bin/sh /usr/bin/startkde
8225   8279           \_ /usr/bin/ssh-agent
8225   8341               \_ kwrapper ksmserver
   1   8316  kdeinit Running...
8316  10842   \_ konqueror [kdeinit] --silent
8316  29663   \_ quanta
8316  30906   \_ /usr/bin/kwrite /home/scott/analysis
8316  17893   \_ /usr/lib/opera/9.0-20060206.1/opera
17893 17960   |   \_ /usr/lib/opera/pluginwrapper
17893 17961   |   \_ /usr/lib/opera/plugincleaner
```

Note that `ps axjf` introduces a key new column, PPID. PPID, the Parent Process ID number, is the number of the process that spawned the PID. Armed with the PID or PPID, you can end runaway processes, as you'll see soon in "End a Running Process."

NOTE: Another way to view a process tree is via the `pstree` command. Not all systems have it, so you might have to install it yourself (to learn how, see Chapter 14, "Installing Software").

View Processes Owned by a Particular User

`ps U [username]`

Up to now, you've been looking at how `ps` gives you a list of all processes on your system. If you want to limit the results to those owned by a single user, simply use the `u` option, followed by the username or number.

```
$ ps U scott
  PID TTY    STAT TIME COMMAND
14928 ?      S    0:00 /usr/lib/openoffice2/program/
➥soffice -writer
14957 ?      Sl   0:42 /usr/lib/openoffice2/program/
➥soffice.bin -writer
 4688 pts/4  S+   0:00 ssh scott@humbug.machine.com
26751 ?      Z    0:00 [wine-preloader] <defunct>
27955 pts/5  R+   0:00 ps U scott
```

Of course, `ps` doesn't include the username in the listing because it was already part of the command.

TIP: Remember, if you don't know the user's number, just look in `/etc/passwd`. Find the username, and the user number is in the third column.

End a Running Process

`kill`
`killall`

Sometimes a program goes rogue, and it won't react to normal attempts to close it. In a GUI like GNOME or KDE, you click repeatedly on the Close button,

but nothing happens, or, in the shell, you press
Ctrl+C but it fails to stop a running command. When
this happens, it's time for the `kill` command.

You can use several signals with the `kill` command,
ranging from "Please shut yourself down, cleaning up
your mess as you do so" to "Shut yourself down as
soon as you can" to "Die *now!*" You're going to focus
on the three most important. When you use `kill`, you
can specify the intensity of the process's death with a
number or a word, as Table 13.1 shows.

Table 13.1   **Common Signals Associated with** `kill`

Signal Number	Signal Word	Meaning
`-1`	`-HUP` (*hang up*)	Controlling process has died. Shut down (if applied to a system service, reload configuration files and restart).
`-15`	`-TERM`	Terminate gracefully, cleaning up stray processes and files.
`-9`	`-KILL`	Stop whatever you're doing and die now!

Normally, you should first try `-15` (in fact, it's the
default if you run `kill` without any option). That
way, you give the program a chance to shut down
any other programs depending upon it, close files
opened by it, and so on. If you've been patient and
waited a while ("a while" is completely subjective, of
course), and the process is still running completely out
of control or still failing to respond, you can bring out
the big guns and use `-9`. The `-9` option is equivalent

to yanking the rug out from under a running program, and while it does the job, it could leave stray files and processes littering your system, and that's never a good thing.

As for -1, or -HUP, that's primarily for services such as Samba or wireless connectivity. You won't use it much, but you should know what it means.

Here's what you would do if gvim (which never has stability problems—this is just for demonstration purposes) seemed to freeze on your system (results truncated, of course).

```
$ ps U scott
  PID TTY    STAT TIME COMMAND
14928 ?      S    0:00 /bin/sh /usr/lib/openoffice2/
➥program/soffice -writer
 4688 pts/4 S+    0:00 ssh admin@bacon.humbug.com
26751 ?      Z    0:00 [wine-preloader] <defunct>
  743 ?      Ss   0:00 /usr/bin/gvim
  833 pts/5 R+    0:00 ps U scott
$ kill 743
$ ps U scott
  PID TTY    STAT TIME COMMAND
14928 ?      S    0:00 /bin/sh /usr/lib/openoffice2/
➥program/soffice -writer
 4688 pts/4 S+    0:00 ssh admin@bacon.humbug.com
26751 ?      Z    0:00 [wine-preloader] <defunct>
  858 pts/5 R+    0:00 ps U scott
```

To kill gvim, you use ps to find gvim's PID, which in this case is 743. Next, you kill that PID (and remember that kill uses the TERM signal by default) and then check again with ps. Yes, gvim is no more.

NOTE: Why didn't you kill PID 26751, which has a STAT of z, indicating that it's a zombie? Because even -9 doesn't work on a zombie—it's already dead; hence, the kill command won't work. A reboot (think of it as shooting the zombie in the head) is the only way to fix that (usually unimportant) problem.

To use kill, you must provide a PID. But what if a program you want to end has several, or even many, PIDs? Using kill with each PID would be tedious, even unpleasant. In that case, use killall instead of kill. The killall command uses process names instead of PIDs, so that makes it a bit easier to use in these situations.

Let's say that cronolog (a program that allows you to control the generation of log files) had gone haywire and you needed to stop it now. On one of my servers, there are 84 processes for cronolog, and I sure don't want to stop each and every one with kill! Here's how I would stop all of them in one swell foop with killall (now, you should not do this unless you absolutely have to, so please use killall—and kill—responsibly).

```
$ ps aux | grep /usr/bin/cronolog| wc -l
84
$ killall cronolog
$ ps aux | grep /usr/sbin/cronolog | wc -l
0
```

I used the ps command from earlier in this chapter and then piped the results to grep (see Chapter 10) to pull out only the actual cronolog processes. I then piped those results to wc -l (discussed in Chapter 7, "Manipulating Text Files with Filters"), which counts the number of lines in the output, giving me 84. I used `killall` with the name of the cronolog process, and then ran the `ps` command again. This time? Nada. Zilch. Bupkus. Zip. Nothin'. Just as I wanted.

View a Dynamically Updated List of Running Processes

```
top
```

On occasion, you'll find that your Linux machine suddenly slows down, apparently for no reason. Something is running on your computer at full tilt, and it's using up the processor. Or perhaps you'll start running a command, only to find that it's using far more of your CPU's cycles than you thought it would. To find out what's causing the problem, or if you just want to find out what's running on your system, you could use `ps`, except that `ps` doesn't update itself. Instead, it provides a snapshot of your system's processes, and that's it.

The `top` command, on the other hand, provides a dynamically updated view of what's running on your system and how many system resources each process is using. It's a bit hard to see in a book because you can't see `top` update its display every second, but here's what you would see at one moment while `top` is running.

```
$ top
top - 18:05:03 up 4 days,  8:03,  1 user,  load
➥average: 0.83, 0.82, 0.97
Tasks: 135 total,   3 running, 126 sleeping,   2
➥stopped,   4 zombie
Cpu(s): 22.9% us,  7.7% sy,  3.1% ni, 62.1% id,
➥3.5% wa,  0.1% hi,  0.7% si
```

```
Mem:    1036136k total,   987996k used,    48140k
➥free,    27884k buffers
Swap: 1012084k total,   479284k used,   532800k
➥free,   179580k cached
  PID USER    PR  NI  VIRT  RES  SHR S %CPU %MEM
➥TIME+  COMMAND
25213 scott   15   0  230m 150m  15m S 11.1 14.9
➥33:39.34 firefox-bin
 7604 root    15   0  409m 285m 2896 S 10.8 28.2
➥749:55.75 Xorg
 8323 scott   15   0 37396 7716 4860 S  2.0  0.7
➥142:50.89 kded
 8491 scott   15   0 45196 9.8m 6156 S  2.0  1.0
➥0:26.30 nautilus
 8378 scott   15   0 37084  10m 7456 S  1.0  1.1
➥13:53.99 kicker
```

The top command gives you a great deal of
information about your system in the first five lines of
its output, and then it focuses on listing each running
process. Note that top automatically sorts the output
by the numbers in the %CPU column, so as programs
use more and then less of your processor, their
position in top changes as well.

TIP: For help controlling and using top to the best
of its abilities, press ? and read the resulting help
screen. It's actually helpful!

If you want to kill programs from within top, just
press k. At the top of the listings, just after the line
that begins with swap:, you'll see the following:

```
PID to kill:
```

Enter the PID for the process you want to end (let's
say 8026), press Enter, and you're asked what signal

number (discussed in the previous "End a Running
Process" section) you want to use:

```
Kill PID 8026 with signal [15]:
```

By default, top wants to use 15. If you're happy with
that, just press Enter; if not, enter the signal number
you want to use and then press Enter. A second or so
later, that process will disappear from top.

To exit top, press q.

The top command is incredibly useful, and you'll find
yourself turning to it often, just to find out what's
happening on your Linux machine. When you have
questions about your computer's activity, top often
provides the answers.

NOTE: People are starting to prefer htop to plain ol'
top. It's scrollable, colorized, menu-driven, and it provides a nice graph of memory usage. To read more, go
to http://hisham.hm/htop/. Really, htop pretty much
kicks top's behind (in fact, htop is what I like to use
on my Linux boxes). However, it typically doesn't come
with standard distro installs, so you'll have to install it
yourself (see Chapter 14 for installation info).

List Open Files

`lsof`

Chapter 1, "Things to Know About Your Command
Line," discussed the fact that everything is a file to
a Linux machine, including directories, network
connections, and devices. That means that even
though from your perspective you only have one file
open—a letter to your Mom—your system actually has

thousands of files open at any one time. That's right—
thousands. To see the complete list of those open files,
use the `lsof` command (short for *list open files*).

Actually, don't. If you just run `lsof` by itself (to get the
full list of results, you need to be root), you'll receive
as output that list of thousands of files. On this system,
there were 5,497 files open and being used. Still, `lsof`
can be a useful way to get an idea of just how much is
going on with your computer at any one time.

Piping the output of `lsof` to `less` gives you the results
one screen at a time.

```
# lsof | less
COMMAND      PID USER   FD   TYPE DEVICE      SIZE  NODE
➡NAME
init           1 root  cwd    DIR    3,1       656     2 /
init           1 root  rtd    DIR    3,1       656     2 /
init           1 root  txt    REG    3,1     31608  2072
➡/sbin/init
init           1 root  mem    REG    0,0                 0
➡[heap]  (stat: No such file or directory)
init           1 root  mem    REG    3,1   1226096 27220
➡/lib/tls/i686/cmov/libc-2.3.5.so
init           1 root  mem    REG    3,1     86596 27536
➡/lib/ld-2.3.5.so
init           1 root  10u   FIFO   0,12              3915
➡/dev/initctl
ksoftirqd      2 root  cwd    DIR    3,1       656     2 /
```

Still, with 5,497 results, that's many screens to page
through. You can also pipe the output of `lsof` to `grep`.
As you'll see in the next few sections, however, `lsof`
contains within itself ways to filter out the data you
don't want to see so you can focus only on a particular
subset of open files that interest you.

NOTE: The lsof command has a truly epic number of options, so many that minuses *and* plusses are used before the same letter options. In other words, there's a +c and a -c, and a +d and a -d, and they all mean different things. That means this can be a complicated command if you start wading into the weeds, so be prepared.

List a User's Open Files

```
lsof -u
```

If you want to look at the files a particular user has open (and remember that those include network connections and devices, among many others), add the -u option to lsof, followed by the username (remember that lsof must be run as root).

```
# lsof -u scott
COMMAND     PID  USER  FD  TYPE     DEVICE      SIZE
➦NODE NAMEP
evolution   8603 scott 37u unix 0xe73dc680
➦13518 socket
evolution   8603 scott 38r FIFO       0,5
➦13520 pipe
evolution   8603 scott 39w FIFO       0,5
➦13520 pipe
evolution   8603 scott 40u REG        3,2      49152
➦181419 /home/scott/.evolution/addressbook/
➦local/system/addressbook.db
opera      11638 scott cwd DIR        3,2       7096
➦6 /home/scott
opera      11638 scott rtd DIR        3,1        656
➦2 /
opera      11638 scott txt REG        3,1 13682540
➦109226 /usr/lib/opera/9.0-20060206.1/opera
```

```
opera      11638 scott mem    REG        0,0
➥0 [heap] (stat: No such file or directory)
opera      11638 scott mem    REG        3,1      34968
➥162978 /usr/lib/X11/locale/common/
➥xomGeneric.so.2.0.0
opera      11638 scott mem    REG        3,1      111724
➥109232 /usr/lib/opera/plugins/libnpp.so
opera      11638 scott mem    REG        3,1      14776
➥27361 /lib/tls/i686/cmov/libnss_dns-2.3.5.so
opera      11638 scott mem    REG        3,1      286620
➥103029 /usr/share/fonts/truetype/
➥msttcorefonts/Arial_Bold.ttf
[Results greatly truncated for length]
```

Even filtering out all users except one, you're left with 3,039 lines in this list. Still, some interesting items are here. For one, it appears that Evolution (an email and personal information manager program) is running all the time, without your knowledge or intention. Also, the Opera web browser is running, which is expected, and one of the web pages it's on is requiring the use of the Arial Bold font, among other files.

If you administer a box used by more than person, try out lsof -u for your users. You might find that they are running programs that they shouldn't. If you're the sole user on your Linux machine, try lsof -u on yourself—you might find that you're running programs of which you were unaware!

List Users for a Particular File

```
lsof [file]
```

In the previous section, you saw what files a particular user had open. Let's reverse that, and see who's using a particular file. To do so, simply follow lsof with the path to a file on your system. For instance, let's take a look at who's using the SSH daemon, used to connect remotely to this computer (remember that lsof must be run as root).

```
# lsof /usr/sbin/sshd
COMMAND    PID   USER   FD TYPE DEVICE   SIZE   NODE
➥NAME
sshd      7814   root  txt  REG    3,1 278492 67453
➥/usr/sbin/sshd
sshd     10542   root  txt  REG    3,1 278492 67453
➥/usr/sbin/sshd
sshd     10548  scott  txt  REG    3,1 278492 67453
➥/usr/sbin/sshd
```

That's the result you wanted: two users, root and scott. If an unexpected user had shown up here—say, 4ackordood—you'd know that you've been compromised.

NOTE: Yes, sshd is a program, but remember, that's from your human perspective. To Linux, /usr/sbin/sshd is just another file.

List Processes for a Particular Program

```
lsof -c [program]
```

In the previous section, you saw who was using /usr/sbin/sshd. The results you received, however, don't tell the whole story. Any particular program is actually comprised of calls to several (perhaps many) other processes, programs, sockets, and devices, all of which appear to Linux as more files. To find out the full universe of other files associated with a particular running program, follow `lsof` with the `-c` option, and then the name of a running (and therefore "open") program. For example, `lsof /usr/sbin/sshd` said that there were only two users and three open files associated with that exact file. But what about the entire `sshd` command?

```
# lsof -c sshd
COMMAND   PID  USER  FD  TYPE       DEVICE   SIZE
➥NODE NAME
sshd   10542  root  mem  REG          3,1   37480
➥27362 /lib/tls/i686/cmov/libnss_files-2.3.5.so
sshd   10542  root  mem  REG          3,1   34612
➥27396 /lib/tls/i686/cmov/libnss_nis-2.3.5.so
sshd   10542  root  mem  REG          3,1   86596
➥27536 /lib/ld-2.3.5.so
sshd   10542  root   0u  CHR          1,3
➥1237 /dev/null
sshd   10542  root   1u  CHR          1,3
➥1237 /dev/null
sshd   10542  root   2u  CHR          1,3
➥1237 /dev/null
sshd   10542  root   3u  IPv6        28186
➥TCP 192.168.0.170:ssh->192.168.0.100:4577
➥ (ESTABLISHED)
sshd   10542  root   5u  unix  0xf2961680
➥28227 socket
sshd   10548  scott cwd  DIR          3,1     656
➥2 /
sshd   10548  scott rtd  DIR          3,1     656
➥2 /
sshd   10548  scott txt  REG          3,1  278492
➥67453 /usr/sbin/sshdp
sshd   10548  scott  3u  IPv6        28186
➥TCP 192.168.0.170:ssh->192.168.0.100:4577
➥ (ESTABLISHED)
[Results truncated for length]
```

In the preceding code, you can see a few of the 94 lines (representing 94 open files) somehow connected with the sshd program. Several are .so files (*shared objects*, akin to DLLs on Windows), and a few even show you that a network connection has occurred between this and another machine (actually, that another machine on this network has connected via SSH to this machine; for more on that process, see "Securely Log In to Another Computer" in Chapter 16, "Working on the Network").

You can find out a tremendous amount by applying lsof to various commands on your computer; at the least, you'll learn just how complicated modern programs are. Try it out with the software you use every day, and you might gain a fresh appreciation for the programmers who worked hard to make it available to you.

NOTE: The lsof command has an amazing number of options, and you're only going to look at a tiny subset. The source code for lsof includes a file named OOQUICKSTART (that's two zeroes at the beginning) that is a tutorial for some of the command's more powerful features. Search Google for that filename and start reading.

Display Information About System RAM

`free`

Nowadays, most computers come with hundreds of megabytes or even gigabytes of RAM, but it's still possible to find your machine slowing down due to a

lot of memory usage or virtual memory swapping. To
see the current state of your system's memory, use the
`free` command.

```
$ free
          total    used    free  shared buffers cached
Mem:   1036136 995852   40284       0   80816 332264
-/+ buffers/cache:   582772 453364
Swap: 1012084 495584 516500
```

By default, `free` shows the results in kilobytes, the
same as if you'd used the `-k` option. You can change
that, however. The `-b` option shows you memory
usage in bytes, and `-m` (which you should probably use
most of the time) uses megabytes.

```
$ free -m
            total used free shared buffers cached
Mem:         1011  963   48      0      78    316
-/+ buffers/cache:       569    442
Swap:              988  483    504
```

From `free`'s output, you can see that this machine
has 1011MB of available physical RAM (actually
1024MB, but `free` displays it as 1011MB because
the kernel takes up the remaining 13MB, so it could
never be made available for other uses). The first line
makes it appear that 963MB of that is in use, leaving
only 48MB of RAM free. There's nearly a gigabyte of
swap, or virtual memory, in place, too, and about half
of that, or 483MB, has already been used. That's how
it appears, anyway.

It's not that simple, however. The important row is the middle one, labeled `-/+ buffers/cache`. Hard drives use buffers (memory Linux has reserved for processes) and cache (recently-accessed files stored in unused memory for quick retrieval) to speed up access, and if a program needs that memory, it can be quickly freed up for that program. From the point of view of the applications running on this Linux machine, 569MB of RAM, is currently used. To get that last number, take 963MB in the first row and then subtract 78MB for buffers and 316MB for cached files. Your total? 569MB, the number shown in the second column as `used`. The total amount of free RAM available right now for use is 442MB (1011MB with 569MB subtracted) And all that is in addition to the swap space you have available. Linux is nothing if not efficient when it comes to managing memory.

TIP: An excellent website with more information on `free` and Linux memory management is LinuxMM, "a wiki for documenting how memory management works and for coordinating new memory management development projects" (http://linux-mm.org). For something a bit less technical, see www.linuxatemyram.com.

Show File System Disk Usage

`df`

The `free` command deals with the RAM you have on your system; likewise, the `df` command (think *disk free*) deals with the amount of hard drive space you have. Run `df`, and you get a list of the disk space that is available to, and used by, every mounted filesystem.

```
$ df
Filesystem 1K-blocks    Used Available Use% Mounted
➥on
/dev/hda1    7678736 5170204   2508532  68% /
tmpfs         518068       0    518068   0%
➥/dev/shm
tmpfs         518068   12588    505480   3%
➥/lib/modules/2.6.12-10-386/volatile
/dev/hda2   30369948 24792784  5577164  82% /home
```

Before looking at these results in more detail, let's
make them a little easier to read. The df command
shows results in kilobytes by default, but it's usually
easier to comprehend if you instead use the -h (or
--human-readable) option.

```
$ df -h
Filesystem     Size  Used Avail Use% Mounted on
/dev/hda1      7.4G  5.0G  2.4G  68% /
tmpfs          506M     0  506M   0% /dev/shm
tmpfs          506M   13M  494M   3% /lib/modules/
➥2.6.12-10-386/volatile
/dev/hda2       29G   24G  5.4G  82% /home
```

"Human-readable" (which is a wonderful term, by
the way) means that kilobytes are indicated by κ,
megabytes by м, and gigabytes by ɢ. You can see those
last two in the preceding listing.

So what do the results mean? You have two partitions
on the hard drive: /dev/hda1, mounted at /, and /dev/
hda2, mounted at /home. The /home partition had 29GB
allocated to it, of which 82% is currently used, leaving
about 5.4GB free. It's not panic time yet when it
comes to disk space for that partition, but many more
CDs worth of MP3s and it might be time to delete
some unnecessary files.

The root partition, or /, has less space available: only
2.4GB out of 7.4GB. That partition isn't as likely
to grow, however, because it contains programs and
other relatively static files. Granted, /var is found
there, and that's where software installers (as you'll
discover in Chapter 14) and other files that change size
and contents, such as logs, are located. But overall,
there's still plenty of space left on that partition,
especially if you're not planning to install enormous
applications or start running a web or database server
on this machine.

The other two partitions are both labeled as tmpfs,
which means they are temporary file systems used by
the virtual memory, or swap space, on your computer.
When you shut down your computer, the contents of
those partitions disappear.

TIP: For more on tmpfs, see the Wikipedia article at
http://en.wikipedia.org/wiki/TMPFS.

Report File Space Used by a Directory

```
du
```

The du command tells you about your entire hard
drive, but what if you just want to know how much
space a directory and its contents are using? The du
command (short for *disk usage*) answers that question.
First, you use the cd command to change directories
to the directory in question, and then run du.

```
$ cd music
$ du
36582     ./Donald_Fagen
593985    ./Clash
145962    ./Hank_Mobley/1958_Peckin'_Time
128200    ./Hank_Mobley/1963_No_Room_For_Squares
108445    ./Hank_Mobley/1961_Workout
382615    ./Hank_Mobley
2662185   .
[Results truncated for length]
```

As with df, results for du are given in kilobytes,
but also like df, you can view them in a more
comprehensible fashion with the -h (or --human-
readable) option.

```
$ cd music
$ du -h
36M      ./Donald_Fagen
581M     ./Clash
143M     ./Hank_Mobley/1958_Peckin'_Time
126M     ./Hank_Mobley/1963_No_Room_For_Squares
106M     ./Hank_Mobley/1961_Workout
374M     ./Hank_Mobley
2.6G     .
[Results truncated for length]
```

This output shows you the space used by each
subdirectory, but directories that contain other
directories also show the total for those contents. Look
at the Hank_Mobley directory, which takes up 374MB
on this filesystem. That total comes from the three
subdirectories contained within Hank_Mobley (since the
actual amount in kilobytes was rounded to display
megabytes, the totals are just a bit off); if the total
for Hank_Mobley was substantially bigger than the total

of its three subdirectories, that would mean that the Hank_Mobley directory contained within it several loose files that were outside of a subdirectory.

Finally, you get a total for the entire music/ directory at the end: 2.6GB. That should keep you busy for a day or two!

TIP: If you want to see a report showing you the sizes of both directories *and* files, use du -a (or --all). If you want a sorted report of file space, use du | sort -rn (or --reverse and --numeric-sort). The du command gives you the numbers, and then sort (covered in Chapter 7) puts them in order. The -r option puts the largest number at the top and sorts from there, while the -n option makes sure that the numbers are sorted correctly (try it without the -n and you'll see). If you're feeling really fancy, redirect to a file (> toomuchcrap.txt) that, as a bonus, will be tab-delimited and ready to be imported into a spreadsheet like you'd create with LibreOffice, which is pretty cool.

Finally, if you're particularly ambitious and decide to do run du on your entire hard drive, don't forget to pipe to grep (see Chapter 10) between the du and sort in order to remove unnecessary directories. For instance: du | grep -v /dev -v /proc | sort -rn.

Report Just the Total Space Used for a Directory

```
du -s
```

If you don't want information about all of a directory's subdirectories, it's possible to ask du to simply report back the grand total by using the -s option.

```
$ cd music
$ du -hs
2.6G    .
```

Short and sweet.

Conclusion

Virtually every command you've looked at in this chapter has GUIs for it. But if your system is nonresponsive, if you're connecting to a machine via SSH (covered in Chapter 16) and can't use a GUI, or if you just want to use the speediest tool, you'll need to use the command line. The commands in this chapter are easy to remember, thanks to well-chosen names:

- ps (view running **p**roce**s**ses)
- kill (kill processes)
- top (top listing of running processes)
- lsof (list [**ls**] **o**pen **f**iles)
- free (free, or available, memory)
- df (**d**isk **f**ree space)
- du (**d**isk **u**sage)

Practice with them on your computer, and don't forget to read the man pages for each one because this chapter could only cover a fraction of their capabilities. There are many options to several of them—in particular, ps, top, and lsof—that allow you to do some truly amazing detective work on the computers under your watch.

14

Installing Software

Linux distributions by default contain thousands of great software packages. Immediately after completing a basic install, you can surf the Net, write reports, create spreadsheets, view and manipulate images, and listen to music. Even with that plethora of software, you're still going to want to add new tools that you run across. Fortunately, Linux makes it easy to install new software onto your computer.

Conventional wisdom about Linux has said you have to compile any software you want to install. You can still do that if you like (and many people do), but it's rarely necessary these days. Instead, you can install any of thousands of packages easily and quickly by using some simple tools.

You need to understand one important thing before proceeding, however. In the Linux world, software packages come in a variety of formats, with two in particular dominating: RPM and DEB (not surprisingly, those are the two we're going to cover in this chapter). RPM is used by distributions such as Red Hat (in fact, RPM stands for *Red Hat Package Manager*), Fedora Core, SUSE, and other RPM-based distributions. DEB is used by Debian-based distributions such as Debian itself, Ubuntu and its many children, Linux Mint, Knoppix, and many others. You should know how both work, but focus on the system that matches your distribution.

In fact, throughout this chapter, I will label sections so you know which package format is discussed: (RPM) for RPM-based distributions and (DEB) for Debian-based distributions. And, just to make sure you don't get confused, let me tell you now that if you see RPM, YUM, or APT, I'm referring to the package management system, but if you see rpm, yum, or apt, I'm referring to the actual commands.

TIP: For a great breakdown of the various package management systems and the distributions that use them, see DistroWatch's "Package Management Cheatsheet" at http://distrowatch.com/dwres.php?resource=package-management.

Install Software Packages (RPM)

```
rpm -ihv [package]
rpm -Uhv [package]
```

The rpm command works with software installers that end in .rpm, which seems entirely logical. To install an RPM package, you need to download it first. Let's use the industry-standard open-source network port scanner nmap as the example. You can download the RPM package for nmap from www.insecure.org/nmap/download.html; after it's on your system, you simply run rpm along with three options: -i (for *install*), -h (to show hash marks so you can watch the progress of the install), and -v (be verbose and tell me what you're doing). The command, which must be run as root (or using sudo, if your distro works with that; see the section "Install Software Packages (DEB)" later in this chapter for more details), would look like this:

```
# rpm -ihv nmap-6.40-4.el7.x86_64.rpm
```

This is actually *not* the command you should run, however. A better choice of options is -Uhv, where -U stands for *upgrade*. Why is -U better than -i? Because -i only installs, while -U upgrades *and* installs. If a package already exists on your system and you're trying to put a newer one on your machine, -U performs an upgrade; if a package doesn't already exist on your system, -U notices that and instead installs it. Therefore, just use -U all the time, and it won't matter if you're upgrading or installing: -U does what needs to be done, and you won't need to worry about it.

```
# rpm -Uhv nmap-6.40-4.el7.x86_64.rpm
Preparing...                ####################### [100%]
Updating / installing...
  1:nmap-2:6.40-4.el7 ##################### [100%]
```

If you want to install more than one RPM, just list them separated by spaces, one after the other:

```
# rpm -Uhv nmap-6.40-4.el7.x86_64.rpm nmap-
➥frontend-6.40-4.el7.noarch.rpm
```

You can also use wildcards if you have many RPMs to install. For instance, if you have 20 .rpm files in a subdirectory named software, just run this command to install them all:

```
# rpm -Uhv software/*.rpm
```

CAUTION: The `-U` option is always better than `-i`, *except* when installing a kernel. Then you want to use `-i` instead. If you upgrade with `-U` and the new kernel doesn't work, you're in a world of hurt. On the other hand, if you install a new kernel with `-i`, the old one is still on your machine as a backup if the new one blows up.

Remove Software Packages (RPM)

```
rpm -e [package]
```

Getting rid of installed RPMs is even easier than installing them. Instead of `-Uhv` to place RPMs on your computer, use `-e` (for *erase*) to remove them.

```
# rpm -e nmap
```

And that's it. The `-e` option is silent, so there's no output. Notice, however, that when you install software using `rpm -Uhv`, you need to specify the filename, otherwise RPM has no way to know what you want to install. When you remove software with `rpm -e`, however, you specify the package name because the files used for installation are now long gone, and RPM knows software by the package name.

NOTE: If you want to find out which packages are installed on your system and how RPM identifies them, use `rpm -qa`. Note that in addition to the package name, you also get the version number as well, which could come in handy.

Install Software Packages and Dependencies (RPM)

```
yum install [package]
```

The rpm command is powerful, but after you use it for a while you'll quickly run into a problem when you try to install a package that has dependencies. In order to install package A, you also need to download and install packages B and C, but in order to install C you also need to download and install packages D and E, but in order to install E…aaaaaggh! You're in dependency hell!

Debian-based distributions (that you'll read about later in this chapter) solved this problem years ago with the powerful and useful APT. RPM-based distributions can use APT, but more commonly they use the yum command. Originally developed for the RPM-based Yellow Dog Linux distribution (hence the name, which stands for *Yellow Dog Updater, Modified*), YUM is now widely used.

The yum command installs, upgrades, and uninstalls software packages by acting as a wrapper around RPM. In addition, YUM automatically handles dependencies for you. For example, if you're trying to install package A from the example in the introductory paragraph, YUM downloads and installs A, B, and C for you. Later, if you decide that you no longer want A on your system, YUM can uninstall it for you, along with B and C, as long as other software packages don't require them. Finally, tools like YUM (and APT, coming up later) provide you with a centralized location for software (kind of like an App Store, but with far fewer restrictions!) so that you don't have to spend hours hunting down individual RPM files.

NOTE: YUM will eventually be replaced with DNF…
maybe. DNF, which stands for Dandified Yum, is
designed to be a better YUM, especially in the area
of performance. At the time I'm writing this (summer
of 2015), Fedora is the only major distro that has
switched to DNF. Will others follow? We shall see. If
they do, I'll cover DNF in this book's third edition. Until
then, you can read about DNF at http://dnf.baseurl.org.

Installing software with YUM is pretty easy. Let's say
you want to install Shotwell, an image organizer. To
install Shotwell, you also need to install a few other
dependencies. With YUM, this process becomes much
less painful than it would be if you were attempting to
install manually using RPM. To start with, you don't
need to find and download the Shotwell package
yourself; instead, YUM downloads Shotwell and any
other necessary dependencies for you.

Unfortunately, yum is pretty verbose as it goes about its
work. The following output has been cut drastically,
yet it's still lengthy. Nevertheless, this gives you a
rough approximation of what you'd see if you were
using the yum command.

```
# yum install shotwell
Resolving Dependencies
--> Running transaction check
---> Package shotwell.x86_64 0:0.14.1-5.el7 will
➥be installed
--> Processing Dependency: libraw.so.5()(64bit)
➥for package: shotwell-0.14.1-5.el7.x86_64
--> Processing Dependency: libgexiv2.so.1()(64bit)
➥for package: shotwell-0.14.1-5.el7.x86_64
--> Running transaction check
```

```
---> Package LibRaw.x86_64 0:0.14.8-5 will be
➥installed
---> Package libgexiv2.x86_64 0:0.5.0-9.el7 will
➥be installed
--> Finished Dependency Resolution


Package     Version         Repository   Size


Installing:
shotwell    0.14.1-5.el7    base         2.8 M
Installing for dependencies:
LibRaw      0.14.8-5        base         250 k
libgexiv2   0.5.0-9.el7     base         61 k


Transaction Summary
Install 1 Package (+2 Dependent packages)
Total download size: 3.1 M
Installed size: 13 M
Is this ok [y/d/N]:
```

After you enter y, YUM downloads and installs the
packages, continuing to inform you about what it's
doing, every step of the way.

```
Downloading packages:
(1/3): LibRaw-0.14.8-5.el7.x86_64.rpm     | 250 kB
(2/3): libgexiv2-0.5.0-9.el7.x86_64.rpm   |  61 kB
(3/3): shotwell-0.14.1-5.el7.x86_64.rpm   | 2.8 MB


Total                         1.9 MB/s | 3.1 MB
Running transaction check
Running transaction test
Transaction test succeeded
Running transaction
  Installing : LibRaw-0.14.8-5.el7.x86_64       1/3
  Installing : libgexiv2-0.5.0-9.el7.x86_64     2/3
  Installing : shotwell-0.14.1-5.el7.x86_64     3/3
```

```
Verifying  : libgexiv2-0.5.0-9.el7.x86_64   1/3
Verifying  : LibRaw-0.14.8-5.el7.x86_64      2/3
Verifying  : shotwell-0.14.1-5.el7.x86_64    3/3

Installed:
  shotwell.x86_64 0:0.14.1-5.el7

Dependency Installed:
  LibRaw.x86_64 0:0.14.8-5.el7
  libgexiv2.x86_64 0:0.5.0-9.el7

Complete!
```

Whew! Shotwell is finally installed and available for
use. Now to find out how to get rid of Shotwell if
you decide you don't like it.

Remove Software Packages and Dependencies (RPM)

```
yum remove [package]
```

One thing in YUM's favor: Its command syntax is
very user friendly. Want to install a package? yum
install. Want to remove? yum remove. So if you're
tired of Shotwell, just run this command:

```
# yum remove shotwell
Resolving Dependencies
--> Running transaction check
---> Package shotwell.x86_64 0:0.14.1-5.el7
➥will be erased
--> Finished Dependency Resolution

Package    Version         Repository  Size
```

```
Removing:
shotwell  0.14.1-5.el7  @base        11 M

Transaction Summary
Remove 1 Package
Installed size: 11 M
Is this ok [y/N]:
```

Even for something as simple as removing a software package, YUM continues its habit of grabbing you by the lapels and telling you at length about its day. Press y to approve the uninstall, and you get a bit more data thrown at you:

```
Downloading packages:
Running transaction check
Running transaction test
Transaction test succeeded
Running transaction
 Erasing    : shotwell-0.14.1-5.el7.x86_64  1/1
 Verifying  : shotwell-0.14.1-5.el7.x86_64  1/1

Removed:
 shotwell.x86_64 0:0.14.1-5.el7

Complete!
```

And now Shotwell is gone. Notice that the dependencies that were installed by yum (detailed in the previous section, "Install Software Packages and Dependencies for RPM-Based Distributions") are not removed along with the shotwell package. Shotwell needed those dependencies to run, but they can still work on your computer with different programs, so YUM allows them to remain. (This is the default behavior of APT as well, as you'll see soon

in "Remove Software Packages and Dependencies
(DEB)" for Debian.)

NOTE: If you want to find out which packages are
installed on your system, and how YUM identifies
them, use `yum list installed`. Note that in addition
to the package name, you also get the version number
as well, which could be very useful.

Upgrade Software Packages and Dependencies (RPM)

```
yum update
```

Your Linux system contains hundreds, if not
thousands, of software packages, and upgrades come
out constantly for one package or another. It would
be a full-time job for you to manually keep track of
every new version of your software and install updates,
but YUM makes the process easy. A simple `yum update`
command tells YUM to check for any upgrades to the
software it's tracking. If new packages are available,
YUM shows you what's available and asks your
permission to proceed with an install.

```
# yum update
Resolving Dependencies
--> Running transaction check
---> Package kernel.x86_64 0:3.10.0-229.11.1.el7
➥will be installed
---> Package openssl.x86_64 1:1.0.1e-42.el7 will
➥be updated
---> Package openssl.x86_64 1:1.0.1e-42.el7.9 will
➥be an update
```

```
---> Package unzip.x86_64 0:6.0-13.el7 will be
↪updated
---> Package unzip.x86_64 0:6.0-15.el7 will be an
↪update
--> Running transaction check
--> Finished Dependency Resolution

Package    Version              Repository  Size

Installing:
kernel     3.10.0-229.11.1.el7  updates     31 M
Updating:
openssl    1:1.0.1e-42.el7.9    updates     711 k
unzip      6.0-15.el7           updates     166 k

Transaction Summary
Install  1 Package
Upgrade  2 Packages
Total size: 32 M
Is this ok [y/d/N]:
```

If you press y at this point, you're giving YUM
approval to download and install three packages. After
lots of output, YUM completes its job, and your
computer is now up to date. Want to live on the
bleeding edge? Run yum update daily. If you're not
desirous of always using the latest and greatest, run
yum update at a longer interval, but be sure to run it
regularly. Security updates for software come out all
the time, and it's a good idea to keep up-to-date.

Find Packages Available for Download (RPM)

```
yum search [string]
yum list available
```

So you know how to install and remove software using YUM, but how do you find software in the first place? Let's say you're interested in Wireshark, the formidable packet analyzer. You want to know if any packages related to Wireshark are available to install using YUM. You could try using `yum search wireshark`, but it wouldn't be a good idea. That command looks for matches to your search term in all package names, descriptions, summaries, and even the list of packagers' names (although I'd love to meet someone named Wireshark!). You could end up with a list about as long as Bill Gates' bank statement.

A better choice is to query the list of packages available through YUM (which would normally produce another crazily long list), but then pipe the results through a `grep` search for your term.

```
$ yum list available | grep wireshark
wireshark.i686              1.10.3-12.el7_0  base
wireshark.x86_64           1.10.3-12.el7_0  base
wireshark-devel.i686       1.10.3-12.el7_0  base
wireshark-devel.x86_64     1.10.3-12.el7_0  base
wireshark-gnome.x86_64     1.10.3-12.el7_0  base
```

Five results—now that's workable. If you really want to perform the complete search, use `yum search`; otherwise, use `yum list available` and `grep`. Most of the time, the latter choice is what you'll really want, and it'll be far easier to work with to boot.

TIP: For a list of graphical package managers, jump forward in this chapter to the Tip in "Find Packages Available for Download (DEB)." Many of those listed there were either designed for RPM-based distros or work beautifully with them (and many other kinds of package formats, too!).

Install Software Packages (DEB)

```
dpkg -i [package]
```

Installing new software is one of the most fun things you can do with a Linux machine. As you'll learn in upcoming sections, Debian has APT, the most flexible and easiest-to-use system for installing software of any Linux distribution. As cool as APT is, much of it is a wrapper around the dpkg program (in the same way YUM is a wrapper around RPM), which does the grunt work of installing and removing software on a Debian-based machine. Before learning how to use APT, you should learn how to use dpkg because APT can't be used to install everything.

Here's a case in point: One of the most popular Voice over IP (VoIP) programs out now is Skype. Due to licensing issues, however, Skype can't be included in the default installs of many distributions. If you want Skype and it's not available through your distro, you have to download it from the company's site, and then manually install it. To get Skype, head over to its home page, at www.skype.com, locate the Downloads page, and find the package for your distribution. In this case, you're going to use the Debian package, which at this time is named skype_debian-4.3.0.37-1_i386.deb.

After the .deb file is downloaded onto your system, it's time to install it. First use cd to change directories to the directory that contains the .deb file, and then use the dpkg command to install it.

NOTE: On most Debian-based distributions, this and all other dpkg commands are run as root. The wildly popular Ubuntu distribution, however, doesn't use root. Instead, commands normally run as root are prefaced with sudo. In other words, Debian would use this:

```
# dpkg -i skype_debian-4.3.0.37-1_i386.deb
```

Ubuntu and other sudo-based distributions would instead use this:

```
$ sudo dpkg -i skype_debian-4.3.0.371.2.0.18-1_
➥i386.deb
```

This book was written using several machines running Ubuntu, so if you see sudo instead of a root prompt, now you know why.

```
$ ls
skype_debian-4.3.0.3-1_i386.deb
$ sudo dkpg -i skype_debian-4.3.0.3-1_i386.deb
Selecting previously deselected package skype.
(Reading database ... 97963 files and directories
➥currently installed.)
Unpacking skype (from skype_debian-4.3.0.3-1_i386.
➥deb) ...
Setting up skype (4.3.0.3-1) ...
```

That's it. The dpkg command is a model of brevity, telling you the important information and nothing more.

Remove Software Packages (DEB)

```
dpkg -r [package]
```

The `-i` option, used to install software on Debian-based machines, stands for *install*; in a similar bit of happy obviousness, the `-r` option, used to uninstall software on Debian-based machines, stands for *remove*. If you get tired of Skype, it's a simple matter to get it off your computer.

```
# dpkg -r skype
(Reading database ... 98004 files and directories
➥currently installed.)
Removing skype ...
```

When you install software using `dpkg -i`, you need to specify the filename, otherwise `dpkg` has no way to know what you want to install. When you remove software with `dpkg -r`, however, you specify the package name because the files used for installation are now long gone, and APT knows software by the package name.

NOTE: If you want to find out which packages are installed on your system, and how `dpkg` identifies them, use `dpkg -l`. Note that in addition to the package name, you also get the version number, architecture (usually 32- or 64-bit), and a short description as well.

Install Software Packages and Dependencies (DEB)

```
apt-get install [package]
```

The dkpg command is powerful, but after you use it for a while you'll quickly run into a problem when you try to install a package that has dependencies. In order to install package A, you also need to download and install packages B and C, but in order to install C you also need to download and install packages D and E, but in order to install E…ugh! (Adopts Rod Serling voice): You, my friend, have stepped into the twi—I mean, the dependency zone, and you need APT, the Advanced Package Tool.

The apt command and its accessories install, upgrade, and uninstall software packages. Best of all, APT automatically handles dependencies for you. For example, if you're trying to install package A from the example in the previous paragraph, APT downloads and installs A, B, and C for you. Later, if you decide that you no longer want A on your system, APT can uninstall it for you, along with B and C, as long as other software packages don't require them.

The apt command was originally developed for use on the Debian distribution as a front end to dpkg. It's now found on every Debian-based distribution—which includes Debian itself, Ubuntu and all of its variants, Knoppix, Linux Mint, and a whole host of others—and it's one of the features that make Debian so easy to use. Other, non-Debian distributions realized how great APT was, and eventually Connectiva ported APT to work with RPMs. (This chapter focuses on APT as it is used with Debian.)

NOTE: Although this chapter centers on APT as it is used with Debian, you can actually use it with some RPM-based distros. For more info, check out http://apt-rpm.org. Dag Wieers provides a nice justification and tutorial at "Using apt in an RPM world" (http://dag.wieers.com/blog/using-apt-in-an-rpm-world). Finally, I wrote an article for *Linux Magazine* back in 2003 called "A Very Apropos apt" that is obviously out of date in many ways, but which still contains a ton of useful tips. You can find it at www.linux-mag.com/id/1476/.

Let's say you want to install the web editor Bluefish using APT. To do it, you go through the following process (and remember that these commands must be run as root):

```
# apt-get update
Get:1 http://security.ubuntu.com trusty-security
➥Release.gpg [933 B]
Ign http://extras.ubuntu.com trusty InRelease
Get:2 http://security.ubuntu.com trusty-security
➥Release [63.5 kB]
Get:3 http://us.archive.ubuntu.com trusty-updates
➥Release.gpg [933 B] Fetched 3,353 kB in 7s (445 kB/s)
Reading package lists... Done
[Results greatly truncated for length]
# apt-get install bluefish
Reading package lists... Done
Building dependency tree
The following extra packages will be installed:
  bluefish-data bluefish-plugins
Suggested packages:
  bluefish-dbg libxml2-utils php5-cli tidy weblint
The following NEW packages will be installed:
  bluefish bluefish-data bluefish-plugins
```

```
0 upgraded, 3 newly installed, 0 to remove and 0
➥not upgraded.
Need to get 2,548 kB of archives.
After this operation, 9,484 kB of additional disk
➥space will be used.
Do you want to continue? [Y/n] y
Get:1 http://us.archive.ubuntu.com/ubuntu/ trusty/
➥universe bluefish-data all 2.2.5-1 [2,134 kB]
Get:2 http://us.archive.ubuntu.com/ubuntu/ trusty/
➥universe bluefish-plugins amd64 2.2.5-1 [172 kB]
Get:3 http://us.archive.ubuntu.com/ubuntu/ trusty/
➥universe bluefish amd64 2.2.5-1 [243 kB]
Fetched 2,548 kB in 3s (831 kB/s)
(Reading database ... 223602 files and directories
➥currently installed.)
Unpacking bluefish-data (2.2.5-1) ...
Unpacking bluefish-plugins (2.2.5-1) ...
Unpacking bluefish (2.2.5-1) ...
Setting up bluefish-data (2.2.5-1) ...
Setting up bluefish-plugins (2.2.5-1) ...
Setting up bluefish (2.2.5-1) ...
```

Let's go over what you just did because you actually
ran two commands. apt-get update downloads a list of
current software packages from APT servers—known as
repositories—that are listed in your APT configuration
file, found at /etc/apt/sources.list (if you want to
see where your repositories are, run cat /etc/apt/
sources.list). If you saw Get at the beginning of a
line after running apt-get update, it means that APT
saw that the list on the repository is newer, so it's
downloading that particular list; Ign, on the other
hand, means that the list on the repository and on
your computer are in sync, so the list is ignored and
nothing is downloaded. By running apt-get update
before you do anything else, you ensure that your list
of packages is correct and up-to-date.

NOTE: If you want to add new repositories, you really shouldn't edit the `sources.list` file, as your additions could be overwritten by a software update at any time. Instead, it's a much better idea to create a separate conf file for each new repo in `/etc/apt/sources.d`. For example, Dropbox is available to download as a `deb`, but I want to add it via APT so that I will automatically get updates. Dropbox has instructions on its website (Google for "dropbox apt repo") for adding its repo.

As root, or using `sudo`, create a file in `/etc/apt/sources.list.d` named `dropbox.list`. In that file, put the following: `deb http://linux.dropbox.com/ubuntu trusty main`. (`Trusty` refers to the system version in Ubuntu's idiosyncratic scheme; if you're not sure which version of Ubuntu you're using, just use `cat /etc/os-release`.) Save the file and close it, and then, before you do anything else, you have to import Dropbox's GPG keys by running `sudo apt-key adv --keyserver pgp.mit.edu --recv-keys 5044912E`. Once you do that, run `sudo apt-get update`. When that's finished, try `apt-cache search dropbox`, and you'll see results for—tada!—Dropbox. As you discover other repos that sound worthy, add them in `sources.list.d` and have fun.

The command `apt-get install bluefish` retrieves the specified package, as well as any necessary dependencies (in this case, `bluefish-data` and `bluefish-plugins`). After they're on your computer, APT (really `dpkg` acting at the behest of APT) installs all of the software for you. Keep in mind that you always use the package name, not the filename. In other words, use `apt-get install bluefish`, not `apt-get install bluefish_2.2.5-1_amd64.deb`. As you saw, if APT does discover additional dependencies for the requested package, as it did for `bluefish`, you'll have to confirm that you want them installed before APT grabs them.

If you want to install more than one package at the same time, just list them all on the command line. For example, if you wanted to install `bluefish` and `pandoc`, you'd do the following:

```
# apt-get install bluefish pandoc
```

Any dependencies for either `bluefish` or `pandoc` are discovered, and you are asked if you want to install them as well. Yes, it's that simple.

TIP: Don't know what `pandoc` is? Oh, but you should! Start by checking out the official website at http://pandoc.org. I've written a bit about how I use it on my blog, Chainsaw on a Tire Swing, at www.chainsawonatireswing.com (do a search there, as I've mentioned it several times).

Remove Software Packages and Dependencies (DEB)

```
apt-get remove [package]
```

If you no longer want a package on your system, APT makes it easy to uninstall it: Instead of `apt-get install`, you use `apt-get remove`. This command works exactly contrary to `apt-get install`: It uninstalls the packages you specify, along with any dependencies. Note, however, that if one of those dependencies is used by another program, it will *not* be deleted, which makes complete sense. Once again, reference the package name, not the filename, so run `apt-get remove sshfs`, not `apt-get remove sshfs_2.5-1ubuntu1_amd64.deb`.

```
# apt-get remove sshfs
Reading package lists... Done
Building dependency tree... Done
The following packages will be REMOVED:
  sshfs
0 upgraded, 0 newly installed, 1 to remove and 54
➥not upgraded.
Need to get 0B of archives.
After unpacking 98.3kB disk space will be freed.
Do you want to continue [Y/n]?
```

Removing a package actually doesn't remove every vestige of a package, however, because configuration files for the removed package stick around on your computer. If you're sure that you want to remove everything, use the --purge option.

```
# apt-get --purge remove sshfs
Reading package lists... Done
Building dependency tree... Done
The following packages will be REMOVED:
  sshfs*
0 upgraded, 0 newly installed, 1 to remove and 54
➥not upgraded.
Need to get 0B of archives.
After unpacking 98.3kB disk space will be freed.
Do you want to continue [Y/n]?
```

Using --purge, the packages that APT is about to remove are marked with asterisks, indicating that associated configuration files are going to be removed as well.

NOTE: If you want to find out which packages are installed on your system, and how APT identifies them, use `apt --installed list`. Note that in addition to the package name, you also get the version number and the architecture (normally 32- or 64-bit).

Upgrade Software Packages and Dependencies (DEB)

`apt-get upgrade`

A modern Linux system has several thousand software packages on it, and it's a sure bet that at least one of those is upgraded by its maintainer every day. With APT, it's quite simple to keep your system up-to-date. The process looks like this (and remember, this command must be run as root or using `sudo`, as I do here):

```
$ sudo apt-get update
Get:1 http://security.ubuntu.com trusty-security
➥Release.gpg [933 B]
Get:2 http://security.ubuntu.com trusty-security
➥Release [63.5 kB]
Get:3 http://extras.ubuntu.com trusty Release.gpg
➥ [72 B]
Get:4 http://us.archive.ubuntu.com trusty-updates
➥Release.gpg [933 B]
Fetched 4,275 kB in 6s (694 kB/s)
Reading package lists... Done
[Results greatly truncated for length]
$ sudo apt-get upgrade
Reading package lists... Done
Building dependency tree
Reading state information... Done
```

```
Calculating upgrade... Done
The following packages have been kept back:
  system-config-printer-gnome
The following packages will be upgraded:
  firefox firefox-locale-en fonts-droid
511 upgraded, 0 newly installed, 0 to remove and 8
➥not upgraded.
Need to get 349 MB of archives.
After this operation, 45.9 MB of additional disk
➥space will be used.
Do you want to continue? [Y/n]
```

Let's figure out what was going on here. Once again,
you want to run apt-get update first so your computer
is in sync with your APT repositories. Then apt-get
upgrade looks for any differences between what you
have installed and what's available on the repositories.
If differences exist, APT shows you a list of all of the
packages that it would like to download and install on
your computer. Of course, the actual list of packages
varies depending on how up-to-date your system is.
In this case, this was a brand new install, so there were
511 packages to upgrade.

If you type y, APT downloads the 511 software
packages to /var/cache/apt/archives and then installs
them after they're all on your machine. If you don't
want to go through with the upgrade, just type n
instead.

That's easy enough, but the most efficient way to
use APT to update your Linux box is to just join the
commands together:

apt-get update && apt-get upgrade

The && makes sure that apt-get upgrade doesn't run
unless apt-get update finishes without errors. Better

yet, make an alias for that command in your `.bash_aliases` file, as was discussed in the "Create a New Permanent Alias" section of Chapter 12, "Your Shell."

```
alias upgrade='apt-get update && apt-get upgrade'
```

Reload your `.bash_aliases` file, and now you just need to type in `upgrade`, press Enter, press `y` to accept any new packages, and you're done. Windows Update, eat your heart out!

NOTE: When you use `apt-get upgrade`, you will be told about packages that were kept back and not upgraded or installed. If you want to automatically install new software and remove installed packages that are no longer needed, then you want to use `apt-get dist-upgrade`. Do not use the `dist-upgrade` command lightly! Pay attention to what it's about to do, for no other reason than keeping abreast with what's about to happen to your system.

Find Packages Available for Download (DEB)

```
apt-cache search
```

We've been talking a lot about installing software using APT, but how do you know what software packages are available in the first place? There's another tool in the APT toolbox that helps you do that: `apt-cache search`, which searches the lists of packages available in your APT repositories. In a nice change of pace, you don't need to be root at all to use `apt-cache search`.

```
$ apt-cache search dvdcss
brasero - CD/DVD burning application for GNOME
ubuntu-restricted-extras - Commonly used restricted
➥packages for Ubuntu
arista - multimedia transcoder for the GNOME Desktop
gxine - the xine video player, GTK+/Gnome user
➥interface
libdvdread4 - library for reading DVDs
python3-dvdvideo - Video DVD reader library
```

Keep in mind several things about how this command searches. It looks for matches to your string—in this case, dvdcss—and not for exact words. Also, your search pattern might appear either in the package name or description. Finally, apt-cache search looks through the entire package list of both installed and uninstalled packages, so the results of your search will show you packages you've already installed as well as new ones.

TIP: There are a plethora of GUIs for package managers that make it easy for you to do virtually everything discussed in this chapter—viewing, managing, updating, installing, uninstalling, and more—but via point-and-click instead of typing. I'm going to provide a list of many of the important ones, but you should keep a few things in mind.

First, graphical package managers created for either GNOME or KDE will of course work with the other desktop environment, provided that the correct libraries are installed. And second, for all of these, Wikipedia is a great start if you want to learn more.

Here they are, in alphabetical order:

- **Apper:** Formerly KPackageKit, this is a KDE app that provides a front end for the PackageKit service, so it works with almost anything related to Linux packages: YUM, APT, Entropy, Portage, urpmi, Pacman, zypp, Hif, and others. Dates back to 2008. Adopted by Fedora, Red Hat, and OpenSUSE.

- **GNOME PackageKit:** GTK-based front end for the PackageKit server (see Apper for more info). Aimed more at power users, while GNOME Software (keep reading!) is for mainstream users.

- **GNOME Software:** Provides a GTK-based front end for the PackageKit service (see Apper for more info). In all-too-typical GNOME fashion, uses a completely generic name that is impossible to find on Google. Released in 2013 and still active.

- **Muon Discover:** Qt-based front end for APT. Found on Kubuntu. Focused on mainstream users.

- **Octopi:** Qt-based front end for Arch Linux's Pacman package manager. Around since 2013 and going strong.

- **Smart:** Ambitious GTK-based project that works with RPM, DPKG, and Slackware packages. Aims to more intelligently manage software installation and upgrades (hence, the name!).

- **Synaptic:** GTK-based front end for APT (or RPM!). Very popular and still widely used, but it's no longer the default graphical package manager on some distros. Very full-featured.

- **Ubuntu Software Center:** GTK-based app for GNOME that works with APT and dpkg. Released in 2009 and is now the default in Ubuntu. Aimed at mainstream users (power users should use Synaptic).

- **Yumex:** Short for YUM Extender, a GTK-based program that provides a front-end for YUM and now DNF (the package manager that Fedora has already switched to).

- **Zero Install:** GTK-based program that downloads programs into their own directories and then uses environment variables so programs can find their libraries. Works on Linux, Mac OS X, UNIX, and Windows. Only one thousand packages available.

Clean Up Unneeded Installation Packages (DEB)

`apt-get clean`

When packages are downloaded and installed using APT, the .deb files are left behind in /var/cache/apt/archives/. Over time, you can take up a lot of disk space with those unnecessary installers. To remove all of the unneeded .deb files, use apt-get clean (once again, this command is run as root):

```
$ ls -1 /var/cache/apt/archives/
bluefish_2.2.5-1_amd64.deb
bluefish-data_2.2.5-1_all.deb
bluefish-plugins_2.2.5-1_amd64.deb
lock
partial/
$ sudo apt-get clean
$ ls -1 /var/cache/apt/archives/
lock
partial/
```

The clean option for apt-get is incredibly useful, but there are two other related options that you show know. When you run apt-get autoclean, only obsolete packages are removed. Likewise, apt-get autoremove gets rid of packages that were installed as dependencies but are no longer needed, like old kernels. All of these help keep your system clean of stuff you just do not need any longer.

Oh—here's one more thing: If a download is interrupted for whatever reason, you might find a partial .deb file in /var/cache/apt/archives/partial/. If you know that all of the updates and upgrades are complete and installed, it's safe to delete the contents of that directory, should you find anything in it.

Troubleshoot Problems with APT (DEB)

Of course, as great as APT is, you might run into problems. Here are some problems and their workarounds.

One simple problem that will result in a smack to your own forehead is the "Could not open lock file" error. You'll try to run apt-get, but instead of working, you get this error message:

```
E: Could not open lock file /var/lib/dpkg/lock -
➥open (13 Permission denied)
E: Unable to lock the administration directory
➥(/var/lib/dpkg/), are you root?
```

The solution to this issue is right there in the second line: You're not logged in as root! Simply log in as root and try again, and everything should work.

NOTE: If you're running Ubuntu, or any other distribution that uses sudo instead of root, the error means that you didn't preface the command with sudo. In other words, you ran this:

```
$ apt-get upgrade
```

You're seeing the error message because you should have run this instead:

```
$ sudo apt-get upgrade
```

The next common issue occurs when APT complains about broken dependencies. You'll know this one's happening when APT encourages you to run `apt-get -f install`. This suggestion is the program's way of telling you that your system has some broken dependencies that prevent APT from finishing its job.

There are a couple of possible solutions. You can follow APT's advice, and run `apt-get -f install`, which tries to fix the problem by downloading and installing the necessary packages. Normally, this solves the problem, and you can move on.

If you don't want to do that, you can instead try running `apt-get -f remove`, which tries to fix the problem by removing packages that APT deems troublesome. These might sound like potentially dangerous steps to take—and they could be if you don't pay attention—but each option gives you the chance to review any proposed changes and give your assent. Just be sure to examine APT's proposals before saying yes.

Finally, APT might warn you that some packages "have been kept back." This warning tells you that APT has found a conflict between the requested package or one of its dependencies and another package already installed on your system. To resolve the issue, try to install the package that was kept back with the `-u` option, which gives you information about exactly what needs to be upgraded.

Conclusion

RPM-based and Debian-based distributions, despite their differences, share some similarities when it comes to package management, in that both are designed to simplify the installation, removal, and management of software. RPM-based distributions use the `rpm` command to install, upgrade, and remove software, while Debian-based distributions use `dpkg` for the same purposes. To solve the headaches of dependency hell, RPM-based distributions have `yum`, a wrapper around `rpm`, while Debian-based distributions have APT, a wrapper around `dpkg`.

In the end, both are still better than what Windows users have to put up with. Windows Update only updates Microsoft's own software and a few third-party hardware drivers, while both APT and YUM handle virtually every piece of software on a Linux system. That's a huge advantage that Linux users have over their Microsoft cousins, and it's one that should make us proud.

Connectivity

Networking has been part of Linux since the OS's beginning a humble kernel hacked on by a small group of programmers, and it's completely central to what makes Linux great. Linux networking most of the time just works, providing you with a rock-solid connection that can be endlessly tweaked and tuned to meet your exact needs.

A transition from the old to the new has been going on for years at this point, and we're still in the middle of it. Some of the tools I cover in this chapter have been around since the Linux Stone Age, and they are now being deprecated: ifconfig, iwconfig, host, ifup, ifdown, and route (ping and traceroute have also been around forever, but they aren't in line for replacement). For instance, in 3.x Linux kernels, route has been deprecated and its replacement—ip route show—can be found in a suite of tools called iproute2. Something similar is true for all the other deprecated commands I mentioned, as you will see.

The problem for me is that most distros (the vast majority, maybe?) still include route, ifconfig, ifup, and the others. Many (again, most, perhaps?—it's very hard to tell) also include iproute2, and the others make it available to download and install. So as I wend my way through this chapter, I will usually try to cover both the old school command and it's younger, hipper replacement. Double the content at the same low price—you are one lucky reader!

Old or new, this chapter is all about testing, measuring, and managing your networking devices and connections. When things are working correctly—and they will for the vast majority of the time—you can use the tools in this chapter to monitor your system's network connections; should you experience problems, this chapter will help you resolve some of the most irksome.

TIP: The information in this chapter assumes that you're using IPv4 addressing, in the format of xxx.xxx.xxx.xxx. IPv6 will eventually replace IPv4, but that's still in the future (it's growing closer all the time here in 2015, but it's still going to be a while). At that time, `route` and many of the other commands you'll be examining will change (unsurprisingly, the newer `ip` command already supports IPv6). For now, though, the information in this chapter is what you need. For more on IPv6, see Wikipedia's "IPv6" (http://en.wikipedia.org/wiki/Ipv6) .

NOTE: When I updated this book for its second edition, I removed the text of the section about using `iwconfig` to configure wireless network interfaces ("Configure a Wireless Network Interface"). I kept the section, however, but I use it to explain why I took the content out. You can find the original text on my website, www.granneman.com/linux-redactions.

View the Status of Your Network Interfaces

```
ifconfig
ip addr show
```

Everything in this chapter depends on your network connection. At the end of this chapter, in "Troubleshooting Network Problems," you're going to learn ways to fix problems with your network connection. Here at the beginning, let's find out what network connections you have in place and their status.

To get a quick look at all of your running network devices, use ifconfig, which stands for *interface configuration*. (If you want to look at all your network devices, even those that aren't currently running, use the -a (for *all*) option.) Here's what you might see on a laptop (note that some distributions require you to log on as root to use ifconfig in this way):

```
$ ifconfig
ath0 Link encap:Ethernet  HWaddr 00:14:6C:06:6B:FD
     inet addr:192.168.0.101  Bcast:192.168.0.255
➥Mask:255.255.255.0
UP BROADCAST RUNNING MULTICAST  MTU:1500
➥Metric:1
lo   Link encap:Local Loopback
     inet addr:127.0.0.1  Mask:255.0.0.0
UP LOOPBACK RUNNING  NTU:16436  Metric:1
 [Listing greatly condensed due to length]
```

Two interfaces are listed here: ath0 (a wireless card) and lo (the loopback interface—more on that in a moment). For each of those, you're told the type of connection, the Media Access Control (MAC) or hardware address, the IP address, the broadcast and subnet mask addresses, and information about received and transmitted packets, among other data. If you had instead used the -a option to see all of the devices, those that were disconnected (like eth0 in this case) would be missing much of that information, such as an IP address and the word UP in the fourth complete line, which makes it pretty obvious.

Let's take the three interfaces in reverse order. lo is the loopback address, which enables a machine to refer to itself. The loopback address is always represented by the IP address of 127.0.0.1. Basically, your system needs it to work correctly. If you have it, don't worry about it; if you don't have it, you'll know it because you will find yourself in a world of hurt.

TIP: For more on the loopback interface and address, see Wikipedia's "Loopback" at http://en.wikipedia.org/wiki/Loopback.

---

eth0 (which wouldn't appear unless the -a option was used) is an Ethernet card, into which you actually plug cables (whaaa? I know! Amazing!). No cables are plugged into the Ethernet card's port currently, so it's not activated, hence the lack of any addresses: IP, broadcast, and subnet mask. Of course, it's possible to have both a wired and wireless interface running at the same time, although it's usually not necessary.

Finally there is ath0, a wireless PCMCIA card. You might also see a wireless card with a name like eth0 if it's the primary network interface, or eth1 if it's secondary. When the wireless card was inserted, Ubuntu automatically recognized it and configured the system to work with it, giving it the ath0 identifier.

Because wireless interfaces are just Ethernet interfaces with some extra wireless goodies, the information you get with `ifconfig` is similar to what you'd see for `eth0` if it was up.

NOTE: You may see other names for your network devices, such as `wlan0` for wireless cards.

As you can see, `ifconfig` is a quick way to check the status of your network interfaces, especially if you need to find your IP address quickly. But that's the old method. Time for a new method using the `ip` command.

You never use `ip` all by itself. Instead, you follow it by an object—the networking device or information that you want to view or change—and then commands for that object. For example, to get the same information as `ifconfig`, you'd do this:

```
$ ip addr show up
1: lo: <LOOPBACK,UP,LOWER_UP> mtu 65536 state
   ➥UNKNOWN
   link/loopback 00:00:00:00:00:00 brd
   ➥00:00:00:00:00:00
   inet 127.0.0.1/8 scope host lo
2: eth0: <BROADCAST,MULTICAST,UP,LOWER_UP> mtu 1500
   ➥state UP
   link/ether 00:14:6C:06:6B:FD brd
   ➥ff:ff:ff:ff:ff:ff
   inet 192.168.0.101/24 scope global dynamic eth0
[Listing condensed due to length]
```

We start with `ip`, and then we specify our object: `addr` (or `address` or even just `a`!). What do we want to do to the address? Why, `show` it. Which ones? The ones that are `up` and running. And there you see the data, just like you would with `ifconfig`. If you wanted to see all the devices, even those that aren't currently connected, you would instead use `ip addr show`, just like `ifconfig -a`.

Verify That a Computer Is Running and Accepting Requests

```
ping
ping -c
```

The `ping` command sends a special kind of packet—an ICMP ECHO_REQUEST message—to the specified address. If a machine at that address is listening for ICMP messages, it responds with an ICMP ECHO_ REPLY packet. (It's true that firewalls can block ICMP messages, rendering `ping` useless, but most of the time it's not a problem.) A successful `ping` means that network connectivity is occurring between the two machines.

```
$ ping www.google.com
ping www.google.com
PING www.l.google.com (72.14.203.99) 56(84) bytes of
➥data.
64 bytes from 72.14.203.99: icmp_seq=1 ttl=245
➥time=17.1 ms
64 bytes from 72.14.203.99: icmp_seq=2 ttl=245
➥time=18.1 ms
64 bytes from 72.14.203.99: icmp_seq=3 ttl=245
➥time=17.9 ms
64 bytes from 72.14.203.99: icmp_seq=4 ttl=245
➥time=16.9 ms
```

```
64 bytes from 72.14.203.99: icmp_seq=5 ttl=245
➥time=17.5 ms

--- www.1.google.com ping statistics ---
6 packets transmitted, 5 received, 16% packet loss,
➥time 5051ms
rtt min/avg/max/mdev = 16.939/17.560/18.136/0.460 ms
```

The `ping` command won't stop until you press
Ctrl+C. This can cause problems if you forget that
you're using `ping` because it will continue forever until
it is stopped or your machine's network connection
stops. I once forgot and left a `ping` session running for
18 days, sending nearly 1.4 million pings to one of my
servers. Oops!

If you want to give `ping` a limit, you can set the
number of packets that `ping` is to send with the `-c`
option, followed by a number. After `ping` sends out
that number of packets, it stops, reporting its results.

```
$ ping -c 3 www.granneman.com
PING granneman.com (216.23.180.5) 56(84) bytes of
➥data.
64 bytes from 216.23.180.5: icmp_seq=1 ttl=44
➥time=65.4 ms
64 bytes from 216.23.180.5: icmp_seq=2 ttl=44
➥time=64.5 ms
64 bytes from 216.23.180.5: icmp_seq=3 ttl=44
➥time=65.7 ms

--- granneman.com ping statistics ---
3 packets transmitted, 3 received, 0% packet loss,
➥time 4006ms
rtt min/avg/max/mdev = 64.515/65.248/65.700/0.510 ms
```

The `ping` command is a standard and speedy way to determine basic network connectivity; even better, if you include the `-c` option, you'll never forget and leave `ping` running accidentally for 18 days. However, be careful—if you ping certain government or military servers, for instance, they might decide that you're attacking them. Best case, you'll be blacklisted from accessing that server; worst case, you'll get a visit from some men in black.

For more about using `ping` to diagnose network connectivity issues, see "Troubleshooting Network Problems" later in the chapter.

Trace the Route Packets Take Between Two Hosts

```
traceroute
```

The `traceroute` command shows every step taken on the route from your machine to a specified host. Let's say you want to know why you can't get to www.granneman.com. You were able to load it just fine yesterday, but today's attempts to load the web page are timing out. Where's the problem?

```
$ traceroute www.granneman.com
traceroute to granneman.com (216.23.180.5), 30 hops
➥max, 38 byte packets
 1  192.168.0.1 (192.168.0.1)  1.245 ms  0.827 ms
➥0.839 ms
 2  10.29.64.1 (10.29.64.1)  8.582 ms  19.930 ms
➥7.083 ms
 3  24.217.2.165 (24.217.2.165)  10.152 ms  25.476
➥ms  36.617 ms
```

```
 4   12.124.129.97 (12.124.129.97)   9.203 ms   8.003
➡ms   11.307 ms
 5   12.122.82.241 (12.122.82.241)   52.901 ms   53.619
➡ms   51.215 ms
 6   tbr2-p013501.sl9mo.ip.att.net (12.122.11.121)
➡51.625 ms   52.166 ms   50.156 ms
 7   tbr2-cl21.la2ca.ip.att.net (12.122.10.14)
➡50.669 ms   54.049 ms   69.334 ms
 8   gar1-p3100.lsnca.ip.att.net (12.123.199.229)
➡50.167 ms   48.703 ms   49.636 ms
 9   * * *
10   border20.po2-bbnet2.lax.pnap.net
➡(216.52.255.101)   59.414 ms   62.148 ms   51.337 ms
11   intelenet-3.border20.lax.pnap.net
➡(216.52.253.234)   51.930 ms   53.054 ms   50.748 ms
12   v8.core2.irv.intelenet.net (216.23.160.66)
➡50.611 ms   51.947 ms   60.694 ms
13   * * *
14   * * *
15   * * *
```

What do those * * * mean? Each one indicates a five-second timeout at that hop. Sometimes that could indicate that the machine simply doesn't understand how to cope with that traceroute packet due to a bug, but a consistent set of * indicates that there's a problem somewhere with the router to which v8.core2.irv.intelenet.net hands off packets. If the problem persists, you need to notify the administrator of v8.core2.irv.intelenet.net and let him know there's a problem. (Of course, it might not hurt to let the administrator of gar1-p3100.lsnca.ip.att.net know that his router is having a problem getting to border20.po2-bbnet2.lax.pnap.net as well, but it's not nearly the problem that intelenet.net is having.)

One other way to get around a problematic `traceroute` is to increase the number of hops that the command will try. By default, the maximum number of hops is 30, although you can change that with the `-m` option, as in `traceroute -m 40 www.bbc.co.uk`.

TIP: Actually, a better `traceroute` is `mtr`, which stands for Matt's traceroute. Think of it as a combination of `ping` and `traceroute`. If `mtr` is available for your Linux distribution, download and try it out. For more information, head over to www.bitwizard.nl/mtr and https://en.wikipedia.org/wiki/MTR_(software).

Query DNS Records

```
host
dig
```

The Domain Name System (DNS) was created to make it easier for humans to access resources on the Internet. Computers work beautifully with numbers—after all, everything a computer does is really a number—but humans can remember and process words much more efficiently. A website might be located at 74.125.227.243, but it would be hard for most people to remember that. Instead, it's much easier to keep in memory that you want to go to www.google.com. DNS is basically a giant database that keeps track of the relationship between 74.125.227.243 and www.google.com, and millions of other IP addresses and domain names as well.

TIP: DNS is a large, complicated, and fascinating topic. For more details, see Wikipedia's "Domain Name System" (https://en.wikipedia.org/wiki/Domain_Name_System) to start, and then dive into the deep waters with Paul Albitz and Cricket Liu's seminal book *DNS and BIND*.

To quickly find the IP address associated with a domain name, use the `host` command:

```
$ host chainsawonatireswing.com
chainsawonatireswing.com has address 68.65.123.160
chainsawonatireswing.com mail is handled by 20
➥alt2.aspmx.l.google.com.
chainsawonatireswing.com mail is handled by 10
➥aspmx.l.google.com.
$ host www.chainsawonatireswing.com
www.chainsawonatireswing.com is an alias for
➥gawain.websanity.com.
gawain.websanity.com has address 23.239.25.194194
```

Notice how different but very similar queries provide completely different answers. Someone might think that chainsawonatireswing.com and www.chainsawonatireswing.com are the same thing, but they definitely are not.

You can also reverse the process—known as a *reverse DNS lookup*—and find out a domain name associated with an IP. Note that this does not always work, however. If there's not a DNS record associated with an IP address, you're not going to get a usable answer back.

```
$ host 23.239.25.19
19.25.239.23.in-addr.arpa domain name pointer
➥li708-19.members.linode.com
$ host 68.65.123.160
Host 160.123.65.68.in-addr.arpa. not found:
➥3(NXDOMAIN)
```

You might also notice how the IP addresses get
reversed in the answer. This is perfectly normal and to
be expected.

The host command has been around for a long time
and it does the job, but there's a new command that
is designed to ultimately replace host: dig (short for
domain information groper). You'll find that dig can do
everything host can, and a lot more.

You can perform several different kinds of lookups with
dig; to do so, you indicate the type you want after the
domain name. Options include, but are certainly not
limited to, a (an IPv4 address), aaaa (an IPv6 address),
cname (a canonical name that points to an A record),
mx (a mail server), soa (Start of Authority: authoritative
information about a domain, such as the primary name
server, the administrator's mail address, and timers
for refreshing the domain's records), and any (which
means literally any that it can find, including A, AAAA,
CNAME, MX, SOA, and several more).

```
$ dig www.chainsawonatireswing.com any
;; ANSWER SECTION:
www.chainsawonatireswing.com. 600 IN CNAME
➥gawain.websanity.com.
;; AUTHORITY SECTION:
chainsawonatireswing.com. 1800 IN NS dns1.registrar-
➥servers.com.
chainsawonatireswing.com. 1800 IN NS dns2.registrar-
➥servers.com.
```

I actually stripped out a lot of extra information there. The example here only has 5 lines of output, but the one I started with has 21! However, there's a way to get just the meat and potatoes with `dig`:

```
$ dig +noall +answer www.chainsawonatireswing.com any
www.chainsawonatireswing.com. 600 IN CNAME
➥gawain.websanity.com.
```

The `+noall` option tells `dig` to clear all other flags for displaying results (there are potentially a lot of those), and `+answer` orders `dig` to just display the answer section and nothing else. Together, you end up with a much shorter, cleaner answer to your query.

Now, what if we leave off the `www` in our command?

```
$ dig chainsawonatireswing.com any
;; ANSWER SECTION:
chainsawonatireswing.com. 3601 IN SOA dns1.
➥registrar-servers.com. hostmaster.registrar-
➥ servers.com. 2015072302 43200 3600 604800 3601
chainsawonatireswing.com. 1800 IN NS
➥dns1.registrar-servers.com.
chainsawonatireswing.com. 1800 IN NS
➥dns2.registrar-servers.com.
chainsawonatireswing.com. 583  IN A
➥68.65.123.160
chainsawonatireswing.com. 600  IN MX 20
➥alt1.aspmx.1.google.com.
chainsawonatireswing.com. 600  IN MX 10
➥aspmx.1.google.com.
chainsawonatireswing.com. 600   IN  TXT
➥"v=spf1 include:_spf.google.com ~all"
```

There were actually 31 lines this time, shortened to only 8 lines here. If you want to know as much as possible about a domain, give `dig` with a type of `any` a try.

And, no surprise, `dig` can also perform reverse lookups. The `-x` performs the real work, but I'm going to also use the other options I discussed a few paragraphs back so we get just the answer and nothing more.

```
$ dig +noall +answer -x 23.239.25.194
194.25.239.23.in-addr.arpa. 86384 IN PTR
➥gawain.websanity.com.
```

As I said earlier, it worked in this instance, but it won't always.

Both host and dig are extremely useful commands. Keep reading to the end of this chapter and you'll find out how `host` and `dig` can help you with "Troubleshooting Network Problems."

Configure a Network Interface

```
ifconfig
ip addr add
ip link set
```

In the first section of this chapter, "View the Status of Your Network Interfaces," you saw how you could use `ifconfig` or `ip` to get details about the status of your network interfaces. The `ifconfig` and `ip` commands are more powerful than that, however, as you can also use them to configure your network interfaces.

NOTE: You can make quite a few changes with `ifconfig` and `ip` (that's putting it mildly!), but you're only going to look at a few (for more details, see `man ifconfig` and `man ip`).

To change the IP address for the Ethernet card found at `eth0` to 192.168.0.125, run this command (virtually all commands associated with `ifconfig` need to be run as root):

```
# ifconfig eth0 192.168.0.125
```

If you're using the `ip` command, you would instead use this (again, you have to be root, for good reason):

```
# ip addr add 192.168.0.125 dev eth0
```

To run certain types of network-sniffing tools, such as the awesome Wireshark (find it at www.wireshark. org), you first need to set your network card to promiscuous mode. By default, `eth0` only listens for packets sent specifically to it, but in order to sniff all the packets flowing by on a network, you need to tell your card to listen to everything, which is known as promiscuous mode.

```
# ifconfig eth0 promisc
```

After you've done that, running `ifconfig` shows you that your card is now looking at every packet it can. See the PROMISC in the last line?

```
# ifconfig eth0
eth0 Link encap:Ethernet  HWaddr 00:02:8A:36:48:8A
     inet addr:192.168.0.143  Bcast:192.168.0.255
➥Mask:255.255.255.0
     inet6 addr: fe80::202:8aff:fe36:488a/64
➥Scope:Link
     UP BROADCAST PROMISC MULTICAST  MTU:1500
➥Metric:1
```

When you're done using Wireshark, don't forget to turn off promiscuous mode (see how PROMISC is gone).

```
# ifconfig eth0 -promisc
# ifconfig eth0
eth0 Link encap:Ethernet  HWaddr 00:02:8A:36:48:8A
     inet addr:192.168.0.143  Bcast:192.168.0.255
➥Mask:255.255.255.0
     inet6 addr: fe80::202:8aff:fe36:488a/64
➥Scope:Link
     UP BROADCAST MULTICAST  MTU:1500  Metric:1
```

For the `ip` command, you enable promiscuous mode by entering this command (be sure to look at the line for `eth0`):

```
# ip link set dev eth0 promisc on
# ip addr show up
1: lo: <LOOPBACK,UP,LOWER_UP> mtu 65536 state
   ➥UNKNOWN
...
2: eth0: <BROADCAST,MULTICAST,PROMISC,UP,LOWER_UP>
   ➥mtu 1500 state UP
```

And now let's change it back:

```
# ip link set dev eth0 promisc off
# ip addr show up
1: lo: <LOOPBACK,UP,LOWER_UP> mtu 65536 state
   ➥UNKNOWN
...
2: eth0: <BROADCAST,MULTICAST,UP,LOWER_UP> mtu 1500
   ➥state UP
```

You can even change (or "spoof") the hardware MAC address for your network device. This is usually only necessary to get around some ISPs' attempts to link Internet service to a specific machine. Be careful with spoofing your MAC address because a mistake can conflict with other network devices, causing problems (although that is *very* unlikely).

If you do decide to spoof your MAC, make sure you use `ifconfig` or `ip addr show up` to first acquire the default MAC address so you can roll back to that later. Then you should bring the device down, make the change, and bring it back up. Don't worry if you don't recognize the command to bring the device down and then up, because you'll learn about them later in this chapter. Finally, you again use `ifconfig` or `ip addr show up` to verify that the MAC address has changed. Oh, and the MAC address shown in this command is completely bogus, so don't try to use it.

```
# ifdown eth0
# ifconfig eth0 hw ether 12:34:56:78:90:aa
# ifup eth0
```

With the `ip` command, you'd do the following:

```
# ip link set dev eth0 down
# ip link set dev eth0 address 12:34:56:78:90:aa
# ip link set dev eth0 up
```

The `ifconfig` and `ip` commands are cornerstones of working with network interfaces. Make sure you understand how they work so you can take maximum advantage of all they have to offer.

View the Status of Your Wireless Network Interfaces

```
iwconfig
nmcli
```

The `ifconfig` command shows the status of your network interfaces, even wireless ones. However, it can't show all the data associated with a wireless interface because `ifconfig` simply doesn't know about it. To get the maximum data associated with a wireless card, you want to use `iwconfig` instead of `ifconfig`.

```
$ iwconfig
lo    no wireless extensions.

eth0 no wireless extensions.

ath0 IEEE 802.11g  ESSID:"einstein"
     Mode:Managed  Frequency:2.437 GHz  Access
➥Point: 00:12:17:31:4F:C6
     Bit Rate:48 Mb/s   Tx-Power:18 dBm
➥Sensitivity=0/3
     Retry:off   RTS thr:off   Fragment thr:off
     Power Management:off
     Link Quality=41/94  Signal level=-54 dBm  Noise
➥level=-95 dBm
     Rx invalid nwid:1047  Rx invalid crypt:0  Rx
➥invalid frag:0
     Tx excessive retries:73  Invalid misc:73
➥Missed beacon:21
```

You can see the data unique to wireless interfaces that `iwconfig` provides, including the type of card (802.11g in this case), the ESSID or network name (this network's ESSID is `einstein`), the mode or kind of network to which you're connected, the MAC address of the wireless access point (here 00:12:17:31:4F:C6), and various details about the quality of the wireless connection.

The combination of `ifconfig` and `iwconfig` tells you everything you need to know about your wireless network interface. And, just as you can also use `ifconfig` to configure your wired cards, you can also use `iwconfig` to configure your wireless cards, as you'll see in the next section.

Just as `ifconfig` has been deprecated in favor of `ip`, so too is `iwconfig` suffering the same fate, even though it's still found in virtually every major distro. A new command is supposed to take its place—`iw`—but so far it's still *very* much under development. In fact, the help for `iw` even says, "Do NOT screenscrape this tool, we don't consider its output stable" [sic]. So I'm not going to cover `iw` at all until the third edition of this book, assuming it survives and grows in the intervening years. If you want to read about it, check out https://wireless.wiki.kernel.org/en/users/documentation/iw.

What to use in the meantime? Most distros now provide a GUI program called NetworkManager that makes it pretty easy for users to connect to, and manage, wired and wireless networks. What's nice for us is that the GUI includes a command line equivalent called `nmcli` (NetworkManager command line interface) that will help us in a big way.

To see the status of your wireless device, use `nmcli` with the `-p` option (for *pretty*, as in, make it extra readable for humans) and point it at the `device` object with a command of `status`:

```
$ nmcli -p device status
=======================================
            Status of devices
=======================================
DEVICE TYPE     STATE       CONNECTION
wlan0  wifi     connected   Home
eth0   ethernet unavailable --
lo     loopback unmanaged   --
```

Now we know that Wi-Fi is connected, but what about the details? You could run `nmcli -p connection show Home` (the `connection` object, with a command

of show and then the name of your connection, like
Home in this case), but that really isn't a good idea.
Oh, you'll get details all right—126 lines of them, in
my case!

Instead, try this, which narrows down the info you'll
get (and keep in mind that I still had to remove a lot
from this listing—it was still 36 lines):

```
$ nmcli -p -f GENERAL,IP4,WIFI-PROPERTIES dev show
➥wlan0
GENERAL.DEVICE         wlan0
GENERAL.TYPE           wifi
GENERAL.VENDOR         Intel Corporation
GENERAL.PRODUCT        PRO/Wireless 5100 AGN [Shiloh]
GENERAL.DRIVER         iwlwifi
GENERAL.HWADDR         12:34:56:78:90:ab
GENERAL.STATE          100 (connected)
GENERAL.CONNECTION     Home
IP4.ADDRESS            ip=192.168.1.100/24,
➥gw=192.168.1.1
IP4.DNS[1]             192.168.1.1
IP4.DNS[2]             208.67.220.220
WIFI-PROPERTIES.WEP    yes
WIFI-PROPERTIES.WPA2   yes
```

In this case, the -f means to show only the selected
fields—GENERAL, IP4, and WIFI-PROPERTIES—of the
device object, in this case, wlan0. There's some very
useful info there: vendor and product ID, driver,
hardware (MAC) address, connected state, connection
name, IP address and associated addresses, and finally
the types of encryption it supports. All good stuff to
know.

Configure a Wireless Network Interface

In the previous edition of this book, I covered the iwconfig command and how you could use it to configure the wireless card on your Linux box. I have taken it out of the second edition of the book, and, as I mentioned at the beginning of this chapter, you can find the original information on my website.

I took this section out for several reasons that I briefly wanted to cover here.

When this book originally came out in 2005, configuring the wireless connection on your Linux computer was still very often a royal pain. This section was an attempt to help readers out with what was often a frustrating exercise. But in 2015, things are very different.

It's extremely rare now for a desktop or laptop Linux user to need to use the command line to configure his wireless connection via the command line (hello, Richard Stallman!). If you're running a server, you're probably using a CLI, but you're also not using Wi-Fi either! You want Ethernet, and that's easy to set up without a GUI.

As I said in the previous section, virtually all desktop Linux distros now ship with NetworkManager, a GUI tool that generally takes all the pain out of configuring Wi-Fi connections. And, importantly, it supports WPA2, the current standard for wireless encryption. Trying to set up a Wi-Fi connection with WPA2 using the command line is still complicated and difficult, and at the least, no fun. The nmcli tool doesn't really help much either in this area. In this case, just fire up NetworkManager (or your distro's equivalent) and use that. You'll be far happier you did.

Grab a New Address Using DHCP

`dhclient`

Most home networks and many business networks use the Dynamic Host Control Protocol (DHCP) to parcel out IP addresses and other key information about the network to new machines joining it. Without DHCP, any new machine must have all of its networking information hard-coded in; with DHCP, a new machine simply plugs in to the network, asks the DHCP server to provide it with an IP address and other necessary items, and then automatically incorporates the DHCP server's reply into its networking configurations.

NOTE: The following discussion assumes that you've already configured your network device to use DHCP instead of hard-coded settings. Various Linux distributions expect that information to be found in different configuration files. Debian-based distributions look for the line `iface [interface] inet dhcp` in `/etc/network/interfaces`. Red Hat–derived distributions instead want to see `BOOTPROTO=dhcp` in `/etc/sysconfig/network-scripts/ifcfg-[interface]`. In these examples, substitute `[interface]` with the name of your interface. For more information, search Google for "dhcp *your-distro*".

Sometimes your machine can't connect at boot to the DHCP server, so you need to manually initiate the DHCP request. Or you might have networking problems that require a new IP address. No matter the reason, the dhclient command attempts to query any available DHCP server for the necessary data (dhclient must be run as root).

```
# dhclient eth0
Internet Systems Consortium DHCP Client V3.0.2
Copyright 2004 Internet Systems Consortium.
All rights reserved.
For info, please visit http://www.isc.org/products/
➥DHCP

Listening on LPF/eth0/00:0b:cd:3b:20:e2
Sending on   LPF/eth0/00:0b:cd:3b:20:e2
Sending on   Socket/fallback
DHCPDISCOVER on eth0 to 255.255.255.255 port 67
➥interval 8
DHCPOFFER from 192.168.0.1
DHCPREQUEST on eth0 to 255.255.255.255 port 67
DHCPACK from 192.168.0.1
bound to 192.168.0.104 -- renewal in 37250 seconds.
# ifconfig eth0
eth0 Link encap:Ethernet  HWaddr 00:0B:CD:3B:20:E2
     inet addr:192.168.0.104  Bcast:192.168.0.255
➥Mask:255.255.255.0
     inet6 addr: fe80::20b:cdff:fe3b:20e2/64
➥Scope:Link
[Results truncated for length]
```

To release, or give up, the IP address that the DHCP server has assigned you, use the -r (for *release*) option.

```
# dhclient -r eth0
Internet Systems Consortium DHCP Client V3.0.2
Copyright 2004 Internet Systems Consortium.
All rights reserved.
For info, please visit http://www.isc.org/products/
➥DHCP

sit0: unknown hardware address type 776
sit0: unknown hardware address type 776
Listening on LPF/eth0/00:0b:cd:3b:20:e2
Sending on   LPF/eth0/00:0b:cd:3b:20:e2
Sending on   Socket/fallback
```

Ideally, the dhclient command should run
automatically when you boot your computer, plug
in a wireless PCMCIA card, or connect an Ethernet
cable to your wired jack, but sometimes it doesn't.
When DHCP doesn't work like it's supposed to,
turn to dhclient. It's especially nice how dhclient is
automatically verbose, so you can see what's going on
and diagnose as necessary.

Make a Network Connection Active

ifup

ip link set

You actually use the ifup command all the time
without realizing it. When you boot your computer to
find that you're successfully connected to the Internet,
you can thank ifup. If you plug in an Ethernet cable
to the port on the back of your Linux box, and a few
seconds later you're able to get email again, it's ifup
that did the heavy lifting. In essence, ifup runs when

it detects a network event, such as a reboot or a cable plugged in, and then executes the instructions found in your network interface configuration files. (If you're curious, a Note in the preceding section discussed the names and locations of those files.)

Sometimes, though, you might experience networking problems and need to run ifup manually. It's incredibly easy to do so: Log on as root, and then follow ifup with the name of the network interface you want to activate.

```
# ifconfig
lo Link encap:Local Loopback
   inet addr:127.0.0.1  Mask:255.0.0.0
   inet6 addr: ::1/128 Scope:Host
   UP LOOPBACK RUNNING  MTU:16436  Metric:1
# ifup eth0
# ifconfig
eth0 Link encap:Ethernet  HWaddr 00:0B:CD:3B:20:E2
     inet addr:192.168.0.14  Bcast:192.168.0.255
➥Mask:255.255.255.0
     inet6 addr: fe80::20b:cdff:fe3b:20e2/64
➥Scope:Link
     UP BROADCAST RUNNING MULTICAST  MTU:1500
➥Metric:1
lo   Link encap:Local Loopback
     inet addr:127.0.0.1  Mask:255.0.0.0
     inet6 addr: ::1/128 Scope:Host
     UP LOOPBACK RUNNING  MTU:16436  Metric:1
[Listing condensed due to length]
```

Notice that ifup doesn't tell you that it was successful. Indeed, like most UNIX apps, ifup is silent upon success, and only noisy if it experiences failure or error. To see what ifup has accomplished, use ifconfig, as shown in the preceding listing.

NOTE: You can also use `ifconfig [interface]`
`up` or `iwconfig [interface] up` to make wired or
wireless connections active. And if you were utilizing
the command line version of NetworkManager, the
equivalent would be `nmcli connection up id name-`
`of-connection` or `nmcli connection down id name-`
`of-connection`.

The new command from `iproute2` for bringing an
interface up is `ip link set eth0 up` (which has to be
run as root, of course).

```
# ip addr show up
1: lo: <LOOPBACK,UP,LOWER_UP> mtu 65536 state
    ➥UNKNOWN
# ip link set eth0 up
# ip addr show up
1: lo: <LOOPBACK,UP,LOWER_UP> mtu 65536 state
    ➥UNKNOWN
2: eth0: <BROADCAST,MULTICAST,UP,LOWER_UP> mtu 1500
    ➥state UP
```

And there ya go!

Bring a Network Connection Down

The `ifup` command makes network connections
active, and the `ifdown` command brings them down.
Why would you need to bring down your network
connection? Most often, it's because you're trying
to bring it up, and `ifconfig` reports that it's already
up, but erroneously configured. So you first bring it
down, and then bring it back up.

```
# ifup eth0
ifup: interface eth0 already configured
# ifdown eth0
# ifup eth0
```

Notice that ifdown, like ifup, is silent upon success.
If you don't see anything after entering ifdown, the
command was successful, and that network interface is
no longer going to work.

NOTE: You can also use ifconfig eth0 down or
iwconfig ath0 down to bring wired or wireless connections down.

The new command from iproute2 for bringing an
interface down is ip link set eth0 down (root or sudo
required).

```
# ip addr show up
1: lo: <LOOPBACK,UP,LOWER_UP> mtu 65536 state
    ➥UNKNOWN
2: eth0: <BROADCAST,MULTICAST,UP,LOWER_UP> mtu 1500
    ➥state UP
# ip link set eth0 down
# ip addr show up
1: lo: <LOOPBACK,UP,LOWER_UP> mtu 65536 state
    ➥UNKNOWN
```

Not so bad, is it? Personally, I find ifup to be easier
to use (and remember), but maybe that's because I
learned it a while ago.

Display Your IP Routing Table

```
route
ip route
```

When you try to use Secure Shell (SSH) to connect to another computer on your LAN (something you'll learn about in Chapter 16, "Working on the Network"), how does your computer know that it should confine the packets to your LAN and not send them to your router to be sent out on the Internet? And if you point your web browser to www.ubuntu. com, how does your Linux box know to send that request to your router and not to another machine next to you?

The answer is that your Linux kernel has a routing table that keeps track of those things. To view your current routing table, simply enter route in your shell (no, you don't have to be root to *view* the routing table, but you do have to be root to *change* it, as you'll see in the next section). There's only one network interface on this machine, so this is a pretty simple routing table. On a laptop that has both an Ethernet port and a wireless card, you'll see additional entries.

```
$ route
Kernel IP routing table
Destination Gateway      Genmask         Flags Metric
➥Ref      Use Iface
192.168.0.0 *            255.255.255.0 U      0
➥0         0 eth0
default     192.168.0.1 0.0.0.0         UG    0
➥0         0 eth0
```

NOTE: This command will provide almost the same output as `route`: `netstat -nr` (or `--numeric` and `--route`). The `netstat` command is ridiculously comprehensive and can be a bit complicated, so search for tutorials on the Web.

An IP address is composed of four octets, giving it the appearance of xxx.xxx.xxx.xxx, as in 192.168.0.124. When you send a packet out of your machine, the IP address that is the destination of that packet is compared to the Destination column in the routing table. The Genmask column works with the Destination column to indicate which of the four octets should be examined to determine the packet's destination.

For example, let's say you enter `ping 192.168.0.124` in your shell. A Genmask of 255.255.255.0 indicates that only the last octet—the number represented by 0—matters. In other words, when looking at 192.168.0.124, only the .124 is important to route packets to that address. Any packets intended for 192.168.0.1 through 192.168.0.255 (the limits of an IP address) match the Genmask and the Destination, so they stay on the Local Area Network and avoid the router. That's why there's an * in the Gateway column next to 192.168.0.0: No Gateway is needed because that traffic is local.

On the other hand, everything else is by default intended for the router, which in this instance is at 192.168.0.1 in the Gateway column. The Genmask in this row is 0.0.0.0, indicating that any IP address not matching 192.168.0.1 through 192.168.0.255 should be sent through 192.168.0.1 (because 192.168.0.1 *is* the Gateway, it's a special case). 72.14.203.99, 82.211.81.166, and 216.23.180.5 all match with 0.0.0.0, so they must all go through the Gateway for the Net.

The other interesting thing about the routing table exposed by route is the Flags column, which gives information about the route. There are several possible flags, but the most common are U (the route is up) and G (use the gateway). In the preceding table, you can see that both routes are up, but only the second is the Gateway.

Now let's learn the new way. On the same machine we just ran route on, we use the following:

```
$ ip route show
default via 192.168.0.1 dev eth0
192.168.0.0/24 dev eth0  proto kernel  scope link
➥src 192.168.0.10
```

The first line is pretty simple: anything on eth0 that is intended to go outside the LAN should by default head for the router, found at 192.168.0.1.

The second line is a bit more complicated. 192.168.0.0/24 is the same thing as the route command's 192.168.0.0 with a Genmask of 255.255.255.0—it's just a different way of saying the same thing (a more difficult way, in my opinion). To check that they're the same thing, do a search on the Web for "ip subnet calculator" and enter in the numbers.

Continuing, dev eth0 is the device and proto kernel describes what created the route in the first place. In this case, kernel means just that—the kernel installed this route thanks to autoconfiguration. Next, scope link tells you the area in which the address is valid, and in this case, link means the address is valid only on this device. Finally, src 192.168.0.10 states the source address that your computer will prefer when sending packets to the destination address. Personally, I find good ol' route to be far easier to quickly grasp. Which you prefer is up to you, but I'd start learning ip route show, as some day it may be the default method.

Change Your IP Routing Table

```
route
ip route
```

The route command can be used not only to view your routing table, but to alter it as well. You need to be careful here, however, as you can break your network connection and effectively landlock your computer.

Let's say your machine keeps dropping the Gateway, effectively making it impossible for any packets to leave your LAN for the Internet (this really happened to me once). Run the route command, verify that the Gateway is missing, and then add it in with route (although viewing the route can be done as a normal user, changes to route requires root access).

```
# route
Kernel IP routing table
Destination Gateway Genmask        Flags Metric Ref
➥Use Iface
192.168.0.0 *      255.255.255.0 U    0      0
➥0 eth0
# route add -net default gw 192.168.0.1 dev eth0
# route
Kernel IP routing table
Destination Gateway   Genmask       Flags Metric
➥Ref   Use Iface
192.168.0.0 *      255.255.255.0 U    0
➥0    0 eth0
default     192.168.0.1 0.0.0.0    UG    0
➥0    0 eth0
```

Let's break down that command. `add` indicates that
you're adding a new route (to remove one, use
`del`). The `-net` option tells the kernel that the target
you're adding is a network, in this case the `default`
destination. `gw` indicates that you want to route packets
matching the destination (here the default, therefore
utilizing a Genmask of 0.0.0.0) using a gateway at
`129.168.0.1`. Finally, `dev eth0` specifies the device to
use, in this case the Ethernet card at `eth0`.

Using the new tools, you would do this:

```
# ip route show
192.168.0.0/24 dev eth0 proto kernel scope link
➥192.168.0.101
# ip route add default via 192.168.0.1
# ip route show
default via 192.168.0.1 dev eth0 proto static
➥metric 1024
192.168.0.0/24 dev eth0 proto kernel scope link
➥192.168.0.101
```

Well, that's easy. Just give the command with the IP
address of the gateway at the end and you're finished.
Not too bad, `ip`.

Let's say that in addition to your Ethernet card at
`eth0`, you also have a wireless card at `ath0`. You want
that wireless card to access resources on a LAN that
uses 10.1.xxx.xxx as its base. You don't want the
wireless card to be able to access the Internet at all.
To add a route matching those criteria, you'd use
these commands:

```
# route
Kernel IP routing table
Destination Gateway    Genmask       Flags Metric
➥Ref   Use Iface
192.168.0.0 *          255.255.255.0 U     0
➥0      0 eth0
default     192.168.0.1 0.0.0.0      UG    0
➥0      0 eth0
# route add -net 10.1.0.0 netmask 255.255.0.0 dev
➥ath0
# route
Kernel IP routing table
Destination Gateway    Genmask       Flags Metric
➥Ref   Use Iface
192.168.0.0 *          255.255.255.0 U     0
➥0      0 eth0
10.1.0.0    *          255.255.0.0   U     0
➥0      0 ath0
default     192.168.0.1 0.0.0.0      UG    0
➥0      0 eth0
```

Here you indicated the wireless card with dev ath0,
and then specified the netmask as 255.255.0.0 so
routing would occur correctly. If you later want to
remove that route, you'd use the following:

```
# route
Kernel IP routing table
Destination Gateway    Genmask       Flags Metric
➥Ref   Use Iface
192.168.0.0 *          255.255.255.0 U     0
➥0      0 eth0
10.1.0.0    *          255.255.0.0   U     0
➥0      0 ath0
default     192.168.0.1 0.0.0.0      UG    0
➥0      0 eth0
```

```
# route del -net 10.1.0.0 netmask 255.255.0.0 dev
↪eth0
# route
Kernel IP routing table
Destination Gateway      Genmask         Flags Metric
↪Ref    Use Iface
192.168.0.0 *            255.255.255.0 U     0
↪0      0 eth0
default     192.168.0.1 0.0.0.0         UG    0
↪0      0 eth0
```

Everything is the same, except you use del instead of add. Now that's easy!

What about ip route? To add a route for the Wi-Fi card that keeps it off the Internet, you do the following:

```
# ip route show
default via 192.168.0.1 dev eth0 proto static
↪metric 1024
192.168.0.0/24 dev eth0 proto kernel scope link
↪192.168.0.101
# ip route add 10.1.0.0/16 dev ath0
# ip route show
default via 192.168.0.1 dev eth0 proto static
↪metric 1024
192.168.0.0/24 dev eth0 proto kernel scope link
↪192.168.0.101
10.1.0.0/16 dev ath0 scope link
```

Just add the route with the IP address of your network along with its netmask of 16 (255.255.0.0) and the name of your device and it shows up.

Deleting it is pretty easy, too:

```
# ip route show
default via 192.168.0.1 dev eth0 proto static
↪metric 1024
```

```
192.168.0.0/24 dev eth0 proto kernel scope link
➥192.168.0.101
10.1.0.0/16 dev wlan0 scope link
# ip route del 10.1.0.0/16 dev ath0
# ip route show
default via 192.168.0.1 dev eth0 proto static
➥metric 1024
192.168.0.0/24 dev eth0 proto kernel scope link
➥192.168.0.101
```

Again, all you're doing is substituting `del` for `add`, and you're back to normal.

Troubleshooting Network Problems

Linux distributions nowadays usually "just work" when it comes to networking, but you might still experience an issue. Following are some basic tips for troubleshooting network problems, based on what I've covered in this chapter.

If your network interface appears to be up and running, but you can't get on the Internet, first try pinging your localhost device, at 127.0.0.1. If that doesn't work, stop and go no further, because you have a seriously damaged system. If that works, ping your machine's external IP address. If that doesn't work, make sure networking is enabled on your machine. If it does work, now try pinging other machines on your network, assuming you have any. If you're not successful, it's your interface (assuming your router is okay). Make sure that your cables are plugged in (seriously). Use `ifconfig` or `ip addr show` if it's wired, or `iwconfig` or `nmcli -p device status` if it's wireless, to verify the status of your interface and use `ifup` or `ip link set eth0 up` to turn the interface on, if necessary. Then try `ping` again.

If your attempt to ping another local computer was successful, next try pinging your router. If you can't get to a router and you're pinging it using its IP address, I would reboot your router and see if that fixes it. If you can get to other machines on your network, but you can't get to your router, time to check your routing tables with `route` or `ip route show` (refer to "Display Your IP Routing Table"). If you're missing items from your routing table, add them, as detailed in "Change Your IP Routing Table."

NOTE: It's much easier to diagnose and fix problems if you have a baseline from which to work. After you know a machine's networking is correct, run `route` and save the results, so you have a stored blueprint if the routing table goes bonkers and you need to restore something later.

If you can get to your router, try pinging a machine you know will be up and running out on the Internet, like www.google.com or www.ubuntu.com. If that doesn't work, try pinging that same machine's IP address. Yes, that means that you need to have some IP addresses on a sticky note or in a text file on your computer for just such an occasion as this. Here are a few that are good right now; of course, they could change, so you really should look these up yourself.

Site	IP Address
www.google.com	74.125.141.106
www.debian.org	128.31.0.62
www.ubuntu.com	91.189.89.115
www.distrowatch.com	82.103.136.226
www.granneman.com	23.239.25.194

NOTE: How do you get those IP addresses? You can ping the machine using its domain name, and `ping` gives you the IP address, or you can get the same info with `traceroute`. A quicker method is with the `host` or `dig` commands, covered earlier in "Query DNS Records."

If you can get to the IP address but can't get to the domain name, you have a DNS problem. If you're using DHCP, it's time to run `dhclient` (refer to "Grab a New Address Using DHCP") to try to renew the DNS information provided by your DHCP server. If you're not using DHCP, find the DNS information you need by looking on your router or asking your administrator or ISP, and then add it manually as root to `/etc/resolv.conf` so that it looks like this, for example:

```
nameserver 24.217.0.5
nameserver 24.217.0.55
```

That's `nameserver` (a required word), followed by an IP address you're supposed to use for the DNS. If your router can handle it, and you know its IP address (192.168.0.1, let's say), you can always try this first:

```
nameserver 192.168.0.1
```

Try `ifdown` and then `ifup` and see if you're good to go. At this point, I need to point out a problem that reader Brian Greer brought to my attention: "When manually adding a nameserver to `/etc/resolv.conf`, it is only a temporary solution since `dhclient` overwrites this file on release or reboot." Thank you, Brian— you are completely correct! If you want your DNS changes to persist across DHCP releases and reboots, you need to follow these steps.

First, start by backing up your current `resolv.conf` in case anything goes bump.

```
$ sudo cp /etc/resolv.conf /etc/resolv.conf.auto
```

Now you need to edit your `dhclient.conf` file, but first you have to find it, as the location of the file depends upon your distro. (On my Ubuntu 14.04 box, it's at `/etc/dhcp/dhclient.conf`.) If you can't easily find it, you can always use the `find` command from Chapter 11, "The `find` Command":

```
$ sudo find /etc -name dhclient.conf
```

Once you've found `dhclient.conf`, edit it with your favorite editor, but be sure you open the editor using `sudo`, or with the ability to authenticate when you point it at `dhclient.conf`, because you need root privileges to edit that file. When it's open, add the following line to the document before the `return subnet-mask` line—and note the semicolon at the end!

```
prepend domain-name-servers 208.67.222.222,
➥208.67.220.220;
```

Save and exit `dhclient.conf`. Bring down the connection and then bring it up again, and then check to make sure your DNS is in place with `cat /etc/resolv.conf`.

NOTE: Instructions for SUSE, Mint, and Cinnamon users can be found at https://support.opendns.com/forums/21618384-Computer-Configuration.

If you're still having problems, time to begin again, starting always with hardware. Is everything seated

correctly? Is everything plugged in? After you're sure
of that, start checking your software. The worst-case
scenario is that your hardware just doesn't have drivers
to work with Linux. It's rare, and growing rarer all
the time, but it still happens.

Wireless cards, however, can be wildly incompatible
with Linux thanks to close-mouthed manufacturers
who don't want to help Linux developers make their
hardware work. To prevent headaches, it's a good
idea to check online to make sure a wireless card
you're thinking about purchasing will be copasetic
with Linux. Good sites to review include Linux
Wireless LAN Support (http://linux-wless.passys.nl)
and the Ubuntu Wiki's WirelessCardsSupported page
(https://help.ubuntu.com/community/WifiDocs/
WirelessCardsSupported).

Oh, and to finish our troubleshooting: If you can
successfully ping both the IP address and the domain
name, stop reading this—you're online! Go have fun!

Conclusion

You've covered a wide selection of networking tools
in this chapter. Many of them, such as `ifconfig`,
`iwconfig`, and `route`, can perform double duty, both
informing you about the status of your connectivity
and allowing you to change the parameters of your
connections. Others are used more for diagnostic
purposes, such as `ping`, `traceroute`, and `host`. Finally,
some govern your ability to connect to a network at
all: `dhclient`, `ifup`, and `ifdown`. If you're serious about
Linux, you're going to need to learn all of them.
There's nothing more frustrating than a network

connection that won't work, but often the right program can fix that problem in a matter of seconds. Know your tools well, and you can fix issues quickly and efficiently as they arise.

16

Working on the Network

Many of the commands in this chapter are so rich in features and power that they deserve books of their own. I can't begin to cover all of the awesome stuff you can do with ssh, rsync, wget, and curl, but I can get you started. The best thing to do with these commands is to try them, get comfortable with the basics, and then begin exploring the areas that interest you. There's enough to keep you busy for a long time, and after you start using your imagination, you'll discover a world of cool purposes for the programs you're going to read about in this chapter.

Securely Log In to Another Computer

```
ssh
```

Because UNIX was built with networking in mind, it's no surprise that early developers created programs that would allow users to connect to other machines so they could run programs, view files, and access resources. For a long time, `telnet` was the program to use, but it had a huge problem; it was completely insecure. Everything you sent using `telnet`—your username, password, and all commands and data—were sent without any encryption at all. Anyone who listened in could see everything, and that was not good.

To combat this problem, SSH (secure shell) was developed. It can do everything `telnet` can, and then a *lot* more. Even better, all SSH traffic is encrypted, making it even more powerful and useful. If you need to connect to another machine, whether that computer is on the other side of the globe or in the next room, use SSH.

Let's say you want to use the `ssh` command from your laptop (named `pound`, and found at 192.168.0.15) to your desktop (named `eliot`, and located at 192.168.0.25) so you can look at a file. Your username on the laptop is `ezra`, but on the desktop it's `tom`. To SSH to `eliot`, you'd enter the following (you could also use domain names such as hoohah. granneman.com if one existed):

```
$ ssh tom@192.168.0.25
tom@192.168.0.25's password:
Last login: Mon Feb 6 22:40:31 2006
➥from 192.168.0.15
```

You're prompted for a password after you connect. Type it in (you won't see what you're typing, in order to prevent someone from "shoulder surfing" and discovering your password) and press Enter. If it's accepted, you'll see some information about the machine to which you just connected, including (it depends on the distro) its name, kernel, date and time, and the last time you logged in. You can now run any command you're authorized to run on that machine as though you were sitting right in front of it. From the perspective of SSH and eliot, it doesn't matter where on earth you are—you're logged in and ready to go.

If this were the first time you'd ever connected to eliot, however, you would have seen a different message:

```
$ ssh tom@192.168.0.25
The authenticity of host '192.168.0.25
➡(192.168.0.25)' can't be established.
RSA key fingerprint is 54:53:c3:1c:9a:07:22:0c:82:
➡7b:38:53:21:23:ce:53.
Are you sure you want to continue connecting
➡(yes/no)?
```

Basically, SSH is telling you that it doesn't recognize this machine, and it's asking you to verify the machine's identity. Type in yes, press Enter, and you get another message, along with the password prompt:

```
Warning: Permanently added '192.168.0.25' (RSA)
➡to the list of known hosts.1
tom@192.168.0.25's password:
```

From here things proceed normally. You only see this message the first time you connect to eliot because

SSH stores that RSA key fingerprint it mentioned in
a file on pound located at ~/.ssh/known_hosts. Take a
look at that file, and you see a line has been added to
it. Depending on whether the HashKnownHosts option
has been enabled in your /etc/ssh/ssh_config file, that
line appears in one of two formats. If HashKnownHosts is
set to no, it looks something like this:

```
192.168.0.25 ssh-rsa SkxPUQLYqXSzknsstN6Bh2MHK5AmC6E
➥pg4psdNL69R5pHbQi3kRWNNNNO3AmnP1lp2RNNNNOVjNN9mu5
➥FZe 16zK0iKfJBbLh/Mh9KOhBNtrX6prfcxO9vBEAHYITeLTMm
➥YZLQHB xSr6ehj/9xFxkCHDYLdKFmxaffgA6Ou2ZUX5NzP6Rct
➥4cfqAY69E 5cUoDv3xEJ/gj2zv0bh630zehrGc=
```

You can clearly see the IP address as well as the
encryption hash, but that's nothing compared to what
you'd see if HashKnownHosts is set to yes:

```
NNNNO3AmnP1lp2RNNNNOVjNNNVRNgaJdxOt3GIrh00lPD6KBIU1k
➥aT6nQoJUMVTx2tWb5KiF/LLD4Zwbv2Z/j/0czCZIQNPwDUf6Y
➥iKUFFC6eagqpLDDB4T9qsOajOPLNinRZpcQoPlXf1u6j1agfJ
➥zqUJUYE+Lwv8yzmPidCvOuCZ0LQH4qfkVNXEQxmyy6iz6b2wp=?
```

Everything is hashed, even the machine's IP address or
domain name. This is good from a security standpoint,
but it's a problem if the OS on eliot should ever
change. In other words, if you ever need to reinstall
Linux on eliot, the next time you log in from pound
you'll see this dire warning:

```
@@@@@@@@@@@@@@@@@@@@@@@@@@@@@@@@@@@@@@@@@@@@@@@@@@@@@@@
@ WARNING: REMOTE HOST IDENTIFICATION HAS CHANGED! @
@@@@@@@@@@@@@@@@@@@@@@@@@@@@@@@@@@@@@@@@@@@@@@@@@@@@@@@
IT IS POSSIBLE THAT SOMEONE IS DOING SOMETHING NASTY
Someone could be eavesdropping on you right now
➥(man-in-the-middle attack)!
It is also possible that the RSA host key has just
➥been changed.
The fingerprint for the RSA key sent by the remote
➥host is
19:85:59:5c:6a:24:85:53:07:7a:dc:34:37:c6:72:1b.
Please contact your system administrator.
Add correct host key in /home/pound/.ssh/
➥known_hosts to get rid of this message.
Offending key in /home/pound/.ssh/known_hosts:8
RSA host key for 192.168.0.125 has changed and you
➥have requested strict checking.
Host key verification failed.
```

The problem is that the SSH key on eliot has
changed since the OS has been reinstalled, and when
SSH checks the key for eliot it has stored in pound's
known_hosts file with the new key, it sees that there's
a mismatch and warns you. To fix this, simply delete
the line in pound's known_hosts that corresponds to
eliot, save the file, and reconnect. To SSH, this is the
first time you've connected, so it asks if you want to
accept the key. Say yes, and things are good again.

TIP: I provide a shell function that makes it pretty dang
easy to remove the problematic line from known_hosts
in Chapter 12's "Create a New Permanent Function."

Securely Log In to Another Machine Without a Password

```
ssh
```

The name of this section might appear to be a misnomer, but it's entirely possible to log in to a machine via SSH, but without providing a password. If you log in every day to a particular computer (and there are some boxes that I might log in to several times a day), the techniques in this section will make you very happy.

Let's say you want to make it possible to log in to eliot (username: tom) from pound (username: ezra) without requiring that you type a password. To start with, create an SSH authentication key on pound using the following command:

```
$ ssh-keygen
Generating public/private rsa key pair.
Enter file in which to save the key
➥(/home/ezra/.ssh/id_rsa):
Enter passphrase (empty for no passphrase):
Enter same passphrase again:
Your identification has been saved in
➥/home/ezra/.ssh/id_rsa.
Your public key has been saved in
➥/home/ezra/.ssh/id_rsa.pub.
The key fingerprint is:
d0:c8:8c:a3:6e:c5:bd:d5:e8:0f:c8:45:6c:75:09:25
➥ezra@pound
The key's randomart image is:
+--[ RSA 2048]----+
|          Eoo.   |
|     + + . o.    |
```

```
|    o = =         |
|    o o + o       |
|    . o . S .     |
|    . . . *       |
|    o   + o       |
|    .       o     |
|        .         |
+------------------+
```

NOTE: You currently have three choices for the type
of key you create using `-t`: `dsa` (short for *Digital
Signature Algorithm*), `rsa` (named for the surnames
of its creators), and `ecdsa` (short for *Elliptic Curve
Digital Signature Algorithm*). DSA is now deprecated by
OpenSSH as of August 2015 due to security issues
(see http://lists.mindrot.org/pipermail/openssh-unix-
announce/2015-August/000122.html), so don't use
that. ECDSA isn't widely supported yet, so you might
want to hold off using that just yet. That leaves RSA,
which is widely-supported and quite secure, provided
you use at least 2048 bits for the key length (the
number after `-t`). If you're really paranoid, go for 3072
or even 4096—just be aware that the longer the key
length, the longer it takes to encrypt and decrypt. With
computers as fast as they are nowadays, however, you
shouldn't notice very much. So, for instance, since
`ssh-keygen` creates RSA keys by default, if you wanted
to generate a 4096-bit key of that type, you'd use `ssh-
keygen -b 4096`.

Accept the default location in which to save the key
by pressing Enter, and leave the passphrase field blank
as well by pressing Enter twice when asked. You just
created a private key at `~/.ssh/id_rsa` and a public key
at `~/.ssh/id_rsa.pub`.

Now you need to transfer the public key—not the
private key!—from pound to eliot. The developers
behind SSH are way ahead of you, and have created
a program that makes this as easy as falling off a log.
To automatically copy your public key from pound to
eliot, just enter the following on pound:

```
$ ssh-copy-id -i ~/.ssh/id_rsa.pub tom@192.168.0.25
```

Now try logging into the machine, with ssh
'tom@192.168.0.25', and check in .ssh/authorized_keys
to make sure you haven't added extra keys that you
weren't expecting.

You're done (although if you want to follow the
advice given by ssh-copy-id, go right ahead). Watch
what happens when you use the ssh command from
pound to eliot now:

```
$ ssh tom@192.168.0.25

Last login: Sun Sep 20 19:52:53 2015 from
➥192.168.0.15
```

Notice that you weren't asked to enter a password,
which is exactly what you wanted.

Some of you are wondering about the security of
this trick. No passwords? Freely exchanging keys?
It's true, but think about it for a moment. True, if
someone gets on pound, he can now connect to eliot
without a password. But that simply means that you
need to practice good security on pound. If pound is
compromised, you have enormous problems whether
or not the attacker realizes that he can also get to
eliot. On top of that, you shoot passwords around
the Internet all the time as you log in to websites. If

an attacker acquires your password, he can do major damage as well. Isn't your private key as important as a password? And aren't you going to back it up and safeguard it? When you think about it in those terms, exchanging keys via ssh is at least as secure as passwords, and in most ways much more secure.

TIP: If working with a passwordless key gives you the willies, then you want to investigate ssh-agent, a program that manages your keys for you. You enter the password for your key and ssh-agent keeps it in memory for you. It's certainly more secure than passwordless keys, but it brings several issues with it that you need to think about. One of the big problems is getting it to run automatically; the best discussion I've seen on that issue is at http://unix.stackexchange.com/questions/90853/how-can-i-run-ssh-add-automatically-without-password-prompt.

Nonetheless, if you prefer to keep using passwords, that's certainly your prerogative. That's what open source and Linux is all about: choice.

Securely Transfer Files Between Machines

`sftp`

In the same way that SSH is a far better choice than telnet, SFTP is far better than FTP. Like telnet, FTP sends your name and password, as well as all the data being transferred, in the clear so that anyone sniffing packets can listen in. SFTP, on the other hand, uses SSH to encrypt everything: username, passwords, and traffic. Other than the fact it's secure (which is a big deal!), it's remarkably similar to FTP in its commands, which should make it easy to learn and use.

NOTE: For a fantastic, thorough, sometimes profane, takedown of FTP and why no one should ever use it, see http://mywiki.wooledge.org/FtpMustDie.

If you can access a machine via SSH, you can also SFTP to it. To use the `sftp` command from `pound` (192.168.0.15; username `ezra`) to `eliot` (192.168.0.25; username `tom`), just use this command:

```
$ sftp tom@192.168.0.25
Connecting to 192.168.0.25...
tom@192.168.0.25's password:
sftp>
```

If you've read the previous section, "Securely Log In to Another Machine Without a Password," you might be wondering why you were prompted for a password. You're correct: The preceding example was taken before a connection that didn't require a password was set. After you've done that, you would instead see a login that looks like this:

```
$ sftp tom@192.168.0.25
Connecting to 192.168.0.25...
sftp>
```

After you're logged in via `sftp`, the commands you can run are pretty standard. Table 16.1 lists some of the more common commands; for the full list, look at `man sftp`.

Table 16.1   **Useful SFTP Commands**

Command	Meaning
cd	Change directory
exit	Close the connection to the remote SSH server
get	Copy the specified file to the local machine
help	Get help on commands
lcd	Change the directory on the local machine
lls	List files on the local machine
ls	List files in the working directory on the remote SSH server
put	Copy the specified file to the remote SSH server
rm	Remove the specified file from the remote SSH server

TIP: When it comes to configuring SSH servers, admins sometimes switch the default port used by SSH from 22 to something else in order to improve security. It's not magic, but it can be a useful speed bump for some script kiddies.

If the SSH server to which you're connecting via sftp has changed the default port, then you're not going to be able to connect. To use the non-default SSH port (or to work with any other special changes to SSH the server admin has made), you pass that option along in your sftp command with -o, followed by the specific SSH option. So, for instance, if the SSH server uses port 2345 instead of 22, you would connect using sftp -oPort=2345 (notice there is no space after -o and the SSH option). If you have to include additional SSH options, just repeat the `-o`, like this: `sftp -oPort=2345 -oPasswordAuthentication=no` (for the full list, look over `man ssh_config`).

Securely Copy Files Between Hosts

`scp`

If you're in a hurry and you need to copy a file securely from one machine to another, `scp` (secure copy) is what you want. In essence, here's the basic pattern for using `scp`:

```
scp user@host1:file1 user@host2:file2
```

This is basically the same syntax as good ole' `cp`, but now extended to the network. An example will make things clearer. Let's say you want to copy `backup.sh` from `pound` (192.168.0.15; username `ezra`) to `/home/tom/bin` on `eliot` (129.168.0.25; username `tom`) using `scp`:

```
$ pwd
/home/ezra
$ ls ~/bin
backup.sh
$ scp ~/bin/backup.sh tom@192.168.0.25/home/tom/bin
backup.sh              100% 8806      8.6KB/s   00:00
$
```

You weren't prompted for a password because you set things up earlier in "Securely Log In to Another Machine Without a Password" so SSH doesn't require passwords to connect from `pound` to `eliot`, and because `scp` relies on SSH, you don't need a password here, either. If you hadn't done that, you would have been asked to enter tom's password before continuing.

Let's say you have several JPEGs you want to transfer from pound to eliot. No problem—just use a wildcard:

```
$ ls -1 ~/covers
earth_wind_&_fire.jpg
handel_-_chamber_music.jpg
smiths_best_1.jpg
strokes_-_is_this_it.jpg
u2_pop.jpg
$ scp *.jpg tom@192.168.0.25:/home/tom/album_covers
earth_wind_&_fire.jpg          100%   44KB  43.8KB/s
handel_-_chamber_music.jpg     100%   12KB  12.3KB/s
smiths_best_1.jpg              100%   47KB  47.5KB/s
strokes_-_is_this_it.jpg       100%   38KB  38.3KB/s
u2_pop.jpg                     100%   9222   9.0KB/
sQ
```

Now let's say you want to go the other direction. You're still on pound, and you want to copy several pictures of Libby from eliot to pound, and into a different directory than the one in which you currently are in:

```
$ scp tom@192.168.0.25:/home/tom/pictures/dog/libby*
➡ ~/pix/libby
libby_in_window_1.20020611.jpg 100%  172KB 172.4KB/s
libby_in_window_2.20020611.jpg 100%  181KB 180.8KB/s
libby_in_window_3.20020611.jpg 100%  197KB 196.7KB/s
libby_in_window_4.20020611.jpg 100%  188KB 187.9KB/s
```

The scp command is really useful when you need to securely copy files between machines. If you have many files to copy, however, you'll find that scp can quickly grow tiresome. In cases like that, you might want to look at SFTP or a mounted Samba share. (You can find information about mounting Samba filesystems on my website, http://www.granneman. com/linux-redactions.)

Securely Transfer and Back Up Files

```
rsync
```

rsync is one of the coolest, most useful programs ever invented, and many people rely on it every day (like me!). What does it do? Its uses are myriad (here we go again into "you could write a book about this command!"), but let's focus on one very powerful, necessary feature: its capability to back up files effectively and securely, with a minimum of network traffic.

Let's say you intend to back up 2GB of files every night from a machine named coleridge (username: sam) to another computer named wordsworth (username: will). Without rsync, you're looking at a transfer of 2GB every single night, a substantial amount of traffic, even on a fast network connection. With rsync, however, you might be looking at a transfer that will take a few moments at most. Why? Because when rsync backs up those 2GB, it transfers only the differences between all the files that make up those 2GB of data. If only a few hundred kilobytes changed in the past 24 hours, that's all that rsync transfers. If instead it was 100MB, that's what rsync copies over. Either way, it's much less than 2GB.

Here's a command that, run from coleridge, transfers the entire content of the documents directory to a backup drive on wordsworth. Look at the command, look at the results, and then you can walk through what those options mean (the command is given first with long options instead of single letters for readability, and then with single letters, if available, for comparison).

```
$ rsync --archive --verbose --compress --rsh=ssh
➥--progress --stats --delete /home/sam/documents/
➥will@wordsworth:/media/backup/documents
$ rsync -a -v -z -e ssh --progress --stats
➥--delete /home/sam/documents/
➥will@wordsworth:/media/backup/documents
```

Of course, you could also run the command this way, if you wanted to combine all the options:

```
$ rsync -avze ssh --progress --stats
➥--delete /home/sam/documents/
➥will@wordsworth:/media/backup/documents
```

Upon running rsync using any of the methods listed, you'd see something like this:

```
building file list ...
107805 files to consider
deleting clientele/Linux_Magazine/do_it_yourself/13/
➥gantt_chart.txt~
deleting Security/diebold_voting/black_box_voting/
➥bbv_chapter-9.pdf
deleting Security/diebold_voting/black_box_voting/
➥bbv_chapter-8.pdf
deleting E-commerce/Books/20050827 ebay LIL ABNER
➥FRAZETTA SUNDAYS 2.txt
deleting E-commerce/Books/20050827 The State We're
➥In.txt
deleting E-commerce/Books/20050811 eBay LIL ABNER
➥DAILIES 6 1940.txt
```

```
Security/electronic_voting/diebold/black_box_voting/
➥bbv_chapter-8.pdf
Security/electronic_voting/diebold/black_box_voting/
➥bbv_chapter-9.pdf
legal_issues/free_speech/Timeline A history of free
➥speech.txt
E-commerce/2005/Books/20050811 eBay LIL ABNER
➥DAILIES 6 1940.txt
E-commerce/2005/Books/20050827 The State We're
➥In.txt
E-commerce/2005/Books/20050827 ebay LIL ABNER
➥FRAZETTA SUNDAYS 2.txt
connectivity/connectivity_info.txt
[Results greatly truncated for length]
Number of files: 107805
Number of files transferred: 120
Total file size: 6702042249 bytes
Total transferred file size: 15337159 bytes
Literal data: 0 bytes
Matched data: 0 bytes
File list size: 2344115
File list generation time: 86.041 seconds
File list transfer time: 0.000 seconds
Total bytes sent: 2345101
Total bytes received: 986

sent 2345101 bytes  received 986 bytes  7507.48
➥bytes/sec
total size is 6702042249  speedup is 2856.69
```

Take a look at those results. rsync first builds a list of
all files that it must consider—107,805 in this case—
and then deletes any files on the target (wordsworth)
that no longer exist on the source (coleridge). In this
example, six files are deleted: a backup file (the ~ is
a giveaway on that one) from an article for *Linux
Magazine*, two PDFs on electronic voting, and then
three text receipts for purchased books.

After deleting files, `rsync` copies over any that have changed, or if it's the same file, just the changes to the file, which is part of what makes `rsync` so slick. In this case, six files are copied over. It turns out that the two PDFs were actually moved to a new subdirectory, but to `rsync` those are new files, so they're copied over in their entirety. The same is true for the three text receipts. The `A history of free speech.txt` file is an entirely new file, so it's copied over to `wordsworth` as well.

After listing the changes it made, `rsync` gives you some information about the transfer as a whole. 120 files were transferred, 15337159 bytes (about 14MB) out of 6702042249 bytes (around 6.4GB). Other data points are contained in the summation, but those are the key ones.

Now let's look at what you asked your computer to do. The head and tail of the command are easy to understand: the command `rsync` at the start, then options, and then the source directory you're copying from (`/home/sam/documents/`, found on `coleridge`), followed by the target directory you're copying to (`/media/backup/documents`, found on `wordsworth`). Before going on to examine the options, you need to focus on the way the source and target directories are designated because there's a catch in there that will really hurt if you don't watch it.

You want to copy the contents of the `documents` directory found on `coleridge`, but not the directory itself, and that's why you use `documents/` and not `documents`. The slash after `documents` in `/home/sam/documents/` tells `rsync` that you want to copy the *contents* of that directory into the `documents` directory found on `wordsworth`; if you instead used `documents`, you'd copy the directory *and* its contents, resulting in `/media/backup/documents/documents` on wordsworth.

NOTE: The slash is only important on the source directory; it doesn't matter whether you use a slash on the target directory.

Now on to the options you used. The `-v` (or `--verbose`) option, coupled with `--progress`, orders rsync to tell you in detail what it's doing at all times. You saw that in the results shown earlier in this section, in which rsync tells you what it's deleting and what it's copying. If you're running rsync via an automated script, you don't need this option, although it doesn't hurt; if you're running rsync interactively, this is an incredibly useful display of information to have in front of you because you can see what's happening.

The metadata you saw at the end of rsync's results— the information about the number and size of files transferred, as well as other interesting data—appeared because you included the `--stats` option. Again, if you're scripting rsync, this isn't needed, but it's sure nice to see if you're running the program manually.

The `-a` (or `--archive`) is the big kahuna, because it's actually short for *seven* other options: `-rlptgoD`. Let's go through those in order.

You've seen the `-r` (or `--recursive`) option many other times with other commands, and it does here what it does everywhere else. Instead of stopping in the current directory, it tunnels down through all subdirectories, affecting everything in its path, enabling you to copy the entire documents directory and all of its contents.

When a soft link is found on the source, the -l (or --links) option re-creates the link on the target. Instead of copying the actual file, which is obviously not what the creator of a soft link intended, the link to the file is copied over, again preserving the original state of the source.

Permissions were discussed in Chapter 7, "Ownerships and Permissions," and here they reappear again. The -p (or --perms) option tells rsync to update permissions on any files found on the target so they match what's on the source and help ensure the backup's accuracy. Likewise with -o (or --owner) and -g (or --groups), which preserve ownership information.

The -t (or --times) option makes rsync transfer the files' modification times along with the files. If you don't include this option, rsync cannot tell what it has previously transferred, and the next time you run the command, all files are copied over again. This is probably not the behavior you want, as it completely obviates the features that make rsync so useful! Finally, as far as the oh-so-powerful -a is concerned, the -D is itself short for two options: --devices and --specials. The former transfers device files (for example, hard drives and optical drives) and the latter sends over special files (for example, named sockets and FIFOs). You probably don't need to worry about it, but -D is part of -a, so it's coming along for the ride.

Even over a fast connection, it's a good idea to use the -z (or --compress) option, as rsync then uses gzip compression while transferring files. On a slow connection, this option is mandatory; on a fast connection, it saves you that much more time.

In the name of security, you're using the -e (or --rsh=ssh) option, which tells rsync to tunnel all of its traffic using SSH. Easy file transfers, and secure as well? Sign me up!

NOTE: If you're using SSH, why didn't you have to provide a password? Because you used the technique displayed in "Securely Log In to Another Machine Without a Password" to remove the need to do so.

We've saved the most dangerous for last: `--delete`. If you're creating a mirror of your files, you obviously want that mirror to be as accurate as possible. That means deleted files on the source need to be deleted on the target as well. But that also means you can accidentally blow away stuff you wanted to keep. If you're going to use the `--delete` option—and you probably will—be sure to use the `-n` (or `--dry-run`) option that is discussed in the following Caution.

CAUTION: There's one option that wasn't listed previously but is still a *very* good idea to include when you're figuring out how your `rsync` command will be structured: `-n` (or `--dry-run`). If you include that option, `rsync` runs, but doesn't actually delete or copy anything. This can be a lifesaver if your choices would have resulted in the deletion of important files. Before committing to your `rsync` command, especially if you're including the `--delete` option from the previous paragraph, do yourself a favor and perform a dry run first!

`rsync` has many other options and plenty of other ways to use the command (the `man` page identifies eight ways it can be used, which is impressive), but the setup discussed in this section will definitely get you started. Open up `man rsync` on your terminal, or search Google for "rsync tutorial," and you'll find a wealth of great information. Get to know `rsync`: When you yell out "Oh no!" upon deleting a file, but then follow it with "Whew! It's backed up using `rsync`!" you'll be glad you took the time to learn this incredibly versatile and useful command.

TIP: If you want to be really safe with your data, set up `rsync` to run with a regular `cron` job. For instance, create a file titled `backup.sh` (`~/bin` is a good place for it) and type in the command you've been using:

```
$ rsync -avze ssh --progress --stats
➥--delete /home/sam/documents/
➥will@wordsworth:/media/backup/documents
```

Use `chmod` to make the file executable:

```
$ chmod 755 /home/scott/bin/backup.sh
```

Then add the following lines to a file named `cronfile` (I put mine in my `~/bin` directory as well):

```
# backup documents every morning at 3:05 am
05 03 * * * /home/scott/bin/backup.sh
```

The first line is a comment explaining the purpose of the job, and the second line tells `cron` to automatically run `/home/scott/bin/backup.sh` every night at 3:05 a.m.

Now add the job to `cron`:

```
$ crontab /home/scott/bin/cronfile
```

Now you don't need to worry about your backups ever again. It's all automated for you—just make sure you leave your computers on overnight!

(For more on `cron`, see `man cron` or "Newbie: Intro to cron" at www.unixgeeks.org/security/newbie/unix/cron-1.html).

Download Files Non-interactively

The Net is a treasure trove of pictures, movies, and music that are available for downloading. The problem is that manually downloading every file from a collection of 200 MP3s quickly grows tedious, leading to mind rot and uncontrollable drooling. The wget command is used to download files and websites without any interference; you set the command in motion and it happily downloads whatever you specified, for hours on end.

The tricky part, of course, is setting up the command. wget is another super-powerful program that really deserves a book all to itself, so we don't have space to show you everything it can do. Instead, you're going to focus on doing two things with wget: downloading a whole mess of files, which is looked at here, and downloading entire websites, which is covered in the next section.

Here's the premise: You find a wonderful website called "The Old Time Radio Archives." On this website are a large number of vintage radio shows, available for download in MP3 format—365 MP3s, to be exact, one for every day of the year. It would sure be nice to grab those MP3s, but the prospect of right-clicking on every MP3 hyperlink, choosing Save Link As, and then clicking OK to start the download isn't very appealing.

Examining the directory structure a bit more, you notice that the MP3s are organized in a directory structure like this:

```
http://www.oldtimeradioarchives.com/mp3/
    season_10/
    season_11/
    season_12/
    . . .
    season_20/
    season_21/
    . . .
    season_3/
    season_4/
    . . .
    season_9/
```

NOTE: The directories are not sorted in numerical order, as humans would do it, but in alphabetical order, which is how computers sort numbers unless told otherwise. After all, "ten" comes before "three" alphabetically.

Inside each directory sit the MP3s. Some directories have just a few files in them, and some have close to 20. If you click on the link to a directory, you get a web page that lists the files in that directory like this:

```
[BACK] Parent Directory      19-May-2015 01:03       -
       1944-12-24_532.mp3    06-Jul-2015 13:54     6.0M
       1944-12-31_533.mp3    06-Jul-2015 14:28     6.5M
       1945-01-07_534.mp3    06-Jul-2015 20:05     6.8M
       1945-01-14_535.mp3    06-Jul-2015 19:53     6.9M
```

So the question is, how do you download all of these MP3s that have different filenames and exist in different directories? The answer is wget!

Start by creating a directory on your computer into which you'll download the MP3 files.

```
$ mkdir radio_mp3s
```

Now use the `cd` command to get into that directory, and then run `wget`:

```
$ cd radio_mp3s
$ wget -r -l2 -np -w 5 -A.mp3 -R.html,.gif
➥http://www.oldtimeradioarchives.com/mp3/
```

Let's walk through this command and its options.

`wget` is the command you're running, of course, and at the far end is the URL that you want `wget` to use: http://www.oldtimeradioarchives.com/mp3. The important stuff, though, lies in between the command and the URL.

The `-r` (or `--recursive`) option for `wget` follows links and goes down through directories in search of files. By telling `wget` that it is to act recursively, you ensure that `wget` will go through every season's directory, grabbing all the MP3s it finds.

The `-l2` (or `--level=[#]`) option is important yet tricky. It tells `wget` how deep it should go in retrieving files recursively. The lowercase `l` stands for *level* and the number is the depth to which `wget` should descend. If you specified `-l1` for level one, `wget` would look in the `/mp3` directory only. That would result in a download of…nothing. Remember, the `/mp3` directory contains other subdirectories: `season_10`, `season_11`, and so on, and those are directories that contain the MP3s you want. By specifying `-l2`, you're asking `wget` to first enter `/mp3` (which would be level one), and then go into each `season_#` directory in turn and grab anything in it. You need to be very careful with the level you specify. If you aren't careful, you can easily fill your hard drive in very little time.

One of the ways to avoid downloading more than you expected is to use the `-np` (or `--no-parent`) option, which prevents `wget` from recursing into the parent directory. If you look back at the preceding list of files, you'll note that the very first link is the parent directory. In other words, when in `/season_10`, the parent is `/mp3`. The same is true for `/season_11`, `/season_12`, and so on. You don't want `wget` to go *up*, however, you want it to go *down*. And you certainly don't need to waste time by going up into the same directory—`/mp3`—every time you're in a season's directory.

This next option isn't required, but it would sure be polite of you to use it. The `-w` (or `--wait=[#]`) option introduces a short wait between each file download. This helps prevent overloading the server as you hammer it continuously for files. By default, the number is interpreted by `wget` as seconds; if you want, you can also specify minutes by appending `m` after the number, or hours with `h`, or even days with `d`.

Now it gets very interesting. The `-A` (or `--accept`) option emphasizes to `wget` that you only want to download files of a certain type and nothing else. The A stands for *accept*, and it's followed by the file suffixes that you want, separated by commas. You only want one kind of file type, MP3, so that's all you specify: `-A.mp3`.

On the flip side, the `-R` (or `--reject`) option tells `wget` what you don't want: HTML and GIF files. By refusing those, you don't get those little musical notes represented by [SND] shown previously. Separate your list of suffixes with a comma, giving you `-R.html,.gif`.

Running wget with those options results in a
download of 365 MP3s to your computer. If, for some
reason, the transfer was interrupted—your router dies,
someone trips over your Ethernet cable and yanks it
out of your box, a backhoe rips up the fiber coming
in to your business—just repeat the command, but add
the -c (or --continue) option. This tells wget to take
over from where it was forced to stop. That way you
don't download everything all over again.

NOTE: The following example doesn't work any longer,
but I kept it in because it explains the concepts so
well. Just don't try it yourself!

Here's another example that uses wget to download
files. A London DJ released two albums worth of
MP3s consisting of mash-ups of The Beatles and
The Beastie Boys, giving us The Beastles, of course.
The MP3s are listed, one after the other, on www.
thebeastles.com. The following command pulls the
links out of that web page, writes them to a file, and
then starts downloading those links using wget:

```
$ lynx -dump http://www.djbc.net/beastles/ |
➥awk '/http/{print $2}' |
➥grep mp3 > beastles ; wget -i beastles
--12:58:12--  http://www.djbc.net/beastles/
➥webcontent/djbc-holdittogethernow.mp3
           => 'djbc-holdittogethernow.mp3'
Resolving www.djbc.net... 216.227.209.173
Connecting to www.djbc.net|216.227.209.173|:80...
➥connected.
HTTP request sent, awaiting response... 200 OK
Length: 4,533,083 (4.3M) [audio/mpeg]
```

```
100%[=========>] 4,533,083    203.20K/s    ETA 00:00

12:58:39 (166.88 KB/s) - 'djbc-holdittogethernow.
➡mp3' saved [4533083/4533083]
[Results truncated for length]
```

Although almost everybody uses a GUI-based Web browser like Firefox, Chrome, or Safari, there's still good call for a command-line text-based browser if you want speed, security, or scriptability. There are many—check out links, elinks, and w3m—but I really like lynx, which comes on many distros. If it isn't already on your computer, you can always install lynx using a package manager (see Chapter 14).

If you invoke lynx with the -dump option and point it at a URL, the links are pulled out of the page and displayed on STDOUT, with each line starting with a number. To get rid of the numbers, you use awk (discussed in Chapter 7's "Print Specific Fields in a File") to filter them out. You pipe those links to grep, asking grep to filter out all but lines containing mp3, and then redirect the resulting MP3 links to a text file named beastles. (Piping and redirecting are covered in Chapter 5, "Building Blocks," and the grep command is covered in Chapter 10, "Finding Files, Directories, Words, and Phrases.")

The semicolon (covered in the "Run Several Commands Sequentially" section in Chapter 5) ends that command and starts a new one: wget. The -i (or --input-file) option tells wget to look in a file for the URLs to download, instead of STDIN. If you have many links, put them all in a file and use the -i option with wget. In this case, you point wget to the beastles file you just created via dog and grep, and the MP3s begin to download, one after the other.

Now really, what could be easier? Ah, the power of the Linux command line!

NOTE: As you've learned, wget is for downloading files. But what if you want to *upload* files non-interactively? That's when you get wput! You can find out more about this command at http://wput.sourceforge.net. It only works with FTP servers, but it's still a neat partner to the mighty wget.

Download Websites Non-interactively

```
wget
```

If you want to back up your website or download another website, look to wget. In the previous section you used wget to grab individual files, but you can use it to obtain entire sites as well.

NOTE: Please be reasonable with wget. Don't download enormous sites, and keep in mind that someone creates and owns the sites that you're copying. Don't copy a site because you want to "steal" it.

Let's say you're buzzing around a site at www.neato.com and you find yourself at www.neato.com/articles/index.htm. You'd like to copy everything in the /articles section, but you don't want anything else on the site. The following command does what you'd like:

```
$ wget -E -r -k -p -w 5 -np
➥http://www.neato.com/articles/index.htm
```

You could have combined the options this way, as well:

```
$ wget -Erkp -w 5 -np
➥http://www.neato.com/articles/index.htm
```

As in the previous section, the command begins with wget and ends with the URL you want to use. You looked at the -w (or --wait=[#]) option before, and that's the same, as well as -np (or --no-parent) and -r (or --recursive). Let's examine the new options that have been introduced in this example.

When you download a site, some of the pages might not end with .htm or .html; instead, they might end with .asp, .php, .cfm, or something else. The problem comes in if you try to view the downloaded site on your computer. If you're running a web server on your desktop, things might look just fine, but more than likely you're not running Apache on your desktop. Even without a web server, however, pages ending in .htm or .html will work on your box if you open them with a web browser. If you use the -E (or --html-extension) option, wget converts every page so that it ends with .html, thus enabling you to view them on your computer without any special software.

Downloading a site might introduce other issues, however, which you can fortunately get around with the right wget options. Links on the pages you download with wget might not work after you open the pages on your computer, making it impossible to navigate from page to page. By specifying the -k (or --convert-links) option, you order wget to rewrite links in the pages so they work on your computer. This option fixes not only links to pages, but also links to pictures, Cascading Style Sheets, and files. You'll be glad you used it.

Speaking of Cascading Style Sheets (CSS) and images, they're why you want to use the -p (or --page-requisites) option. In order for the web page to display correctly, the web developer might have specified images, CSS, and JavaScript files to be used along with the page's HTML. The -p option requires that wget download any files needed to display the web pages that you're grabbing. With it, looking at the page after it's on your machine duplicates what you saw on the Web; without it, you might end up with an almost unreadable file.

The man page for wget is enormously long and detailed, and it's where you will ultimately end up if you want to use wget in a more sophisticated way. If you think wget sounds interesting to you, start reading. You'll learn a lot.

Download Sequential Files and Internet Resources

`curl`

At first blush, wget and curl seem similar: Both download files non-interactively. They each have one large difference distinguishing them, however, among many smaller ones: curl supports sequences and sets in specifying what to download, which wget does not, while wget supports recursion, a feature missing from curl.

NOTE: The programs have plenty of other differences. The full list of curl's features can be seen at "Features—What Can curl Do" (http://curl.haxx.se/docs/features.html), while some of wget's are listed at "Overview" (www.gnu.org/software/wget/manual/html_node/Overview.html). The cURL site has a chart comparing curl to other, similar programs at "Compare cURL Features with Other FTP+HTTP Tools" (http://curl.haxx.se/docs/comparison-table.html); while informative, the chart is (unsurprisingly) a bit biased toward curl.

Here's an example that uses curl's capability to support sequences in specifying what to download. The excellent National Public Radio show *This American Life* makes archives of all of its shows available for download on its parent website in Real Audio format (why they chose Real and not a more open format is a mystery). If you want to download 10 of these Real Audio files, just use the following:

```
$ curl -O http://www.wbez.org/ta/[1-10].rm
[1/10]: http://www.wbez.org/ta/1.rm --> 1.rm
--_curl_--http://www.wbez.org/ta/1.rm

[Results greatly truncated]
```

Notice how you used [1-10].rm to specify that you wanted to download 1.rm, 2.rm, 3.rm, and so on. If WBEZ had instead named the files one.rm, two.rm, and three.rm, for example, you could have used a part set instead:

```
$ curl -O http://www.wbez.org/ta/{one,two,three}.rm
```

The -O (or --remote-name) option is absolutely required. If you don't use it, curl writes the output of the download to STDOUT, which means that your terminal will quickly fill with unusable goobledygook. The -o asks curl to write out what it downloads to a file, and to use the name of the file being downloaded as the local filename as well.

NOTE: The previous example also is out of date and will no longer work, but I kept it because it shows the usefulness of curl.

We've barely scratched the surface of curl. Its man page, while not as long as wget's, is also full of useful information that you need to read if you're going to maximize your use of curl. Consider it required reading.

Conclusion

The commands in this chapter are some of my personal favorites, as they allow me to accomplish tasks that would otherwise be overly tedious, unsafe, or difficult. All of them make the network just another avenue for your data, your programs, and your imagination, and that's really where Linux shines. By making tools as powerful as ssh, rsync, wget, and curl freely available to users, Linux encourages innovation and safety in a way that's just not possible on another operating system that many people are forced to use. Jump in and learn ssh so you can securely connect to other computers, master rsync for safe and automated backups, and rely on wget and curl to specifically download needed content in as efficient a manner as possible. You'll be glad you did!

Index

Symbols

A